D1311252

UK/US
GAAP
COMPARISON

UK/US GAAP COMPARISON

A COMPARISON BETWEEN UK AND US

ACCOUNTING PRINCIPLES

Ernst & Young

KOGAN
PAGE

First published in 1990

Kogan Page Limited
120 Pentonville Road
London N1 9JN

© Ernst & Young

British Library Cataloguing in Publication Data

A CIP record for this book is available from the British Library.

ISBN 0-7494-0343-8

Printed and bound in Great Britain by
Biddles Ltd, Guildford and King's Lynn

*This book is dedicated to
the memory of Richard J Keeling,
Director of International Accounting
of Ernst & Young in New York,
who died suddenly on September 15, 1990.
Richard was a great friend of the firm's
Technical Services Department in London,
and made a substantial contribution
to this publication and its predecessor editions.*

PREFACE

Financial reporting requirements can differ greatly between countries because of different national, legal, commercial and cultural environments. The business environments in the United Kingdom and the United States are similar in many respects, and such differences as exist have not resulted in the development of fundamentally divergent accounting concepts; nonetheless there are numerous differences in the detailed application of accounting principles in the two countries. As a result, material changes to reported earnings and owners' equity will usually arise if accounts prepared under the rules of one country are recast so as to comply with the requirements of the other.

This book compares generally accepted accounting principles in the UK and the US, as they apply to general commercial enterprises: the requirements of specialised industries are beyond its scope. The first three chapters of the book describe the background to financial reporting in the two countries and how their various accounting standards have been developed, thereby establishing a framework for the comparison contained in the later chapters. Chapter 4 highlights the principal differences between the two countries and Chapter 5, the major part of the book, comprises a detailed side-by-side comparison of the requirements which govern each accounting topic.

The comparison extends on the one hand to the accounting principles established by the Accounting Standards Committee in the UK together with the requirements of the Companies Act 1985 and of the International Stock Exchange, and on the other hand to generally accepted accounting principles in the US, derived from numerous sources including the Financial Accounting Standards developed by the FASB and equivalent statements by its predecessors. Where appropriate, reference is also made to accounting rules and regulations of the US Securities and Exchange Commission and to likely future developments in UK accounting standards and major FASB projects. Ernst & Young's companion volume, *UK GAAP — Generally Accepted Accounting Practice in the United Kingdom*, provides a much more detailed analysis and discussion of financial reporting in the UK.

The book has been prepared by members of the Technical Services Department of Ernst & Young, principally Vivian Pereira, but with important contributions from several others including Matthew Curtis, Mike Davies, Richard Jenkins, Ron Paterson and Allister Wilson. Thanks are due to Nigel Bankhead of Clay & Partners for his helpful comments on the pensions sections in this book.

London, September 1990   Ernst & Young

LIST OF CHAPTERS

DETAILED CONTENTS

DETAILED CONTENTS

DETAILED CONTENTS

DETAILED CONTENTS

DETAILED CONTENTS

DETAILED CONTENTS

DETAILED CONTENTS

DETAILED CONTENTS

DETAILED CONTENTS

DETAILED CONTENTS

DETAILED CONTENTS

DETAILED CONTENTS

DETAILED CONTENTS

DETAILED CONTENTS

ABBREVIATIONS

The following abbreviations are used in this book:

PROFESSIONAL AND REGULATORY BODIES:

AICPA   American Institute of Certified Public Accountants

APB   Accounting Principles Board (of the AICPA)

ASB   Accounting Standards Board

ASC   Accounting Standards Committee (a former committee of the CCAB)

CCAB   Consultative Committee of Accountancy Bodies in the UK

FASB   Financial Accounting Standards Board (successor to the APB)

ICAEW   The Institute of Chartered Accountants in England and Wales

ISE   The International Stock Exchange of the United Kingdom and the Republic of Ireland Limited

SEC   The US Securities and Exchange Commission

REFERENCES TO AUTHORITATIVE LITERATURE IN THE UK:

CA 85   The Companies Act 1985

ED   Exposure draft of a SSAP

SSAP   Statement of Standard Accounting Practice (issued by the CCAB)

TC   City code on Take-overs and Mergers issued by the Panel on Take-overs and Mergers

TR   Technical Release (normally issued by the ICAEW)

SI 90/355 Statutory Instrument (year and number). SIs are regulations issued by the Secretary of State or persons authorised by him that amend or supplement certain aspects of CA 85.

YB   The Yellow book of the ISE

ABBREVIATIONS

REFERENCES TO AUTHORITATIVE LITERATURE IN THE US:

AIN-APB   Accounting Interpretation of the AICPA

APB   Opinion of the APB

ARB   Accounting Research Bulletin (issued by the Committee on Accounting Procedure)

ASR   Accounting Series Release (issued by SEC; later codified into FRR 1)

CON   Statement of Financial Accounting Concepts (issued by the FASB)

EITF   Consensus of the Emerging Issues Task Force of the FASB

FAS   Statement of Financial Accounting Standards (issued by the FASB)

FIN   Interpretation of the FASB

FRR   Financial Reporting Release (issued by the SEC)

SAB   Staff Accounting Bulletin (interpretations/practices of the SEC staff)

SAS   Statement on Auditing Standards (issued by the Auditing Standards Board of the AICPA))

SOP   Statement of Position (issued by the Accounting Standards Division of the AICPA)

S-K   Regulation S-K (SEC regulations on non-financial statement disclosures)

S-X   Regulation S-X (SEC regulations governing the form, content and periods to be covered in financial statements included in registration statements and periodic reports)

TB   Technical bulletins (issued by the staff of the FASB)

Q&A   A special report issued by FASB staff addressing questions on implementing a particular standard.

AUTHORITATIVE LITERATURE

UK

The content of this book takes into account all the implications of the Companies Act 1989 and all the SSAPs and Exposure Drafts issued by the ASC before it handed over its responsibilities to the ASB on August 1, 1990. It covers all authoritative literature and company law extant at August 31, 1990, up to and including the following:

- SSAP 25 and ED 55.

- The Companies Act 1985, as amended by the Companies Act 1989.

US

This book takes into account authoritative literature published up to and including:

- FAS 105 and CON No. 6.

- FIN 38 and TB 88-2.

- SAB 88 and FRR 36.

- SOP 90-5.

INTRODUCTION

1.1 SCOPE OF THIS BOOK

This book compares financial accounting practices in the UK and the US. The comparison is based primarily, for the UK, on the accounting principles established by the Accounting Standards Committee and the requirements of the Companies Act 1985 and the International Stock Exchange and, for the US, on the SEC's rules and regulations and US generally accepted accounting principles (US GAAP); it excludes the special accounting practices that apply in certain industries (e.g. banking, insurance, oil and gas etc.) and is not intended to be a guide to all the requirements of the SEC that apply to UK companies which are registered with the SEC.

Chapter 2 deals with the development of accounting standards in the UK, discusses the concept of true and fair and the statutory accounting and disclosure requirements and offers a definition of UK generally accepted accounting practice.

Chapter 3 deals with the background to financial reporting in the US, discusses the influence of the SEC on the standard-setting process and the development of accounting standards in the US, and provides an explanation of the sources of US accounting principles.

Chapter 4 comprises a description of the principal differences between UK generally accepted accounting practice and US GAAP in so far as a general commercial enterprise is concerned.

Chapter 5 comprises a detailed side-by-side comparison between UK accounting and disclosure requirements (on the left hand pages) and US GAAP, including certain SEC requirements (on the right hand pages). The chapter illustrates in considerable detail, the rules in force in the UK and in the US for most of the usual balance sheet and profit and loss account items and other frequently encountered accounting topics.

1.2 SETTING THE SCENE IN THE UK

The Companies Act 1985 (CA 85) regulates the constitution and conduct of nearly all British business corporations (i.e. limited liability and unlimited companies). Unincorporated entities, such as partnerships, are not subject to the CA 85. This important legislation represents almost one hundred and fifty years of continuous development of British company law and its provisions are extensive, covering, inter alia, company formation, company administration and procedure, the allotment of shares and debentures, the increase, maintenance and reduction of share capital, accounts and audit and the distribution of profits and assets. Its development has been largely influenced by the Government, the courts, changes in the structure and operation of the markets for companies' securities and, more recently, membership of the European Community (EC). There have been several major legislative changes introduced over the years, the most recent being actuated by the need to introduce into British legislation the series of EC Directives for the harmonisation of Community company law. The most significant directives in the area of corporate financial reporting are the Fourth and Seventh. The principal objective of the Fourth Directive was to achieve harmonisation in respect of formats of financial statements, valuation rules and note disclosure, whilst the Seventh established a requirement for EC parent companies to prepare consolidated accounts on a common basis.

The CA 85 requires all limited companies to prepare annual financial statements which give a 'true and fair view' of the state of the company's affairs and profit or loss for the year. Where a company has one or more subsidiary undertakings at the balance sheet date, a similar requirement also applies to its consolidated accounts, unless the company is exempt from the requirement to prepare consolidated accounts. The term 'true and fair' is not defined but can perhaps be paraphrased as requiring that the accounts be factually correct in all material respects and fairly presented in accordance with generally accepted accounting practice in the UK, which embraces both proper accounting measurement as well as adequacy of disclosure.

Annual financial statements (individual company as well as consolidated financial statements) must be audited in accordance with UK auditing standards and filed with the Registrar of Companies, where they are available for public inspection. Certain concessions are available in the case of small and medium-sized companies (as defined in the CA 85 — a public company is specifically excluded from being a small or medium-sized company) regarding the content of financial statements filed with the Registrar. The Registrar does not perform a quality control function but is intended to serve as a depository. Companies are also required to file an annual return with the Registrar. The disclosures to be given in this return are prescribed by the CA 85 and include disclosures about the company's principal business activities, details of its share capital, a list of shareholders and certain particulars of the directors and company secretary.

Limited companies may be either public (designated as public limited company or 'p.l.c.') or private. One of the important legal differences between public and private companies is that a public company can offer its securities to the public directly or indirectly whereas a private company cannot. Public companies whose securities are traded on The International Stock Exchange of the United Kingdom and the Republic of Ireland Limited (the London Stock Exchange or

ISE) or traded on its Unlisted Securities Market (the USM is the ISE's market for smaller companies) have to comply with stringent rules as to the content of prospectuses, issue and quotation procedures and the conduct of their affairs. Whilst the ISE's requirements for obtaining and maintaining a listing or quotation for a company's securities are embodied in legislation, there are a number of supplementary requirements and obligations of listed and USM companies which are imposed only by the ISE's own rules.

Listed companies and also those whose securities are traded on the Unlisted Securities Market must comply with some additional disclosure requirements, as outlined in the ISE booklets 'Admission of Securities to Listing' (known as the Yellow Book) and 'Unlisted Securities Market' (known as the Green Book). These include both supplementary disclosures in their annual statutory financial statements and also separate statements/circulars to shareholders on various other matters of financial significance, such as the effects of major acquisitions and disposals. They are also required to issue an unaudited statement of their results for the first six months of the financial year and to make a preliminary announcement of their results for the full year in advance of the publication of their final accounts.

Foreign companies seeking a listing in the UK are subject to the specific requirements for such companies contained in Section 8 of the Yellow Book. Companies subject to the filing requirements of the US Securities and Exchange Commission (SEC) may be able, following consultation with the ISE, to incorporate in their prospectus documents published in connection with their SEC filing.

1.3 SETTING THE SCENE IN THE US

Unlike the position in the UK, there is no federal company law in the US. Companies are subject to the corporation law of their state of incorporation. The scope of the company laws of each of the US states is generally limited to matters of corporate governance; financial reporting is rarely covered except in general terms. Most state company laws do not require the audit and publication of annual financial statements. However, many of the state securities laws (the so-called 'blue-sky laws') do contain various financial reporting requirements. Except for those companies whose securities have been publicly offered or sold in the US and those subject to regulation at federal or state level due to the industry in which they operate (e.g. banking, insurance, utility companies), the only audit requirement often stems from bank lending agreements or from other financing agreements. Virtually none of the federal, state and local taxing authorities use general purpose US GAAP financial statements for tax assessment or reporting purposes.

Companies whose securities are sold publicly in the US are subject to extensive regulation, usually at both federal and state level. The SEC, an independent agency of the federal government, is the body charged with enforcing and administering the federal securities laws subject to the oversight of Congress. Virtually all of the states also have Securities Commissions regulating securities transactions within their jurisdictions. Nevertheless, securities transactions involving interstate commerce would, in the absence of a statutory exemption, be subject to SEC regulation.

Before a security (which is extremely broadly defined in the US) can be offered in a public interstate transaction by a non-exempted issuer, it must be registered with the SEC pursuant to the Securities Act of 1933, as amended. This Act exempts, inter alia, US banks and insurance companies regulated by other federal and/or state agencies, from its registration requirements. More recently, the SEC issued Rule 144A under the 1933 Act which will allow offers of unlisted securities to qualified institutional investors without SEC registration or regulation. The Securities Exchange Act of 1934 separately requires registration with the SEC of securities before they can be listed for trading on a US stock exchange, specifies the subsequent annual and interim reporting obligations of a registrant and governs proxy solicitations in respect of shareholder meetings as well as tender and other offers to purchase.

Since the early 1980s, the 1933 and 1934 Acts have been administered under an integrated approach. Essentially this means that the disclosures required under each Act have, wherever practicable, been conformed — with the result that a registrant under the 1934 Act can use its reports under that Act to fulfil its disclosures under the 1933 Act if a transaction subject to registration under the 1933 Act is contemplated. For larger companies who have filed timeously under the 1934 Act, who have been registrants for some time and who are not in default under the terms of any outstanding debt or preferred stock, a highly abbreviated 1933 Act registration statement can be used. Such 'short-form' registration statements, often in the form of 'shelf-registrations', incorporate by reference all reports filed under the 1934 Act and as a result can be extremely brief.

While the integrated disclosure system has simplified and streamlined the registration process, the specific disclosure requirements, for both registration statements and periodic disclosure reports, are nevertheless significantly more extensive and detailed than the requirements in most other countries. The principal rules and regulations governing disclosure in such filings are Regulation S-X, which deals with the form and content of financial statements and periods to be covered thereby and Regulation S-K, which deals with the non-financial statement disclosures. Where SEC rules require audited financial statements to be filed, the audit must be generally conducted in accordance with US generally accepted auditing standards. In practice, the SEC will not accept a filing containing an audit qualification due to a departure from GAAP or to management imposed scope limitations.

The main reporting obligation under the 1934 Act is an annual report (on Form 10-K) due within 90 days of the year end which must, amongst many other matters, include audited financial statements and applicable supplementary analytical financial statement schedules for the three most recent financial years. The other main 1934 Act reports are the quarterly report (on Form 10-Q) due in respect of the first three quarters of each financial year within 45 days of the quarter-end, and the current events report (on Form 8-K) due in respect of any material events to which the registrant is a party (for example, the material acquisition or disposition of assets or businesses) usually within 15 days of the event reported. In most cases, there is no difference between the financial statement requirements under the 1933 and 1934 Acts.

Eligible non-US companies (meeting the definition of a 'foreign private issuer') similarly must register with the SEC if they wish to enter the US public equity and debt capital markets. Such non-US companies are required to provide a broadly similar level of information to that provided by US companies in their SEC registration statements and periodic reports (their annual reports are filed on Form 20-F, which is due 180 days after the year end) but certain reliefs from the domestic SEC regime are available:

- the consolidated financial statements can be in accordance with the registrant's home-country accounting practices provided that, in the case of most 1933 Act registrations, all the disclosures required by US GAAP are added and provided that reconciliations of reported net income and shareholders' equity to their approximate amounts had US GAAP been applied are presented.

- when a 1934 Act registration is planned and in the case of 1934 Act reporting, certain reliefs from the full gamut of US GAAP disclosure are permitted — though no relief from the reconciliations to US GAAP is available.

Other reliefs available to such non-US companies include exemption from the SEC's proxy rules, the ability to provide half-yearly interim financial

5

information in only as much detail as their various stock exchange listing agreements specify (except in the case of most 1933 Act registrations) and the need to present aggregate data only for their directors'/executive officers' remuneration (as compared to the detailed data for the five highest paid directors/executive officers required to be disclosed by a US company in its proxy materials).

THE DEVELOPMENT OF UK GAAP

2.1 THE DEVELOPMENT OF ACCOUNTING STANDARDS

Prior to 1970, there were no mandatory requirements in the UK outside company law governing the presentation of financial statements of companies; and even those company law provisions which did exist comprised only the basic minimum, which was inadequate for the purpose of achieving a satisfactory standard of financial reporting. Consequently, accounting practices were varied, inconsistent and sometimes inappropriate; inter-firm and inter-period comparisons were difficult as companies altered accounting treatments and resorted to such practices as 'window-dressing' and 'reserve accounting' to achieve desired results in order to present a picture of profitability and growth. Certain professional accounting bodies such as the Institute of Chartered Accountants in England and Wales (ICAEW) had issued a series of recommendations on accounting principles — but these recommendations were not mandatory.

2.1.1 The ASC

By 1969 it had become apparent that the basic accounting requirements contained in company law needed the support of more authoritative pronouncements than the recommendations that were being issued. Consequently, the Council of the ICAEW set up the Accounting Standards Steering Committee in 1970 with the object of developing definitive standards for financial reporting. The Institute of Chartered Accountants of Scotland and the Institute of Chartered Accountants in Ireland became co-sponsors of the Committee almost immediately afterwards; the Chartered Association of Certified Accountants and the Chartered Institute of Management Accountants joined subsequently in 1971 and the Chartered Institute of Public Finance and Accountancy in 1976. With effect from February 1, 1976, the Committee became the Accounting Standards Committee (ASC) and was reconstituted as a joint committee of these six accountancy bodies who now comprise the Consultative Committee of Accountancy Bodies (CCAB).

The ASC essentially comprised a voluntary part-time committee of 21 voting members from the accounting profession and private and public industry and commerce. The ASC formed working parties to develop accounting standards and adopted a structured approach to standard setting. This included consultation with representatives of commerce, industry and government, as well as others concerned with financial reporting (e.g. the London Stock Exchange). Exposure drafts of future accounting standards were issued for comment as part of its standard-setting process.

By July 31, 1990 the ASC had developed 25 Statements of Standard Accounting Standards (SSAPs), 3 of which had been withdrawn and nine of which had been revised, and a total of 55 exposure drafts (EDs). SSAPs, which were issued upon approval by all six CCAB member bodies, deal only with matters of major and fundamental importance that affect most UK companies. Another kind of pronouncement, a Statement of Recommended Practice (SORP) was issued where there was a need for guidance on a specific topic that did not meet the criteria for a SSAP. Although companies are encouraged to comply with SORPs, compliance is (unlike SSAPs) not mandatory. A specific type of SORP known as a 'franked SORP' was issued where the topic was of limited application (e.g. dealing with a specific industry). Franked SORPs were developed by working parties drawn mainly from the industry concerned, but their work was reviewed by the ASC before publication. At July 31, 1990 the ASC had issued 2 SORPs and franked 15 other statements that had been developed by specific industry bodies (7 of which have been superseded). A list of the SSAPs and SORPs extant at August 31, 1990 and also of the EDs in issue which had not yet been converted into SSAPs is provided in Appendix A.

2.1.2 *The need for a review of the standard-setting process*

As the complexities of accounting issues and requirements for more sophisticated levels of financial reporting mounted, the increased demands placed on the ASC clearly indicated that it was unable to satisfactorily fulfil the standard setting role that it was expected to perform. The ASC had to endure mounting criticism for being unable either to respond quickly to changing needs or to deal adequately with fundamental issues such as inflation accounting, off-balance sheet transactions and goodwill. As companies are required to report in a fast-moving and increasingly complex environment, it was becoming apparent that the existing standard-setting process was no longer appropriate.

Consequently, in November 1987 the CCAB appointed a Review Committee under the chairmanship of Sir Ronald Dearing, to review and make recommendations on the standard-setting process. The Committee proposed, inter alia, a three tier framework under which accounting standards would be issued by an independent accounting standards board, overseen and advised by a separate financial reporting council, and enforced by a review panel.

2.1.3 *The implementation of the Dearing proposals*

The recommendations of the Dearing Committee were greeted favourably and they have now been substantially implemented.

Financial Reporting Council

A Financial Reporting Council (FRC) has been established under the chairmanship of Sir Ronald Dearing himself, covering at high level a wide constituency of interests. The objectives of the Council are to guide the standard-setting body on work programmes and issues of public concern; to see that the work on accounting standards is properly financed; and to act as a powerful proactive public influence for securing good accounting practice.

The Council is expected to meet three to four times a year, and has approximately 20 members. The membership comprises an even mix of accountants (some in practice, as well as some from industry, commerce and the public sector) and others drawn from all other relevant areas of interest. The UK and Irish Governments have nominated members or observers.

Accounting Standards Board

On August 1, 1990 the Accounting Standards Board (ASB) succeeded the ASC. The ASB has a full-time Chairman and Technical Director and its total membership cannot exceed nine. The ASB is able to issue accounting standards on its own authority, instead of requiring the approval of the Councils of all the six accountancy bodies which make up the CCAB (see 2.1.1 above). A majority of two-thirds is required for the approval of an accounting standard.

The accounting standards developed by the ASC prior to its disbandment have been adopted by the ASB and it is widely expected that most of the unfinished projects of the ASC (namely the EDs that were issued by the ASC prior to its disbandment) will also be assumed by the ASB.

Review Panel

A Review Panel has been established, with the objective of achieving 'good financial reporting', to examine any identified or alleged material departures from accounting standards. The findings of the Review Panel will stipulate what revisions to the financial statements or what additional information it considered should be made available to users to provide an acceptable set of financial statements giving a true and fair view.

Two of the more significant changes to company law which were recommended by the Dearing Committee were recently introduced into the CA 85 (by the Companies Act 1989). In particular:

(a)   the financial statements of large companies will have to state whether they have been prepared in accordance with applicable accounting standards and give details of, and the reasons for, any material departures. Small and medium-sized companies (as defined in the CA 85) are exempt from this disclosure requirement; and

(b)   the Dearing Committee recommendation that the Secretary of State or other authorised persons (possible candidates include the FRC and the Stock Exchange) should be able to apply to the court for an order requiring the revision of defective financial statements has been implemented in the CA 85. The CA 85 also seeks to enable financial statements to be revised without the necessity for court action, by providing procedures both for the voluntary revision of financial statements and for the Secretary of State to notify directors of apparent defects in financial statements, thus giving them the opportunity to revise the financial statements or explain why they believe no revision is required.

2.2 THE ROLE OF THE COMPANIES ACT 1985

The directors of every UK registered company (the CA 85 applies to limited liability companies — private or public, as well as to unlimited companies) have a duty to prepare annual financial statements. A directors' report must also be prepared. The financial statements comprise a balance sheet and profit and loss account (including notes), together with consolidated financial statements (if applicable). They should also contain a statement of source and application of funds unless turnover or gross income is less than £25,000. In the case of active companies, the financial statements must be audited and an auditors' report prepared.

2.2.1 The true and fair concept

While the CA 85 contains detailed requirements that apply to the preparation of financial statements (see below), there is an overriding requirement that the balance sheet must give a true and fair view of the state of affairs of the company and that the profit and loss account must give a true and fair view of the company's profit or loss. Similar requirements exist for consolidated financial statements. This 'true and fair' test overrides any more particular requirements in the Act. However, any departure from such a requirement on true and fair grounds should be a rare occurrence and must be explained in a note to the financial statements.

The meaning of true and fair

The true and fair requirement was first introduced in British legislation over forty years ago. Because it is a legal concept, the definitive explanation of what constitutes a true and fair view will be that laid down by the courts. However, there is an absence of definitive court pronouncements on the subject.

Clearly, it is legitimate to presume that the courts would, almost as a prerequisite, expect compliance with the accounting and disclosure requirements of the CA 85 when assessing whether or not a set of accounts gives a true and fair view. However the fact that, depending upon the circumstances, those rules must be departed from or supplemented (using the true and fair override) indicates that the system of statutory rules set out in CA 85 for giving effect to the true and fair concept is incomplete.

Accounting standards developed by the ASC serve as authoritative statements on accounting practice which members of the professional bodies which make up the CCAB are required to adhere to. One question which therefore arises is what is the legal relationship between accounting standards and the true and fair concept? As indicated in its Explanatory Foreword to accounting standards, the ASC regarded its standards as authoritative pronouncements on what is true and fair. Moreover, legal opinion and case law to date indicate that it appears highly probable that they will have a very persuasive effect in the courts' interpretation as to whether or not a company's financial statements present a true and fair view. This status will have been further reinforced by the new statutory requirement (described at 2.1.3 above) that any departures from accounting standards be explained in the financial statements.

However rigid adherence to the SSAPs alone may not be enough. The ASC adopted a broad fundamental approach to standard-setting and thus, almost inevitably, there will be areas of accounting which require a considerable measure of judgment to be exercised in the application of the rules established or that are simply not addressed in the SSAPs. As the Explanatory Foreword explains, SSAPs '... are not intended to be a comprehensive code of rigid rules. They do not supersede the exercise of an informed judgment in determining what constitutes a true and fair view in each circumstance. ..... A justifiable reason may therefore exist why an accounting standard may not be applicable in a given situation, namely when the application would conflict with the giving of a true and fair view. In such cases, modified or alternative treatments will require to be adopted.'

The purpose of the true and fair view requirement (which is also embodied in the EC Fourth Directive) is to establish a standard of financial reporting for the protection of the interests of the members of companies and third parties. In determining the standard of reporting that is implicitly demanded because of the true and fair requirement, the courts are likely to consider the accounting and disclosure requirements of the CA 85, the SSAPs, other authoritative statements and refer to generally accepted accounting practice existing at the time as persuasive points of reference. The concept of true and fair is a nebulous one which is not static but changes in the light of the current thinking of the accounting profession at any particular time and as a result, it is not possible to translate the concept into a rigid framework or system of rules.

2.2.2 Statutory disclosure requirements

The CA 85 contains fairly extensive disclosure requirements, which in part reflect the requirements of the EC's Fourth and Seventh Directives on company law. Precise rules specify the format of consolidated and individual company financial statements (i.e. both the accounts headings which must be included and the order in which they must appear). Companies may choose from four profit and loss account formats and two balance sheet formats. However, once a format has been adopted it should be used in all subsequent years unless there is a special reason for a change, which must be explained in a note to the financial statements. Companies have discretion to provide more analysis than is required, but not less. The legislation requires corresponding amounts for the immediately preceding financial year to be shown and prohibits the set-off of asset items and liability items in the balance sheet and income and expenditure items in the profit and loss account.

Considerably more information than is set out in the balance sheet and the profit and loss account must be provided by way of notes to the financial statements. This includes disclosure of the accounting policies adopted in the preparation of the financial statements, information supplementing the balance sheet and profit and loss account, information concerning certain undertakings that are related to the reporting entity and particulars of directors' emoluments, compensation for loss of office, loans and other transactions.

Banking and insurance companies are not subject to all the general rules regarding the form and content of their financial statements. Certain exemptions apply to these companies, which are allowed to prepare their financial statements in accordance with special rules that are contained in the legislation. These rules are not addressed any further because accounting practices applicable to such specialist companies are beyond the scope of this book.

2.2.3 Accounting principles and rules

Basic principles

The CA 85 specifies certain accounting principles which a company must follow in the preparation of its financial statements. These are :

- the company should be presumed to be a going concern;

- accounting policies should be applied consistently from year to year;

- the amount of any item should be determined on a prudent basis and, in particular, only profits realised at the balance sheet date should be included in the profit and loss account and all liabilities and losses which have arisen or are likely to arise in respect of the financial year to which the financial statements relate should be accrued;

• the financial statements should be prepared on an accruals basis;

• in determining the aggregate amount of any item, the amount of each individual asset and liability should be determined separately.

The directors may depart from any of these accounting principles if there are special reasons for so doing and the financial statements give a true and fair view. In the event of any departure from these principles, particulars of the departure, the reasons for it, and its effect must be given in a note to the financial statements.

The legislation defines realised profits (and realised losses) by reference to 'principles generally accepted', which is clearly a wider concept than one based solely on accounting standards. The term 'principles generally accepted' is not defined in the CA 85 and in the light of this, the CCAB issued guidance stating that profits which are required by SSAPs to be recognised in the profit and loss account should normally be treated as realised unless the SSAP specifically indicates otherwise. The guidance also permits recognition of profits in the profit and loss account in circumstances that are not the subject of a SSAP or exceptionally in accordance with a policy which is contrary to a SSAP provided that the policy adopted is consistent with the above accounting principles.

Asset valuation rules
The CA 85 contains rules determining the amount at which items included in the financial statements should be stated. There are two sets of rules — the historical accounting rules (which are based, not surprisingly, on the historical cost convention) and the alternative accounting rules which permit the inclusion of certain assets in the financial statements at a revaluation or on a current cost basis. These two sets of rules, which address the accounting treatment of various categories of fixed and current assets, are not mutually exclusive — selective revaluations of assets under the alternative accounting rules are permitted. The rules contained in the legislation deal, inter alia, with such matters as determining the cost of assets, accounting for revaluation surpluses, depreciation and provisions for diminutions in value of fixed assets.

Consolidated financial statements and business combinations
The legislation requires group financial statements to be in consolidated form and contains rules on the preparation of consolidated financial statements as well as certain disclosure requirements. Definitions of subsidiary undertakings

(which with a few exceptions have to be consolidated) and associated undertakings (which should be equity accounted) are provided in the CA 85. The CA 85 imposes conditions on the use of merger accounting and provides a description of what the acquisition and merger methods of accounting for business combinations entail. Specific disclosures are required to be made in respect of acquisitions and disposals of subsidiary undertakings.

Miscellaneous provisions

The Companies Act rules significantly affect a number of other areas of accounting including, inter alia, accounting for the purchase or redemption of a company's own shares and permitting certain costs to be written off against the share premium account (i.e. excess of paid in capital over par value).

2.3 WHAT IS UK GAAP?

2.3.1 *'Principles' or 'practice'?*

In the UK, the expression 'GAAP' is used far more loosely than in most other countries; the reason for this is that GAAP does not have any statutory or regulatory authority or definition, as is the case in the US. Consequently, references to GAAP are rarely found in the literature in the UK, and where the expression is used, it is done without adequate explanation or definition.

GAAP is a dynamic concept which requires constant review, adaptation and reaction to changing circumstances. The use of the term 'principle' gives GAAP an unjustified and inappropriate degree of permanence. GAAP changes in response to changing business and economic needs and developments. As circumstances alter, accounting practices are modified or developed accordingly. This is recognised in the Explanatory Foreword to the SSAPs which states that accounting standards 'are not intended to be a comprehensive code of rigid rules'. Accordingly, the boundaries of UK GAAP extend far beyond the accounting principles contained in the SSAPs; it includes the requirements of the Companies Act and of the London Stock Exchange, as well as any other acceptable accounting treatments not incorporated in the official literature.

2.3.2 What is 'generally accepted'?

It is often argued that the term 'generally accepted' implies that there must exist a high degree of practical application of a particular accounting practice. However, this interpretation raises certain practical difficulties. For example, what about new areas of accounting which have not, as yet, been generally applied? What about different accounting treatments for similar items — are they all generally accepted?

The view that 'generally accepted' does *not* mean 'generally adopted or used' is widely held. In the UK context, GAAP refers to accounting practices which are regarded as permissible by the accounting profession. The extent to which a particular practice has been adopted is not the overriding consideration. Any accounting practice which is legitimate in the circumstances under which it has been applied should be regarded as GAAP. The decision as to whether or not a particular practice is permissible or legitimate would depend on one or more of the following factors:

(a) Is the practice consistent with the needs of users and the objectives of financial reporting?

(b) Is the practice addressed either in the accounting standards, statute or other official pronouncements?

(c) If the practice is not addressed in UK accounting standards, is it dealt with in International Accounting Standards, or the standards of other countries such as the US?

(d) Does the practice have authoritative support in the accounting literature?

(e) Is the practice being applied by other companies in similar situations?

(f) Is the practice consistent with the fundamental concept of 'true and fair'?

THE DEVELOPMENT OF US GAAP

3.1 BACKGROUND TO PUBLIC FINANCIAL REPORTING

Before the 1930s, there were no authoritative or enforceable US standards governing corporate financial reports. Because of the lack of any statutory underpinning, the accounting profession had no authority to establish ground rules which corporations had to follow in their financial statements. However, the abuses in stock exchange practices, financing of securities and corporate reporting which were revealed after the 1929 stock market crash led Congress to enact the Securities Act of 1933, the Securities Exchange Act of 1934, and several other securities laws.

Under this legislation, among numerous other requirements, companies offering new issues of securities for inter-state sale, other than for certain exempted issuers and certain exempted securities, and all companies whose securities are traded publicly, must register and file periodic reports with the Securities and Exchange Commission (SEC). These laws, taken together, emphasise full disclosure by issuers of securities and others acting in the US securities markets and are intended to provide investors with information about the issuer of a security as well as the terms of the security being offered, so that informed decisions on the investment merits of securities can be made and to ensure that fair trading practices prevail in the primary and secondary markets. The SEC, though given wide power to require that full disclosures are made, was not empowered to pass judgment on the quality or merit of an investment.

3.2 THE SEC

The SEC was created under the 1934 Act to enforce and administer the federal securities laws subject to the oversight of Congress. Securities sold, exchanged or traded solely in intrastate transactions are subject to the separate securities laws of the state concerned, but not ordinarily to the federal securities laws. The SEC is composed of five commissioners, one of whom serves as the chairman. Each commissioner is nominated by the President for a five-year term (the persons nominated must be confirmed by Congress in open proceedings). The chairman and no more than two of the other commissioners can be from the same political party as the President. It has a staff of lawyers, accountants, engineers and financial analysts and employs under 3,000 persons. Despite its relatively small size (by US federal standards) the SEC has earned a reputation as one of the most ably administered federal regulatory agencies. Its small size has been achieved, in part, through transferring the burden of monitoring compliance with its regulations to securities issuers and their professional advisers, through severe legal penalties backed up by vigorous enforcement activities, and through various discretionary powers — principally the sole right to 'accelerate' the effective date of a registration statement — granted by Congress. Though many other federal regulatory agencies are involved in various aspects of financial reporting, particularly in the financial services sector of the US economy, none has the pervasive influence of the SEC.

3.2.1 The influence of the SEC

The SEC was given statutory power to set US generally accepted accounting principles (US GAAP) for companies subject to the federal securities laws; however, with limited exceptions, it has allowed the private sector (e.g. at present the Financial Accounting Standards Board (FASB)) to establish financial accounting standards and has viewed generally accepted accounting principles as those which have 'substantial authoritative support'. This term was first introduced in the SEC's Accounting Series Release (ASR) No. 4, which was issued in 1938 and stated that 'in cases where financial statements filed with the Commission ... are prepared in accordance with accounting principles for which there is no substantial authoritative support, such financial statements will be presumed to be misleading or inaccurate despite disclosures contained in the certificate of the accountant or in footnotes to the statements provided the matters involved are material'. In 1973, the SEC updated ASR 4 to recognise the establishment of the FASB.

The separate accounting rules and regulations of the SEC have been on the whole concerned with disclosure and classification rather than with the establishment of basic measurement principles. In many areas, these rules have required accounting disclosure by registrants beyond that specified for general purpose US GAAP financial statements. The SEC has stated that disclosures required by US GAAP set a minimum standard of disclosure to which should be added such further material information as is necessary to make financial statements filed with the SEC, in the light of the circumstances under which they are prepared, not misleading. Besides audited financial statements of the issuer, the SEC rules can also necessitate the presentation of other financial statements in defined circumstances. Such other financial statements, which must also be audited, are most frequently encountered when the security offered is guaranteed by another party, when the issuer has acquired other businesses and when investees of the issuer accounted for under the equity method are significant to its consolidated financial statements.

Whilst the SEC has adopted an indirect but still active role in the development of measurement principles, it has nevertheless exerted significant direct influence on the development of measurement principles whenever it has believed that accounting principles were not being addressed by the private sector in a timely or appropriate manner. Two examples of situations where the SEC prodded the accounting standard-setting authorities are in 1973, when it required lessees to disclose the present value of their financing lease obligations and the effect of capitalising such leases on net income and in 1974, when it imposed a moratorium on interest capitalisation until the FASB could act on the issue.

The content of US financial statements is designed for the general use of investors, creditors and regulators. Accordingly, they do not include financial information not considered necessary for a fair presentation of financial position and results of operations. For the most part, the SEC's proxy and other rules cover financial data not included in the basic US GAAP financial statements and in many cases this can be quite extensive. The SEC has always considered consolidated financial statements to be more meaningful and parent company financial statements to be relatively unimportant — unless there are contractual or other restrictions on a parent's ability to receive funds by dividend, loan or otherwise from its subsidiaries. In general, US GAAP are applicable to all legal forms of an entity (e.g. partnerships, trusts, charities) and this approach is followed also by the SEC.

Financial statements are widely used, distributed and understood in the US, and the litigious US environment has resulted in numerous court cases and legal opinions regarding their content and purpose. Releases following an SEC enforcement investigation and activities of the SEC Practice Section of the American Institute of Certified Public Accountants (the AICPA) (for example, Peer Reviews and other quality control procedures), additionally support the objectives of fair and consistent financial reporting in the US. It is essential that any inconsistency in applying accounting principles or other lack of comparability between accounting periods be clearly disclosed.

3.3 THE STANDARD SETTERS IN THE US

As noted in 3.2.1 above, although the SEC is empowered to establish GAAP, it has looked to the private sector including the accounting profession to set up standard-setting institutions. The SEC however, has never delegated its responsibility to ensure that appropriate standards are developed and that appropriate financial information is provided to investors. It carefully monitors the activities and decisions of the private sector standard-setting bodies and on rare occasions has overruled the decisions made by such bodies (e.g. in 1978, the SEC overruled the FASB's choice of the successful efforts method of accounting as the only appropriate method of accounting for oil and gas producers).

Since 1939, there have been three private sector standard-setting bodies which have had the opportunity to establish accounting standards in the US; the Committee on Accounting Procedure (1939-1958), the Accounting Principles Board (1958-1973) and the Financial Accounting Standards Board (1973 to the present).

3.3.1 The Committee on Accounting Procedure

The Committee on Accounting Procedure was established by the AICPA partly in response to the creation of the SEC and the preference of the US accounting profession for the detailed accounting standard-setting process to remain a private sector activity. During its existence, the Committee on Accounting Procedure issued a series of Accounting Research Bulletins (ARBs); in 1953, the first 42 ARBs were revised and restated as a consolidated ARB No. 43 and, thereafter, a further eight ARBs were issued.

These ARBs, several of which are still operative, represent the first documented series of US generally accepted accounting principles; however, the Committee met with criticism over its failure to deal with contemporary accounting issues such as leasing and business combinations.

3.3.2 The Accounting Principles Board

As a direct response to the criticism of the Committee on Accounting Procedure, the President of the AICPA set up the Special Committee on Research Program in 1957; in 1958 the Committee recommended the formation of the Accounting Principles Board (APB), and the appointment of a director of research with a permanent research staff. The Special Committee also recommended that 'an immediate project of the accounting research staff should be a study of the basic postulates underlying accounting principles generally, and the preparation of a brief statement thereof. There should be also a study of the broad principles of accounting. ... The results of these, as adopted by the [Accounting Principles] Board, should serve as the foundation for the entire body of future pronouncements by the Institute on accounting matters, to which each new release should be related.'

The APB issued 31 Opinions between 1962 and 1973 and the majority of these statements still form part of US GAAP. For example, the basic rules on business combinations, accounting for intangible assets and accounting for investments under the equity method are contained in APB Opinions. Besides the Opinion statements, the APB also issued several Accounting Research Studies and other statements with the objective of developing a conceptual framework. Much of this work has been superseded by subsequent FASB studies but certain statements still remain extant, for example, APB Statement No. 4 — *Basic*

Concepts and Accounting Principles Underlying Financial Statements of Business Enterprises.

3.3.3 The Financial Accounting Standards Board

In 1971, in response to continued criticism of the APB due to the lack of a conceptual framework and a growing demand within the financial community for the involvement of a wider constituency of interests in the development of accounting standards, the AICPA announced the formation of two study groups better known by the names of their chairmen: the Wheat Committee and the Trueblood Committee. The Wheat Committee published its report in 1972, resulting in the establishment of the FASB in 1973 as the successor to the APB. This had the effect of taking the responsibility for setting accounting standards away from the accounting profession and placing it in the hands of an independent body in the private sector.

The FASB comprises seven members appointed by the Financial Accounting Foundation (FAF), and is funded by the sale of publications and from contributions made to the FAF. The Board of Trustees of the FAF is appointed by its six sponsoring organisations, which include, inter alia, the American Accounting Association and the AICPA. The AICPA designated the FASB as the successor to the APB in establishing accounting principles for purposes of rule 203 of the AICPA Code of Professional Conduct (see 3.5 below).

By the time the FASB came into existence, the Trueblood Committee were nearing completion of its work on the objectives of financial statements. The FASB was clearly aware that accounting standards had to regain the credibility of public opinion which had been lost as a result of the many perceived abuses of financial reporting during the 1960s. Conscious of the threat of 'unjustified government regulation' in the area of financial reporting, the FASB used the Trueblood Committee's report to embark immediately upon a conceptual framework project as the means of enhancing the credibility of financial statements in the eyes of the public. This project yielded 6 concepts statements (see 3.4 below).

Since its formation in 1973, the FASB has issued 105 accounting standards and various interpretations and technical bulletins. For a proposed accounting standard to pass, it must currently obtain the votes of four of the members; however, with effect from January 1, 1991, the votes of five of the seven members of the Board will be required. In drafting its standards, the FASB has adopted a distinctive style: they are very detailed, prescriptive and proscriptive; dissenting FASB members explain their objections; each standard includes a basis for conclusions which gives the background to the project, as well as the

FASB consideration and reasoning for the position taken, reflecting the comments of its constituents. This means that, with definitions and examples, a FASB standard can be several hundred pages in all.

3.4 THE FASB CONCEPTUAL FRAMEWORK

As discussed in 3.3.3 above, the FASB has, since its inception, been engaged in the development of a series of Statements of Financial Accounting Concepts (CONs) which are intended to establish the objectives and concepts that the FASB will use in developing standards of financial reporting. A discussion of whether the FASB has, unlike its predecessors, managed to establish a satisfactory conceptual framework is beyond the scope of this book. However, a brief description of the composition of its conceptual framework follows.

The conceptual framework was expected to:

(a) guide the body responsible for establishing standards;

(b) provide a frame of reference for resolving accounting questions in the absence of a specific promulgated standard;

(c) determine bounds for judgment in preparing financial statements;

(d) increase financial statement users' understanding of and confidence in financial statements; and

(e) enhance comparability.

To date, the FASB has issued six concepts statements, of which one (CON No. 4) deals with the objectives of financial reporting by non-business organisations, whilst another (CON No. 3) dealing with elements of financial statements by business enterprises, has been superseded by CON No. 6, which expands the scope of CON No. 3 to encompass not-for-profit organisations.

The remaining four CONs, which were issued by the FASB between November 1978 and December 1985, are :

(1) CON No. 1 — *Objectives of Financial Reporting by Business Enterprises*, which established eight objectives of financial reporting by business enterprises, all of which focus on providing information needed by current and prospective investors and creditors of a business enterprise in their decision making. Primary emphasis is placed on information regarding an enterprise's earnings.

(2) CON No. 2 — *Qualitative Characteristics of Accounting Information*, which examines the characteristics that make accounting information

useful to the users of that information. The statement views these characteristics as 'a hierarchy of accounting qualities', which then form the basis for selecting and evaluating information for inclusion in financial reports.

(3)   CON No. 5 — *Recognition and Measurement in Financial Statements of Business Enterprises,* which sets forth recognition criteria and guidance on what information should be incorporated into financial statements and when.

(4)   CON No. 6 — *Elements of Financial Statements,* which was issued as a replacement to CON No. 3, *Elements of Financial Statements of Business Enterprises,* having expanded its scope to encompass not-for-profit organisations. The statement defines ten 'elements' of financial statements that are directly related to the measurement of performance and financial status of an entity. However, the elements are very much interrelated, as six of them are arithmetically derived from the definitions of assets and liabilities.

Although these four CONs comprise the FASB's 'conceptual framework' of financial accounting and reporting and are intended to provide a sound and consistent basis for the development of financial accounting standards, they are not generally accepted accounting principles per se. Instead, they set forth fundamentals on which financial accounting and reporting are based, and state the objectives and concepts the FASB uses in developing standards of financial accounting and reporting. CONs are intended to serve the public interest within the context of the role of financial accounting and reporting in the economy. That is, they attempt to provide a coherent rationale on which standards of accounting may be developed that will result in evenhanded financial and other information which, together with information from other sources, will facilitate efficient functioning of capital and other markets and otherwise assist in promoting efficient allocation of scarce resources in the economy. APB Statement No. 4 continues to serve as the conceptual basis for those standards and practices existing prior to the issuance of these CONs.

3.5   WHAT IS US GAAP ?

US GAAP encompasses the conventions, rules, and procedures necessary to define accepted accounting practice at a particular time and includes not only broad guidelines of general application, but also detailed practices and procedures. Whilst US GAAP may be promulgated by authoritative bodies such as the SEC and those noted in 3.3, it also includes principles contained in pronouncements of bodies of recognised stature (e.g. the Accounting Standards

Division of the AICPA) as well as practices that have achieved acceptance through common usage.

3.5.1 *The sources of US accounting principles*

Extensive literature exists addressing virtually all types of business endeavour as well as non-business and state and local government activities. However the determination whether a particular accounting principle is generally accepted will sometimes involve judgment because no single reference source exists for all such principles. The present sources of established accounting principles are generally the following, in descending order of importance:

- The most authoritative accounting principles are those promulgated by a body designated by the AICPA Council to establish such principles, pursuant to Rule 203 of the AICPA Code of Professional Conduct. These officially established accounting principles include:

  - FASB Statements of Financial Accounting Standards (FASs);

  - FASB Interpretations (FASIs);

  - APB Opinions;

  - AICPA Accounting Research Bulletins (ARBs); and

  - Statements and interpretations of the Governmental Accounting Standards Board (GASB) for financial statements of state and local governmental entities.

  Rule 203 provides that an auditor should not express an unqualified opinion if the financial statements upon which he is reporting contain a material departure from such principles unless, due to unusual circumstances, adherence to the pronouncements would make the statements misleading. Additionally the SEC, in ASR No. 150, stated that principles, standards and practices issued by the FASB and its predecessors (the Committee on Accounting Procedure and the APB) are presumptively required to be applied in financial statements filed with the SEC and that financial statements applying contrary accounting principles are unacceptable in the absence of an SEC ruling to the contrary.

- When the accounting treatment of a transaction or event is not specified by a pronouncement covered under the authoritative sources noted above, accountants consider pronouncements of bodies composed of expert accountants that follow a due process procedure (which includes broad distribution of proposed accounting principles for public comment) when establishing accounting principles or describing existing practices that are generally accepted. These pronouncements include:

- AICPA Industry Audit and Accounting Guides;

- AICPA Statements of Position;

- Technical Bulletins issued by the FASB or GASB; and

- AICPA Accounting Interpretations.

Accountants also refer to practices that are widely recognised and prevalent in the industry and the SEC's Financial Reporting Releases (FRRs) and ASRs. When there is a conflict between sources, accountants consider which treatment better presents the substance of the transaction in the circumstances.

- In the absence of established accounting principles developed by authoritative bodies discussed above, accountants may consider other accounting literature, depending on its relevance in the circumstances. Other accounting literature includes, for example, APB Statements, AICPA Issues Papers, Practice Bulletins issued by the Accounting Standards Executive Committee (AcSEC) of the Accounting Standards Division of the AICPA, minutes of the FASB Emerging Issues Task Force (EITF consensuses), FASB Statements of Financial Accounting Concepts, Concepts Statements of the GASB, SEC Staff Accounting Bulletins (SABs), International Accounting Standards Committee Statements of International Accounting Standards, pronouncements of other professional associations or regulatory agencies (including SEC enforcement releases), and accounting textbooks and articles. The appropriateness of other accounting literature as a source of established accounting principles depends on its relevance to particular circumstances, the precision of the guidance, and the general recognition of the issuer or author as an authority. For example, FASB Statements of Financial Accounting Concepts would normally be more influential than accounting textbooks or articles.

On occasion, established accounting principles may not exist for recording and presenting a specific event or transaction because of developments such as new legislation or the evolution of a new type of business transaction. In certain instances, it may be possible to account for the event or transaction on the basis of its substance by selecting an accounting principle from an analogous event or transaction.

3.5.2 *Points of reference*

The sources of US GAAP are varied because of the many objectives US GAAP must achieve and the nature of the accounting issues. Following are brief descriptions of certain of the significant sources of US GAAP mentioned above.

- *SEC ASRs, FRRs, SABs and Regulation S-X.* The *Codification of Financial Reporting Policies* is a compendium of ASRs and FRRs which presents the SEC's views and interpretations relating to financial reporting. SEC staff administrative policies followed in administering the SEC's rules and regulations are communicated in SABs. Regulation S-X is the basic accounting regulation of the SEC. It prescribes rules for the form and content of financial statements included in registration statements and periodic reports. Although it contains some prescribed accounting methods, it is predominantly a document requiring disclosures in addition to those required by US GAAP.

- *FASB Statements and Interpretations* generally address accounting and reporting issues with pervasive and persistent implications. FASB statements may significantly change practice in an area. Prior to being issued, FASs are subject to extensive due process including debate of provisions of proposed statements by the FASB in a forum open to public observation, exposure of draft statements for comment by the FASB's constituents, and public hearings where constituents can present oral arguments to the FASB on the issues in the proposed statement. FASIs relate to FASs, CONs, ARBs, or APB Opinions, and are issued to clarify, explain or elaborate on one of those pronouncements as an aid to its understanding. FASIs need not be subject to due process.

- *FASB Technical Bulletins* (Bulletins) provide guidance for applying standards in ARBs, APB Opinions, and FASB Statements and Interpretations and for resolving accounting issues not directly addressed in those standards. Bulletins are generally issued when the guidance is not expected to cause a major change in accounting practice for a significant number of entities, the administrative cost involved in implementing the guidance is not expected to be significant, and the guidance does not conflict with a broad fundamental principle or create a novel new accounting practice. They are subject to public exposure and comment and public hearings by the FASB prior to issuance. A Bulletin will not be issued if a majority of FASB members object to the guidance contained in the Bulletin.

- *AICPA Industry Audit and Accounting Guides* are issued by the AICPA and generally contain descriptions of, and recommendations on, specialised industry accounting and reporting principles and practices. The descriptions and recommendations may refer to an FASB statement or interpretation, an APB opinion, or an ARB. They are subject to public exposure and comment and review by the FASB prior to issuance.

- *Statements of Position* (SOPs) are issued by AcSEC, which is the senior technical body of the AICPA authorised to speak for it in the areas of financial accounting and reporting. SOPs generally address accounting and reporting issues with broad applicability usually within specialised industries and frequently amend industry audit and accounting guides. They are subject to public exposure and comment and review by the FASB prior to issuance.

- *Practice Bulletins* are issued by AcSEC to disseminate its views on narrow financial accounting and reporting issues. The issues dealt with are those that have not been and are not being considered by the FASB or the GASB. Practice Bulletins present the views of at least two-thirds of the members of AcSEC on the issues addressed. Practice Bulletins are not subject to public exposure and comment.

- *EITF Consensuses*. The FASB established the Emerging Issues Task Force (the EITF) in July 1984 to assist the FASB in the early identification of emerging issues affecting financial reporting and of problems in implementing authoritative pronouncements. Its membership is composed of individuals who are both knowledgeable in accounting and financial reporting and are in positions to be aware of emerging problems as they develop. Issues addressed by the EITF are generally very narrow in scope. Agreement among EITF members is recognised as a consensus if no more than two of its fifteen members disagree with a position. The SEC will challenge any accounting that differs from a consensus of the EITF because the consensus position represents the best thinking on areas for which there are no specific standards.

A list of effective authoritative pronouncements of the ARBs, APB Opinions and the FASB Statements extant at August 31, 1990 is provided in Appendix B to illustrate the broad scope of topics addressed by US GAAP.

PRINCIPAL DIFFERENCES BETWEEN UK AND US GAAP

4.1 INTRODUCTION

Differences between UK and US GAAP may be broadly categorised into those arising from differences in measurement standards and those pertaining to differences in disclosure standards. In addition, however, there are also many differences between UK and US financial reporting practice. For example, the balance sheet and profit and loss account (known as the income statement in the US) formats are quite different in each country, the terminology and technical terms used are often not consistent and a number of financial statement items are classified differently.

This chapter concentrates mainly on the more commonplace measurement differences that can significantly affect a company's financial statements and covers GAAP differences that are frequently reported in SEC filings by UK companies. Other measurement and disclosure differences can be identified by referring to the side-by-side comparison in Chapter 5. Differences in industry related accounting practices adopted by specialist companies such as insurance companies, banks, other financial institutions, oil and gas companies etc. have not been addressed as they are beyond the scope of this book. The ordering of the topics dealt with below is alphabetical, and not intended to emphasise or prioritise the significance of the GAAP differences that are noted.

4.1.1 The fundamental accounting concepts

The broad basic assumptions or fundamental accounting concepts which underlie financial reporting in both countries are essentially the same. The fundamental concepts of going concern, accruals, consistency and prudence are described in some detail in the CA 85 and SSAP 2 in the UK and the conceptual statements issued by the APB and the FASB in the US. The US conceptual statements also refer to a fifth concept, that of substance over form, which although missing from SSAP 2 has been applied in the requirements relating to the capitalisation of finance leases in the financial statements of lessees under SSAP 21, and forms the basis of the approach adopted by the ASC in ED 49 in its attempt to deal with off-balance sheet finance.

In practice, the application of these fundamental concepts to business transactions gives rise to difficulties. The main difficulty arises from the fact that many business transactions have financial effects spreading over a number of years. Accounting for such transactions requires consideration of future events of uncertain financial effect and ultimately a judgment between the matching concept and the prudence concept. The development of accounting standards in both the UK and the US is often a tug-of-war between these two concepts. Not surprisingly, the attitudes of the accounting standard setting bodies in both countries have not always coincided and, consequently, differences in emphasis in the application of the accounting concepts has given rise to significant differences in generally accepted accounting principles in the two countries.

4.2 BUSINESS COMBINATIONS

4.2.1 Merger/Pooling-of-interests accounting

Whilst the techniques of accounting for a merger (or pooling-of-interests accounting in US terminology) are similar in both countries, the circumstances under which such accounting is permitted are substantially different.

UK approach

At present, the underlying principle for when merger accounting can be adopted in the UK is that a business combination occurs involving a substantial exchange of equity shares (as defined) and no significant resources leave the combining entities as a result of the combination. SSAP 23 — *Accounting for acquisitions and mergers* and the Companies Act contain detailed criteria for permitting a business combination to be treated as a merger. However, even if all these conditions are met, the combination does not have to be accounted for as a merger; there is a choice of using either merger or acquisition accounting when the criteria are met.

The UK criteria for merger accounting depend very much on the form of the transaction being undertaken and it is quite possible to vary the form in order to bring a transaction within these rules. The focus is on the combining companies and not on their owners. For example, a frequent practice has been the use of 'vendor rights' or 'vendor placings' as a means of coming within the merger criteria although still offering cash to the vendors. This involves offering shares to the vendor in exchange for his shares in the company being acquired, but with a separate arrangement where, if the vendor would prefer to receive cash, the shares will be simultaneously placed (immediately before closing or shortly after) either with the acquirer's own shareholders (vendor rights) or with third parties (vendor placings) and the proceeds passed on to the vendors.

The UK approach to merger accounting is presently under fundamental review and an exposure draft (ED 48) was published by the ASC before its disbandment. The ED revises the definition of a merger and intends to restrict the use of merger accounting to rare situations. The new conditions are based on the criteria laid down in Canadian GAAP. Although the conditions are closer in some respects to the conditions that have to be satisfied for the use of pooling accounting in the US, significant differences in the conditions still remain. Under the ED, merger accounting would no longer be optional when the conditions were met. The content of the ED's proposals is discussed further in Chapter 5, section 2.

US approach

The US standard on pooling of interest accounting also requires that the combination is effected through an exchange of ordinary shares (with substantially the same rights and privileges as the shares already outstanding) but is based on the concept of continuation of shareholder groups for mutual risks and rewards; arrangements that favour in any way one group of shareholders (or individual shareholders) as compared to others will negate the ability to apply pooling of interests accounting. This basic idea is supported by a series of very detailed rules that are designed to prevent abuses.

In contrast to the flexibility available in the UK, the purchase method (or acquisition accounting in UK terminology) and pooling of interests accounting are not alternatives for the same business combination. If the criteria set have been satisfied, then the combination must be accounted for as a pooling. The SEC rigorously apply the pooling of interests rules and its staff have issued a number of SABs on the subject. It would be a mere coincidence if a UK merger qualifies as a pooling of interests under the US rules though US poolings would invariably qualify as mergers under the UK rules.

4.2.2 Acquisition accounting/the purchase method
The fair value exercise

The basic principles governing acquisition accounting in the UK and the purchase method in the US are broadly similar. The requirement to base the cost of an acquisition on the fair value of the purchase consideration and its allocation among the identifiable assets of the subsidiary for consolidation purposes has been established in UK GAAP for many years; nevertheless there is hardly any authoritative guidance which explains in detail how fair values are to be allocated in an acquisition. As a result, certain practices have developed in a number of areas of fair value accounting which are at variance with US GAAP. These include, inter alia:

- Provisions for reorganisation costs and future trading losses — in practice, companies make provisions for reorganisation costs and also expected trading losses as part of the fair value exercise. Such provisions are usually made irrespective of whether the costs/expenditure will be incurred by the acquired company or the acquiring company.

- Fair value allocation period — there is no set limit on the period of hindsight that the acquirer has by which to complete and finalise the allocation of fair values. In the US, the allocation period available should normally not extend beyond one year from the acquisition date.

- Intangible assets — under US GAAP, there is a requirement to allocate part of the acquisition cost to specifically identifiable intangible assets; no amounts should be allocated to intangible assets that lack specific identification (i.e. that are not distinguishable from goodwill). Concerned by the small net asset totals or negative net assets figures often disclosed in their financial statements as a result of writing off goodwill against shareholders' equity, a number of UK companies have sought to distinguish various forms of intangible assets, such as brand names, publishing titles, or copyright interests from goodwill. In certain cases, the intangible assets recognised during the fair value exercise are not readily distinguishable from goodwill. Moreover, unlike the position in the US (where there is a specific standard on accounting for intangible assets which requires amortisation over their useful life not exceeding 40 years), several UK companies do not charge any amortisation on certain intangible assets on the grounds that they have an infinite economic life.

- Contingent consideration — unlike the position in the US, most UK companies simply disclose their liabilities for contingent consideration rather than providing for the probable amount payable.

In July 1990, the ASC published an exposure draft ED 53 — *Fair value in the context of acquisition accounting*. In general, the ED's proposals will bring practice in the UK much more in line with US practice if converted to a SSAP in its current form. The ASC has also published another exposure draft, ED 52 — *Accounting for intangible assets*. Its proposals contain recognition criteria for intangible assets and proposes that intangible assets recorded in the balance sheet should be amortised over their useful economic life. This should not usually exceed 20 years but a longer life of up to a maximum of 40 years is permitted in exceptional circumstances. As these amortisation rules are the same as those proposed for goodwill in ED 47 — *Accounting for goodwill* (see below), it is hoped that the current incentive to distinguish other intangibles from goodwill will disappear.

Accounting for goodwill

The present UK standard on goodwill, SSAP 22 — *Accounting for Goodwill*, allows two alternative methods of accounting for goodwill. The preferable treatment is immediate write-off to reserves on acquisition. Alternatively, the standard permits capitalisation and amortisation through the profit and loss account on a systematic basis over its estimated useful economic life. The standard does not require that the same choice of accounting policy be applied to different acquisitions.

Most UK companies have chosen to write goodwill off immediately against equity rather than bear future amortisation charges in the profit and loss account. Not surprisingly, this policy will depress net assets in comparison to the amounts that would have otherwise been reported under the amortisation route; in some cases, major acquisitions have led to negative net worth figures being disclosed in the acquirers' consolidated accounts.

Under US GAAP, intangibles including goodwill should be amortised on a straight line basis over their estimated useful life not exceeding 40 years; a period of 40 years should be used if the useful life is greater than 40 years.

The ASC recently issued ED 47 — *Accounting for goodwill* which would revise the existing standard on goodwill. ED 47's proposed changes would require UK companies to capitalise goodwill and amortise the balance through the profit and loss account over its useful economic life. This should not exceed 20 years except in rare circumstances, when a life of up to 40 years may be used.

Accounting for negative goodwill
SSAP 22 requires that negative goodwill should be credited directly to reserves. Under US GAAP, negative goodwill should be allocated to reduce proportionately the values assigned to non-current assets (other than marketable investments) in determining their fair values. Any remainder should be classified as a deferred credit and amortised to income over the period estimated to be benefited but not in excess of 40 years.

ED 47 proposes an amortisation treatment for negative goodwill, equivalent to that proposed for goodwill, that is that it should be amortised as a credit to the profit and loss account.

4.2.3 *Comment*
Substantial differences exist between current UK and US accounting practice in the area of accounting for business combinations; for example, merger accounting, acquisition or purchase accounting (i.e. the treatment of goodwill, the fair value exercise etc.), accounting for reverse acquisitions, common control transactions, leveraged buyout transactions. Whilst there are specific rules on each of these areas under US GAAP, the UK standards primarily focus on accounting for mergers and acquisition accounting (M&A accounting). This book concentrates on M&A accounting primarily because mergers and acquisitions are the more common forms of business combinations in practice

and often give rise to dramatic adjustments to earnings and net assets figures. In general, UK GAAP earnings will be adjusted downwards and net assets upwards if converted to a US GAAP basis (and vice versa for a switch from US GAAP to UK GAAP).

As indicated above, many areas of M&A accounting are in a state of flux in the UK. The various EDs that have been recently issued by the ASC have been inherited by the new ASB. Clearly, if the exposure drafts are adopted in their present form, some major differences between UK and US practice would be eliminated. However, there is much resistance to the proposed changes (particularly, the proposals on goodwill and intangibles) and it is particularly difficult to predict what the final position will be.

4.3 CASH AND FUNDS FLOW STATEMENTS

4.3.1 UK requirements

In the UK, companies are required by SSAP 10 to prepare a statement of source and application of funds (sometimes known as a funds statement). There are numerous interpretations of 'funds' in practice but those most commonly used are net liquid funds, working capital or net borrowings.

The standard does not prescribe a specific format to be used. In practice, funds statements are largely a reconciliation of balance sheet changes. Typically, an analysis is provided of sources and applications of funds as follows:

- funds generated from operations — this is derived from the profit on ordinary activities before taxation with adjustments for items which do not involve funds flows;

- funds from other sources — these include funds raised from medium or long term loans, share issues and disposals of fixed assets;

- application of funds — including acquisitions of fixed assets, repayment of medium or long term loans and dividends paid.

Applications are deducted from sources leaving a residual amount. Generally the residual amount indicates the company's interpretation of 'funds' and thus usually represent the change in either net liquid funds, working capital or net borrowings.

In July 1990, the ASC published an exposure draft ED 54 — *Cash flow statements* which seeks to introduce a requirement to produce a cash flow statement, similar to that required by FAS 95, in place of a statement of source and application of funds.

4.3.2 US requirements

FAS 95 requires the preparation of a statement of cash flows (as opposed to a funds flow statement). The primary purpose of such a statement is to provide relevant information about the cash receipts and cash payments of an enterprise during a period.

FAS 95 cash flow statements classify the cash receipts and cash payments experienced in the year as resulting from investing, financing or operating activities. The standard provides guidance including examples of what investing, financing and operating activities comprise. The entire focus is on the change during the period in cash and cash equivalents, rather than working capital; ambiguous terms such as 'funds' are prohibited. The total amounts of cash and cash equivalents at the beginning and end of the period shown in the statement of cash flows will be the same amounts as presented in the balance sheets as of those dates.

4.4 CAPITALISATION OF BORROWING COSTS

4.4.1 UK position

There is no accounting standard on capitalisation of interest in the UK. The Companies Act permits, but does not require, interest on capital borrowed to finance the production of assets to be included in the production costs to the extent that it relates to the period of production. Although the treatment is optional, it is an increasingly common practice. If interest is so capitalised, the amount involved must be disclosed in the notes to the accounts.

4.4.2 US requirements

Under US GAAP, FAS 34 makes capitalisation of interest costs compulsory for certain assets requiring a period of time to get them ready for their intended use. These are referred to as 'qualifying assets' and are defined to include, inter alia:

- assets that are constructed or otherwise produced for an enterprise's own use (including assets constructed or produced for the enterprise by others for which deposits or progress payments have been made);

- assets intended for sale or lease that are constructed or otherwise produced as discrete projects (e.g. ships or real estate developments).

Inventories that are routinely manufactured or otherwise produced in large quantities on a repetitive basis, assets that are in use or ready for their intended use and assets not in use which are not being prepared for use are specifically excluded from the definition of qualifying assets.

FAS 34 contains specific guidelines for determining the amount of interest that should be capitalised. Under these guidelines, the amount to be capitalised is the interest cost which could theoretically have been avoided if the expenditure on the qualifying asset were not made. The interest cost capitalised cannot exceed the interest cost incurred by the enterprise and is determined by applying an interest rate (the 'capitalisation rate') to the average amount of accumulated expenditure for the asset during the financial year.

Whereas in the UK, the CA 85 does not provide a definition of the 'period of production', under US GAAP the period during which interest should be capitalised is defined in terms of the following three conditions:

•   expenditures for the asset must have been made;

•   activities that are necessary to get the asset ready for its intended use are in progress; and

•   interest cost is being incurred (including the imputation of interest on certain types of payables in accordance with APB Opinion No. 21 — *Interest on Receivables and Payables*).

The capitalisation period begins when all three conditions are present and continues as long as they remain present. The capitalisation period ends when the asset is substantially complete and ready for its intended use.

4.4.3 Comment
Although an increasing number of UK companies do capitalise borrowing costs, there is still a potential for divergence between UK and US practice in this area due to different interpretations being placed on the meaning of qualifying assets, the interest capitalisation rate and capitalisation period.

A recent exposure draft issued by the ASC, ED 51 — *Accounting for fixed assets and revaluations* deals with, inter alia, the capitalisation of borrowing costs. The ED neither requires nor prohibits the practice of capitalising borrowing costs incurred in financing the production of a fixed asset but says that where such a policy is adopted it should be applied consistently. The proposed requirements are not very detailed and largely serve to endorse current UK accounting practice. The proposals are consistent with the approach of FAS 34 but far less prescriptive.

4.5 CHANGES IN ACCOUNTING POLICY

In the UK, changes in accounting policy are generally accounted for by means of a prior year adjustment. This requires restatement of prior years' figures and as a result, adjustment of the opening balance of retained profits.

Under US GAAP, the general rule is that where a company voluntarily changes an accounting policy, the cumulative effect of the change should be disclosed in the profit and loss account for the year of the change after the profit or loss on extraordinary items, and referred to as the 'cumulative effect on prior years of a change in accounting policy ..... '. The effect on earnings per share should be disclosed prominently on the face of the profit and loss account. Although prior year figures are not restated, pro forma comparatives (and per share amounts) should be disclosed for the profit or loss before extraordinary items and the net profit or loss for the year.

However, there are certain specific exceptions to this general rule. A new accounting standard may specify transitional provisions (e.g. in the case of the recent pensions and deferred tax standards) which dictate the method of accounting for the changes to be introduced. In certain other specified circumstances the effect of a change in accounting policy must be accounted for retroactively as a prior period adjustment (i.e. as in the UK). These are as follows:

- a change from the LIFO method of stock valuation to another method;

- a change in the method of accounting for long-term construction-type contracts;

- a change from the 'full cost' method in the oil and gas and similar extractive industries.

4.6 DEFERRED TAXATION

4.6.1 UK treatment - SSAP 15

General approach

In the UK, provision is made for deferred tax only to the extent that it is probable that a liability will arise in the future. The focus is entirely on the balance sheet and not on the profit and loss account. To this end, the deferred tax effects of timing differences existing at the balance sheet date is calculated under the liability method (i.e. using tax rates likely to apply in the future when the timing differences reverse) with partial provision.

The partial provision approach

Under the partial provision approach, the amount of deferred tax to be provided is the liability that is expected to arise in the future based on a projection of the extent to which the cumulative timing differences existing at the balance sheet date are expected to reverse. In judging whether net reversals are likely, timing differences are considered on a combined basis (for each different tax or tax jurisdiction) rather than individually and the future reversals of timing differences existing at the balance sheet date are offset by new originating timing differences that can be predicted with sufficient certainty to arise in the future. In this way, provision is made for the aggregate tax effects of timing differences existing at the balance sheet date only to the extent that it is probable that a liability will crystallise in the future.

Deferred tax assets

Deferred tax net debit balances should not be carried forward as assets, except to the extent that they are expected to be recoverable without replacement by equivalent debit balances. In other words, the tax accelerated by the effect of timing differences is accounted for only to the extent that it is probable that an asset will crystallise in the future.

The accounting treatment for tax losses which have been incurred depends upon the particular way in which the loss is to be relieved:

- if the loss is to give a refund of tax previously paid, then the amount of the refund is recorded in the balance sheet as a debtor.

- if the loss is to be carried forward to be utilised against taxable profits which arise in the future, any deferred tax liability provided in the financial statements should be reduced to the extent of the tax effect of the available losses so long as offset would be possible in practice.

    When the amount of the loss is so great that the set off against deferred tax is such that the loss would be carried as an asset, the rules are framed so as to ensure that an asset is only recognised when its recoverability is assured with a very high degree of certainty. In practice the conditions set can seldom be met.

4.6.2 US treatment - APB 11

In the US, deferred tax accounting has reached a hiatus. In December 1987, the FASB issued FAS 96 to supersede APB 11. However, FAS 103 has delayed the effective date of FAS 96 to accounting periods beginning after December 15, 1991. This means that companies currently have the option of continuing to apply the provisions of APB 11, or of adopting FAS 96 early. FAS 96 has been severely criticised in view of its complexity, cost of implementation and the counterintuitive answers that it sometimes produces. As a consequence, the FASB is presently reassessing the problem areas which include the criteria for recognition and measurement of deferred tax assets. However, despite the uncertainty surrounding the future of FAS 96, companies that have already implemented the new standard cannot revert back to APB 11.

General approach
APB 11 requires full provision for deferred tax (except for certain specific exceptions defined in APB 23 & APB 24) using the deferral method. Its objective is to match initial tax effects of timing differences with related income and expense recognised in pre-tax profits. Such an approach focuses on obtaining matching in the profit and loss account with the result that the balance sheet figure does not necessarily relate to the amount of taxes payable or refundable in future years.

The deferral approach
The computation of deferred tax on originating timing differences is conducted using the 'with-and-without' approach (i.e. with and without the inclusion of the transaction representing the timing difference). Reversals of timing differences are calculated using either the 'net change' method (i.e. at current tax rates) or the 'gross change' method (i.e. the rates at which the originating timing difference was recorded).

Deferred tax assets
The treatment of tax losses is generally the same as in the UK. However, when the tax benefit of an operating loss carry-forward is realised in full or in part in a subsequent period, and was not previously recognised in the loss period, the tax benefit should be reported as an extraordinary item in the results of operations of the period in which realised.

4.6.3 US treatment - FAS 96
General approach
FAS 96 requires a liability approach, focusing on the balance sheet amounts in order to allocate tax between different accounting periods. Under this approach, deferred tax represents tax payable or refundable in future years as a result of existing differences between the book and tax bases of the company's assets and liabilities. Such differences are described as 'temporary differences' — and are defined to include timing differences as well as differences between assigned fair values of assets and liabilities recognised in an acquisition and their tax bases.

The FAS 96 approach

The annual computation of the deferred tax liability or asset in the balance sheet involves:

- scheduling the temporary differences existing at the balance sheet date over the years when they are expected to result in taxable or tax deductible amounts; and

- carrying out pro-forma tax computations for each future year assuming no other taxable or tax deductible amounts will occur in those years.

In respect of each tax jurisdiction, separate scheduling is necessary for each different tax (for example, in the UK context, corporation tax, petroleum revenue tax, etc.) and also for items which are subject to the same tax but assessed under different headings (for example, income assessed under Schedule D Case I and capital gains and losses). Qualifying hypothetical tax planning strategies which would reduce the deferred tax liability or increase the recognised amount of tax benefits for net deductible amounts as much as possible must be considered in the deferred tax calculations.

When calculating the tax payable for each future year, enacted tax rates and tax law as at the balance sheet date should be used, which means, for example, that no account can be taken of changes proposed in a Tax Bill, but not enacted by the year-end.

Deferred tax assets

A deferred tax asset can be recognised generally in circumstances where tax paid in the current or a prior year is refundable. Thus, an asset should be recognised in respect of the tax benefits associated with net deductible amounts expected to reverse in a future year only to the extent that they can be carried back either to reduce the current deferred tax liability, or to result in a refund of taxes paid in the current or prior years. No asset is recognised for any unused 'net deductible amounts' or in respect of any unused tax losses carried forward, regardless of the probability that they will be realised in the future.

4.6.4 Comment

The application of the partial provision approach in the UK is the significant difference between the UK and US requirements for deferred tax accounting. In contrast to the APB 11 and FAS 96 approach which require full provision, the partial provision approach offers much more flexibility when calculating deferred tax. It usually results in lower deferred tax provisions in the balance sheet and lower tax charges against earnings thus improving the company's gearing and earnings per share respectively. Although the reduction of the rates of capital allowances available to UK companies and the decline in the rates of UK corporation tax over recent years has dampened the potential impact of this GAAP difference, material adjustments relating to deferred tax are still a feature of most UK/US GAAP reconciliations presented by UK companies.

4.7 DISCONTINUED OPERATIONS OF A BUSINESS SEGMENT

Where a discontinuance of a business segment has occurred, there is no requirement in the UK to distinguish between the continuing and discontinued operations of the company except that the closure costs and the trading results of the closed operations, after the date at which implementation of the decision to close commences, should be classified as extraordinary. The SSAP suggests that the trading results for the period before the implementation date (which are included as part of the trading results for the year) may require separate disclosure to enable the results of the continuing operations to be ascertained. In practice, the definition of business segment (note under both UK and US GAAP, the definition of a business segment in this context is not necessarily the same as that applied in the context of segmental reporting) is interpreted quite widely compared with practice in the US particularly with regard to the interpretation of what comprises a separate major line of business as distinct from a product line.

In the US, however, the income statement must be completely reclassified (prior years' amounts as well) so that the results of discontinued operations of a business segment are segregated from the results of continuing operations of the company/group. In practice, the definition of a business segment is much more strictly applied. The results of the discontinued business segment up to the date when the decision to close or sell was taken (net of applicable taxes) and the gain or loss on disposal of those activities (net of applicable taxes) should be disclosed separately after the results of continuing operations but not as extraordinary items. Earnings per share data should be adjusted accordingly (see 4.9 below).

4.8 DIVIDENDS PAYABLE

In the UK, dividends are usually linked to the year's profits. The directors of public companies frequently declare interim dividends at the time the half-yearly results of the company are announced and will propose a final dividend for the year, usually after the year end once the annual results for that year are known. The proposed dividend has to be approved by the shareholders at the annual general meeting of the company (agm). The amount of the proposed dividend is nevertheless required by the CA 85 to be recorded and disclosed. Dividends are shown in the profit and loss account after the 'profit for the financial year' figure so as to arrive at the 'retained profit for the year'.

41

In the US, the directors may declare and pay a dividend whenever they think it is appropriate subject to the laws of the state of incorporation and the articles of the company (known as the bye-laws of the company). Common dividends for public companies are usually declared by directors on a quarterly basis. Dividends are not attributable to any particular period's earnings and so are accounted for as a charge to retained earnings at the point in time that they are formally declared by the board of directors. Applying this principle to the UK position, a proposed final dividend for a particular year would not be accounted for until the following year under US GAAP.

4.9 EXTRAORDINARY ITEMS

Although extraordinary items are defined almost identically in the respective accounting standards in the UK (SSAP 6) and the US (APB 30) (see Chapter 5, section 24), the definition is interpreted far more strictly in the US. The differences in interpretation arise because APB 30 provides a more detailed interpretation of the definition of 'extraordinary' and supplements this with specific examples of items which would not be regarded as extraordinary under the definition. Hence in practice, most items which would often be classified as extraordinary in the UK would not be treated as such under US GAAP. The reverse can also apply since certain US standards expressly require that certain gains or losses (e.g. those arising from early extinguishment of debt) are be disclosed as extraordinary.

The differences that exist between the calculation and disclosure of earnings per share (EPS) under UK and US financial reporting practice could also be attributed as a reason for the inconsistency in interpretation of the definition of an extraordinary item noted above . In the UK, the basic EPS is computed without taking account of extraordinary items. Hence, whether an item is classified as extraordinary or not directly affects the EPS figure reported by a company.

In contrast under US requirements, EPS data is presented for:

- income from continuing operations;

- income before extraordinary items;

- the cumulative effect of a change in accounting principle; and

- net income.

Such EPS data is disclosed prominently on the face of the profit and loss account.

4.10 FIXED ASSETS

The basic accounting requirements with regard to tangible fixed assets/property, plant and equipment (PPE) are generally the same in both countries with the following notable exceptions.

4.10.1 Revaluations

The basic accounting rule in the US is that PPE must be recorded at historical cost and depreciated where appropriate. The results of increases in the appraisal value resulting from revaluations may not in most cases be recognised in the financial statements. Recognition of such PPE appraisal can arise in certain rare situations; for example, when applying 'push-down accounting' (this relates to the practice of incorporating or pushing-down the fair value adjustments which have been made by the acquiring company into the financial statements of the acquired subsidiary) in certain situations under the SEC rules.

In the UK also, financial statements are almost invariably prepared using the historical cost accounting convention. However, the Companies Act permits the inclusion of certain assets at a revaluation or on a current cost basis. Many UK companies have used this modification to the historical cost framework; fixed assets and in particular land and buildings are frequently reported at revalued amounts. The revaluation surpluses are recorded in a separate reserve as part of shareholders' equity but are not available for distribution. Depreciation on revalued assets is based on their carrying amounts which means that in general there should be a larger charge for depreciation in the profit and loss account (see 4.10.3).

4.10.2 Investment properties

Investment properties (defined as properties which are not owner occupied and are held for their investment potential) owned by UK companies have to be included in the balance sheet at their open market value. Such properties are not depreciated except for leasehold property which are depreciated at least over the last twenty years of the lease period.

In the US, this treatment is not permitted except in the case of investment companies or those companies that prepare their accounts using a mark to market model (e.g. broker dealers, mutual funds, pension funds). General commercial companies and real estate companies record such properties at cost less any provisions for depreciation and diminution in value.

4.10.3 Depreciation

The basic principles with regard to accounting for depreciation of fixed assets are the same in the two countries. In the US, the costs of all fixed assets (less ultimate salvage value, if any) are depreciated over their estimated useful lives in a systematic and rational manner. 'Salvage' is analogous to the residual value concept mentioned in the UK standard on depreciation.

Under UK GAAP, there is a similar requirement to depreciate all fixed assets (except investment properties). However, in contrast to the position in the US, there is a growing number of UK companies (primarily brewers, retailers and companies in the financial sector, notably banks) which no longer depreciate freehold and long leasehold (over 50 years unexpired) buildings on the grounds that the combination of a very long life and a high residual value (costs are incurred to maintain these properties to high standards) mean that the amount of depreciation is insignificant.

4.11 FOREIGN CURRENCY TRANSLATION

The requirements of the UK and the US pronouncements on foreign currency translation (SSAP 20 and FAS 52) are very similar. This is not surprising because prior to the issue of the respective exposure drafts of both standards, there was a long period of consultation between the standard-setting bodies of both countries, together with Canada.

The main differences between the requirements of both standards that frequently come to light in practice are outlined below. Further information on these standards (including guidance contained in FAS 52 on issues such as accounting for the results of entities that operate in hyperinflationary economies and accounting for forward exchange contracts) can be found in Chapter 5, section 10.

4.11.1 Accounting for the results of foreign enterprises

Where the closing rate/net investment method is being used when consolidating foreign enterprises, SSAP 20 allows a choice of translating the operating results of the foreign enterprise either at the closing rate of exchange or at an average rate for the period.

In contrast, FAS 52 requires the revenues, expenses, gains and losses of foreign enterprises whose functional currency differs from that of the parent to be translated at the rates of exchange ruling when those elements are recognised or at an appropriate weighted average rate for the period.

4.11.2 Foreign currency translation reserve

FAS 52 requires the translation adjustments which result from translating a foreign enterprise's financial statements to be taken to a separate component of equity if its functional currency differs from that of the parent. As a result, the cumulative exchange differences will be apparent from the financial statements.

44

In addition, FAS 52 requires an analysis of the movements within this reserve to be disclosed in the financial statements.

SSAP 20 does not require such exchange differences to be taken to a separate reserve and, therefore, the cumulative exchange differences will be not be apparent from the financial statements.

4.11.3 Disposal of an investment in a foreign enterprise
Under FAS 52, where all or part of an investment in a foreign enterprise is sold, or it is substantially liquidated, the cumulative exchange differences included in the separate component of equity relating to the part which is sold or liquidated is included in the net profit for the period as part of the gain or loss on the sale or liquidation.

SSAP 20 does not contain any provisions as to what should happen to the cumulative exchange differences included in reserves in such an event.

4.12 INVESTMENTS IN MARKETABLE EQUITY SECURITIES
Under UK GAAP, current asset investments in marketable equity securities should be considered individually and recorded in the balance sheet at the lower of cost and net realisable value. Alternatively, they may be included at their current cost with any gain being credited directly to a separate reserve called the revaluation reserve, which forms part of shareholders' funds. Fixed asset investments in marketable equity securities should also be considered on an individual basis and recorded at cost less any provisions for permanent diminution in value. Alternatively, they may be stated at market value and unrealised gains and losses (so long as the latter are not indicative of a permanent diminution in value) taken directly to the revaluation reserve. The gain or loss on disposal of a revalued investment (current or non-current) can be measured by reference to its revalued amount or to its original cost.

Under US GAAP, the current portfolio of investments in marketable equity securities is carried at the lower of aggregate cost and market value at the balance sheet date. If the market value of the portfolio is less than the aggregate cost, this deficit (known as the valuation allowance) is shown as a deduction from aggregate cost in the balance sheet. Changes in the valuation allowance are included in net income of the period in which they occur. A similar approach is adopted when accounting for a non-current portfolio except that the accumulated changes in the valuation allowance (reflecting the unrealised losses on the portfolio) should be included in a separate reserve in the stockholders' equity section of the balance sheet.

The ASC published ED 55 — *Accounting for investments*, shortly before its disbandment. The ED is a general statement on the subject and intended to apply to all enterprises. It preserves existing practice in most areas with two notable exceptions; it proposes that all readily marketable investments held as current assets should be marked to market with all gains and losses dealt with in the profit and loss account, and also that the gain or loss on disposal of a revalued non-current investment should be measured by reference to its revalued amount and not its original cost.

4.13 PENSION COSTS — DEFINED BENEFIT PLANS
4.13.1 UK treatment - SSAP 24
Overview

The accounting objective of SSAP 24 is that the cost of providing pensions should be recognised on a 'systematic and rational' basis over the working lives of the employees in the scheme. The standard does not prescribe a particular actuarial valuation method to attribute cost to individual years (known as regular cost) but leaves it to the employer (with the benefit of actuarial advice) to ensure that the method chosen can fulfil the accounting objective. However, the actuarial assumptions and method, taken as a whole, have to be compatible and lead to the actuary's best estimate of the cost of providing the pension benefits promised.

Broad approach

In determining the regular pension cost for the year, pension liabilities are discounted using an interest rate representing the expected long-term return on scheme assets. The regular cost so determined can be regarded as that amount which the actuary considers as sufficient contribution to the scheme to provide the eventual pensions to be paid in respect of future service, assuming present actuarial assumptions about the future are borne out in practice. This approach gives implicit recognition of the reduction in the ultimate cost of providing pension benefits due to the return expected on the assets that the employer has set aside to meet the obligations of the scheme when they fall due for payment.

Variations

The basic rule is that variations from the regular cost (which arise because the assumptions made in the course of the actuarial process are not borne out in practice or due to changes made to the terms of the scheme) should, in general, be allocated over the expected remaining service lives of current employees in the scheme. No precise method of allocation is prescribed. There are certain exceptions to the basic rule (see Chapter 5, section 17.4.4).

Benefit improvements for past service

The standard encourages provision in advance of expected increases in pensions by their inclusion in the actuarial assumptions.

Transition asset or liability

The actuarial surplus or deficit existing at the date the standard is first adopted (determined by comparing the pension liabilities discounted at the expected long-term return on scheme assets with the actuarial value of the scheme assets often valued on a discounted income flow basis) adjusted to take account of any previously recognised pension related amounts recorded in the balance sheet is recognised by means of a prior year adjustment or alternatively, spread through the profit and loss account over the remaining service lives of the members of the scheme.

4.13.2 US treatment - FAS 87 & FAS 88

Overview

The fundamental objective of FAS 87 is to recognise in each accounting period the cost of providing the pension benefits earned by employees in that period. FAS 87 requires a particular actuarial approach to be used for measuring pension cost (service cost) — the projected unit method (in the US, this is known as the projected unit credit method) and in general prescribes tightly drawn rules as to the computation of pension figures in the accounts. The standard requires that each of the significant assumptions made in valuing the scheme should be the best estimate, in relation to that individual aspect in isolation.

Broad approach

The overall approach of FAS 87 is different from that of SSAP 24. The service cost is the cost of benefits earned by employees during the year (computed actuarially). In determining the service cost for the period, FAS 87 requires the pension liabilities to be assessed without any regard of the company's pension funding arrangements. Pension liabilities should be discounted using a rate of interest (called the discount rate) which reflects the cost of insuring the liabilities at the beginning of year (e.g. at a rate implicit in the price of annuities that could be purchased at the valuation date to settle the liabilities). This rate is also used to calculate a second component of pension cost namely interest cost. The interest cost component is the cost of increasing the pension liabilities existing at the beginning of the year, at the discount rate, to the year end.

The annual investment return that is expected to be earned by the scheme assets should be offset against these two components of pension cost. In order to compute the annual investment return, an estimate should be made of the expected long-term rate of return on scheme assets (which is not the discount rate). That rate of return has to be applied to a 'market-related' value (defined to be either fair market value or a calculated value that smoothes the effect of short term market fluctuations over a period of up to 5 years) of the scheme assets to obtain the investment earnings component of pension cost for the year.

Variations

In general, variations may be deferred and amortised over a number of years. FAS 87 specifies in detail the methods of amortising variations that arise. In general, SSAP 24's exceptions to the basic rule on spreading the effects of variations forward would not be permitted under FAS 87. In particular:

•   accounting for refunds from the scheme in the profit and loss account when the cash is received would not be allowed;

•   FAS 88 prescribes the method for determining the amount to be recognised in the profit and loss account when a pension obligation is curtailed (e.g. when defined benefit accruals for the future services of present employees have been eliminated). Where the curtailment is not connected with the disposal/discontinuance of a business segment, the effect would be recognised immediately under FAS 88 whereas under SSAP 24 it would be dealt with in the periods in which the contributions to the scheme were adjusted as a result of the curtailment.

Benefit improvements for past service

The cost of all 'retroactive' benefit improvements is amortised over the working lives of the members after the increase is awarded.

Transition asset or liability

The difference between the value of the pension liabilities based on the discount rate and the fair market value of the scheme assets at the date the standard is first adopted (adjusted to take account of any previously recognised pension related amounts in the balance sheet) is amortised on a straight-line basis over the average remaining working lives of the employees.

4.13.3 Comment

Whilst the UK standard allows a considerable degree of flexibility, the FASB's requirements are much more tightly defined — the prescription of a specific actuarial method for the measurement of cost, the requirement to use an insurance interest rate for valuing pension obligations and the use of a current fair value for valuing pension fund assets can, conjunctively, give rise to potentially material differences. The FASB pension cost can be regarded as a 'current' cost of providing pension benefits to employees based on current value accounting for the scheme liabilities and assets held off-balance sheet. The use of current values has the potential of introducing great volatility in the profit and loss account charge and therefore is in direct conflict with the objective of SSAP 24 — which is to recognise the cost of providing pensions on a systematic and rational basis over the employees' service lives. Hence, it is highly unlikely that FAS 87 figures would fulfil the requirements of SSAP 24 and vice versa.

4.14 REVENUE RECOGNITION

4.14.1 UK requirements

The guidance on revenue recognition issues in the UK is not as extensive as that available in the US. There are a number of industry SORPs which provide some guidance on revenue recognition issues arising in certain specialist industries (e.g. insurance, oil and gas, banking); the SSAPs in issue contain very limited guidance on the subject. For example, SSAP 2 contains a general requirement for accounts to be prepared on a prudent basis; it defines prudence as follows — 'revenue and profits are not anticipated, but are recognised by inclusion in the profit and loss account only when realised in the form of either cash or of other assets the ultimate cash realisation of which can be assessed with reasonable certainty'. SSAP 9 — *Stocks and long term contracts,* contains guidance on revenue recognition for long-term contracts. SSAP 21 — *Accounting for leases and hire purchase contracts,* contains guidance on revenue recognition issues arising in leasing transactions including sale and leaseback deals.

The CA 85 contains a requirement that 'only profits realised at the balance sheet date should be included in the profit and loss account'. The Act suggests that in establishing whether or not profits of a company should be treated as 'realised profits', reference should be made to 'principles generally accepted with respect to the determination for accounting purposes of realised profits'. However as noted above, the SSAPs are of limited assistance in this area. For this reason, revenue recognition issues tend to be dealt with very much on an ad hoc basis and reference is often made to authoritative literature that exists internationally (primarily, the international accounting standards and also US standards) to provide a basis for tackling practical revenue recognition issues.

4.14.2 US requirements

The general rule in the US (contained in the FASB's Concepts Statement No. 5) is that revenues are not recognised until they are (a) realised or realisable and (b) earned. According to the Statement, revenues are realised 'when products (goods or services), merchandise, or other assets are exchanged for cash or claims to cash', and are realisable 'when related assets received or held are readily convertible to known amounts of cash or claims to cash'. The characteristics of 'readily convertible assets' are that they have '(i) interchangeable (fungible) units and (ii) quoted prices available in an active market that can rapidly absorb the quantity held by the entity without significantly affecting the price'. Revenues are considered to have been 'earned' when the entity 'has substantially accomplished what it must do to be entitled to the benefits represented by the revenues'.

In contrast to the position in the UK, there is an abundance of authoritative literature on the subject of revenue recognition. For example, there are a number of FASB Statements which deal with either the recognition of certain forms of revenue, or the recognition of revenue in certain specific industries. These include FAS 45 — *Accounting for Franchise Fee Revenue*, FAS 50 — *Financial Reporting in the Record and Music Industry*, FAS 48 — *Revenue Recognition When Right of Return Exists*, and FAS 66 — *Accounting for Sales of Real Estate* (see Chapter 5, section 22 for more detail).

In addition, the SEC has issued several Accounting and Auditing Enforcement Releases addressing specific revenue recognition issues faced by registrants, detailing why in their opinion the issue had not been accounted for properly and citing their preferred accounting treatment. There are also several AICPA Industry Audit and Accounting Guides and Statements of Position that deal with revenue recognition, and the Emerging Issues Task Force of the FASB has released several consensuses on a number of revenue recognition areas.

4.15 STOCKS/INVENTORY
The major difference between UK and US accounting requirements for stocks (inventory in the US) is that the last in first out (LIFO) method of stock valuation is fairly widely used in the US but is ordinarily not permitted to be used by SSAP 9.

The fairly wide usage of LIFO by US companies is partly because many believe that this method gives a better portrayal of their operating results in their situation and partly tax driven — the Internal Revenue Codes of 1938 and 1939 officially recognised LIFO as an acceptable method for the computation of tax, provided that it was used consistently for tax and financial reporting purposes. Thus, where LIFO is used by individual companies in a group for tax purposes, it must also be used for reporting purposes in the financial statements of those companies as well as in the group financial statements. In contrast, LIFO is not acceptable for tax purposes in the UK.

DETAILED COMPARISON

INTRODUCTION

This chapter presents UK and US accounting measurement and disclosure requirements on a range of specific accounting topics (in so far as a general commercial enterprise is concerned) in a manner that facilitates quick comparison. For this purpose, the requirements in the UK are based on the SSAPs developed by the ASC and the requirements of the CA 85 and the London Stock Exchange. The corresponding requirements in the US are derived from the accounting principles which have substantial authoritative support (comprising primarily accounting standards and practices promulgated by the FASB and its predecessor bodies – see Chapter 3.3). Where appropriate, we have also made reference to the accounting rules and regulations of the SEC.

The chapter is divided into 35 sections, each of which allows a line-by-line comparison of a specific accounting topic. The UK accounting and disclosure requirements are summarised on the left-hand pages and the corresponding requirements in the US on the right-hand pages. In order to keep the size of this book down to a manageable level, we have avoided repetition of areas of common practice and concentrated on highlighting areas where there are differences in accounting practice or disclosure requirements. As a result, the text is not exhaustive, and reference should therefore be made to the original accounting literature for detailed guidance on any specific area. The relevant authoritative literature is indicated at the beginning of each section and specific references thereto are given in the respective margins.

As noted in Chapter 1, the special accounting practices that apply in certain industries (for example, banking, insurance, oil and gas etc.) are outside the scope of this book. Consequently, certain accounting standards issued by the FASB and the Accounting and Auditing Industry guides issued by the AICPA which deal with specialised industries are not covered. Reference should be made either to these pronouncements where the issue relates to a specialised industry that is the subject of an accounting standard or to other relevant guidance issued by the AICPA. The SEC also has special provisions in Industry Guides governing statistical data and other financial data for registrants with significant banking, insurance or oil and gas operations. Reference should be made to Regulation S-X for these.

LIST OF SECTIONS

General topics

Profit and loss account

Balance sheet

Cash and funds flow statements

1 ACCOUNTING CHANGES

1.1 AUTHORITATIVE PRONOUNCEMENT
- SSAP 6

1.2 CHANGE IN ACCOUNTING POLICY

This is addressed almost exclusively by SSAP 6. The exceptions relate to changes in accounting policy made in conformity with:

- SSAP 21 (see section 15);

- SSAP 24 (which may be implemented using an alternative approach to that required under SSAP 6 - see section 17.4.9); and

SI 1990/355   • amended CA 85 requirements on group accounts (see section 13).

1.2.1 When can a change in policy occur?

SSAP 6.18   The new policy should be preferable to the one it replaces.

1.2.2 Reporting a change in accounting policy

SSAP 6.18,39   The change must be retroactively effected with the result that the comparative figures will be restated except on the introduction of a new standard which permits an alternative method of implementation (e.g. SSAP 24). The effect of the change on the results of the preceding year should be disclosed where practicable. In addition, historical summaries should be restated where practicable.

ACCOUNTING CHANGES

1.1 AUTHORITATIVE PRONOUNCEMENTS

- APB 9

- APB 20

- FAS 16

- FAS 32

- FIN 20

1.2 CHANGE IN ACCOUNTING POLICY

Accounting changes made in conformity with APB Opinions, AICPA Industry Guides or FASB Statements and Interpretations issued in the past or in the future should be implemented in accordance with guidance provided in those pronouncements. Accordingly guidance contained here will not apply in those circumstances unless the pronouncement does not specify the manner in which a change in accounting principle to conform with its recommendations should be reported.

APB 20.4

FIN 20.5

1.2.1 When can a change in policy occur?

An enterprise must justify the use of an alternative accounting principle as being preferable and the nature and justification of the change must be disclosed. Domestic SEC registrants must obtain a preferability letter from the auditor.

APB 20.16-17

The issuance of a new accounting standard that expresses a preference for an accounting principle or rejects a specific accounting principle or adoption of accounting principles or practices contained in many AICPA Statements of Position and Guides (see Chapter 3) is sufficient support for a change in accounting principle.

FAS 32.11

1.2.2 Reporting a change in accounting policy

A Cumulative catch up adjustments

With the exception of a few specific situations (discussed below), a change of accounting principle should be recognised by a cumulative 'catch-up' adjustment, which is included in current year income in the year of the change and disclosed between the captions 'extraordinary items' and 'net income'. Although prior period statements are not restated, the income before extraordinary items and net income computed on a pro-forma retroactive basis should be shown for all periods presented.

APB 20.19,21

ACCOUNTING CHANGES

SSAP 6.35   A statement of reserves should (even where there is no change in accounting policy) immediately follow the profit and loss account or be included in a note referred to on the face of the profit and loss account. This would show the effect of an accounting change on the opening balance of retained profits.

There is no requirement to show the effect of a change on the earnings per share (e.p.s.) figure but e.p.s. for prior years should be restated.

SSAP 12.21   Changes in the method of depreciation or estimates of useful life should not be applied retroactively. The unamortised cost should be depreciated over the remaining useful life using the new method and the effect of the change should be disclosed if material.

ACCOUNTING CHANGES

Earnings per share amounts for income before extraordinary items and net income computed on a pro-forma basis should normally be disclosed on the face of the income statement.

A change in method of depreciation should be accounted for as an accounting change and the retroactive effect should be included in net income of the year of the change as a cumulative 'catch-up' adjustment if the new method is to be applied to previously recorded assets.

APB 20.24

B   Retroactive restatement

As mentioned earlier, certain changes in accounting principles should be reported by restatement of financial statements of all prior periods. The following changes should be accounted for by retroactive restatement:

APB 20.27

* a change from the LIFO method of inventory valuation

* a change in method of accounting for long-term contracts

* a change to or from the 'full cost' method in the extractive industries.

The effect of the change on income before extraordinary items, net income, and the related per share amounts should be disclosed for all periods presented either on the face of the income statement or in the notes.

APB 20.28

The effect on opening retained earnings must be shown in the financial statements.

APB 20 App B

A retroactive restatement may be made for a change in accounting policy by a company whose securities are not currently widely held and where financial statements are first issued for the purpose of obtaining equity capital, registering securities or effecting a business combination. This would normally be the support for retroactive restatement by a UK company when it first prepares a reconciliation of earnings computed under US GAAP.

APB 20.29

ACCOUNTING CHANGES

1.3 CHANGE IN ACCOUNTING ESTIMATE

SSAP 6.17   A change in estimate should not be given retroactive effect by restatement of prior periods; the effect should be included in the determination of the result for the current year and, where appropriate, future years.

If material, the nature and size of change should be disclosed.

1.4 CHANGE IN REPORTING ENTITY

SSAP 23.19   The most common example of 'a change in reporting entity' in the UK is when two groups of shareholders continue or are in a position to continue their shareholdings as before but on a combined basis (i.e. a merger). When merger accounting is adopted, the prior period accounts should be adjusted as if the group was always constituted as it is now (see section 2.3.2).

1.5 CORRECTION OF AN ERROR IN PREVIOUSLY ISSUED
FINANCIAL STATEMENTS

SSAP 6.19   A fundamental error is one of such significance as to destroy the presentation of a true and fair view, and hence the validity of, prior period accounts, and which would have led to their withdrawal had the error been recognised at the time.

ACCOUNTING CHANGES

1.3 CHANGE IN ACCOUNTING ESTIMATE

Prior periods should not be restated nor should pro-forma amounts be disclosed. The effect should be included in current and, where applicable, future years' income and the effect on income should be disclosed if material.

APB 20.31-33

The effect on income before extraordinary items and net income of the current period should be disclosed for a change in estimate that affects several future periods (e.g. estimate of economic lives of fixed assets or actuarial assumptions affecting pension costs).

APB 20.33

1.4 CHANGE IN REPORTING ENTITY

A change in reporting entity is limited mainly to the following situations:

APB 20.12

• consolidated or combined statements are presented in place of statements of individual companies

• there is a change in the specific subsidiaries comprising the group of companies for which consolidated statements are presented, (e.g. last year a subsidiary was not consolidated, this year it is consolidated)

• there is a change in the companies in combined financial statements (see section 13.7) (includes pooling of interests).

Note that business combinations accounted for under the purchase method and disposals of subsidiaries should not be accounted for as a change in reporting entity.

Where there has been a change in the reporting entity and the financial statements are in effect those of a different reporting entity, all prior periods presented should be restated. The nature of the change and the reasons for it should be disclosed.   The effect of the change on income before extraordinary items, net income and related per share data should also be disclosed for all periods presented.

APB 20.34-35

1.5 CORRECTION OF AN ERROR IN PREVIOUSLY ISSUED FINANCIAL STATEMENTS

Errors in financial statements which result from mathematical mistakes, mistakes in the application of accounting principles, or oversight or misuse of facts that existed at the time the financial statements were prepared should be accounted for as prior period adjustments (as in the UK).

APB 20.13
FAS 16.11

ACCOUNTING CHANGES

Such errors should be accounted for by restating prior years, with the result that the opening retained profits will be adjusted.

ACCOUNTING CHANGES

Disclosures should be given of the nature of the error and the effect of its correction on income before extraordinary items and net income and the related per share effects in the period in which the error was discovered and corrected.

APB 20.36-37

APB 9.18,26

Where financial statements for more than one period are given, the effect on the net income of prior periods should also be disclosed. Such disclosure should include the amounts of tax applicable to the prior period adjustments.

2 BUSINESS COMBINATIONS

2.1 AUTHORITATIVE PRONOUNCEMENTS

- CA 85

- SSAP 23

- SSAP 22

- SSAP 14

COMMENT

During 1990 the ASC issued the following exposure drafts:

- ED 47 — Accounting for goodwill, and ED 48 — Accounting for acquisitions and mergers, which are intended to replace SSAPs 22 and 23;

- ED 50 — *Consolidated accounts,* which is intended to replace SSAPs 1 and 14; and

- ED 53 — *Fair value in the context of acquisition accounting,* which aims to provide the first mandatory guidance in this area.

The main changes proposed by these EDs are noted at appropriate points in the text.

2.2 GENERAL APPROACH

SSAP 23 Business combinations is the generic term for transactions which result in one company joining a group by becoming the subsidiary of another. Acquisition accounting and merger accounting are both acceptable in accounting for business combinations and are not necessarily mutually exclusive options.

COMMENT

ED 48 seeks to make merger and acquisition accounting mutually exclusive

2.3 MERGER ACCOUNTING

SSAP 23.2-3 The main criterion used to determine the appropriate method/methods of accounting is whether or not the combination is based principally on a share for share exchange. Merger accounting is considered to be an appropriate method of accounting when two groups of shareholders continue, or are in a position to continue, their shareholdings as before but on a combined basis. The concept of 'no material resources leaving the group' is key to the definition of a merger.

BUSINESS COMBINATIONS

2.1 AUTHORITATIVE PRONOUNCEMENTS

- APB 16 (including AIN-APB 16)

- FAS 38

- FAS 72

- FAS 79

- FAS 87

- FAS 96

2.2 GENERAL APPROACH

The purchase method (acquisition accounting) and the pooling-of-interests method (merger accounting) are both acceptable in accounting for business combinations, but not as alternatives. A business combination either qualifies for the pooling-of-interests method or must be accounted for as a purchase. Special rules (not covered in this book) apply in the case of reverse acquisitions and certain leveraged buyout (LBO) transactions.

APB 16.24,70
EITF 88-16

2.3 THE POOLING-OF-INTERESTS METHOD

The conditions for using the pooling-of-interests method are very extensive and are intended to :

APB 16.54

- present as a single interest the interests of two or more shareholder groups that were previously independent and also the combined rights and risks represented by those interests; and

- reflect the essence of a pooling, namely that shareholder groups neither withdraw nor invest assets but in effect exchange voting common stock in a ratio that determines their respective interests in the combined enterprise.

BUSINESS COMBINATIONS

2.3.1 Conditions for merger accounting

CA 85 Sch 4A.10 Merger accounting may be used if the following conditions are met:

SSAP 23.11
- there has been an offer to all equity and voting shareholders which has at least 90% acceptance;

- at least 90% of the fair value of the consideration is in the form of equity share capital;

- consideration other than in the form of equity share capital does not amount to more than 10% of the nominal value of the equity share capital issued; and

- immediately prior to the offer, the offeror does not hold more than 20% of the equity (or 20% of the votes) of the offeree.

The above criteria for merger accounting do not impose any restriction on what happens to shareholdings before and after the merger. For example, vendor placings do not preclude merger accounting. A vendor placing is a transaction whereby the acquirer issues renounceable letters of allotment to the vendor who immediately transfers them to a middle man (e.g. a merchant bank) who then places the shares either with third parties or the shareholders of the acquiring company.

COMMENT

ED 48 seeks to restrict merger accounting to 'genuine' mergers, distinguished by such features as the lack of an obvious dominant party in the merged entity. However, if the criteria for a genuine merger were satisfied, merger accounting would be required, rather than permitted as at present.

BUSINESS COMBINATIONS

The SEC stresses that sharing of rights and risks among constituent shareholder groups is an essential element of poolings. A business combination which does not meet this essential concept cannot be accounted for as a pooling.

ASR 130

2.3.1 Conditions for pooling

A business combination must meet all of the following criteria to be accounted for as a pooling of interests. The conditions for pooling may be categorised under the following broad headings:

* attributes of the combining companies;

* manner of the combination; and

* absence of planned transactions.

A   Attributes of the combining companies

(a) Autonomy

APB 16.46

Each of the combining companies is autonomous and has not been a subsidiary or division of another company within two years before the plan of combination is initiated (i.e. in general, a plan of combination is initiated on the date the major terms of the plan are formally communicated to shareholders of one of the combining companies).

(b) Independence

Each of the combining companies is independent of the other. This requires that at any time from the date the merger is initiated until it is consummated (i.e. the date that ownership of the issuing company's common stock passes to the stockholders of the combining company in exchange for a majority (greater than 50%) of the stock or net assets of the combining company — the consummation usually coincides with the legal closing), the combining companies do not hold investments in each other exceeding 10% in total of the outstanding voting common stock of any combining company. The application of the 10% independence rule becomes more complex if the combining companies have reciprocal holdings of each other's common stock.

B   Manner of the combination

(c) Single transaction

APB 16.47

The combination is effected in a single transaction, or in accordance with a specific plan within one year after the plan is initiated.

BUSINESS COMBINATIONS

BUSINESS COMBINATIONS

(d) Substantial exchange of shares

The issuing company offers and issues only common stock with rights identical to those of the majority of its outstanding voting common stock in exchange for substantially all of the voting common stock interest of another company at the date the merger is consummated. Substantially all of the voting common stock means 90% or more for this condition. Note that intercorporate investment (either way) will make it more difficult to overcome the 90% test.

> **COMMENT**
>
> Some companies may not have a controlling class of common stock owing to the existence of one or more classes of voting preferred stock. In such cases, a business combination may be accounted for as a pooling of interests only if the issuing company exchanges its common stock for substantially all of the voting common and preferred stock of the other combining entity.

EITF 87-27

(e) Change in equity interests

APB 16.47

No changes in the equity interests of the voting common stock of any combining company may be made in contemplation of a pooling-of-interest either

•   within two years prior to the merger being initiated; or

•   between the dates the merger is initiated and consummated.

Changes in contemplation of effecting the combination may include distribution to stockholders (except for those that are no greater than normal dividends), additional issuances, exchanges and retirements of securities.

Generally, the reacquisition of voting common stock (see section 32.4.1) during the aforementioned periods will, in most cases, result in 'tainted' treasury shares. However, there are some limited exceptions but these are subject to numerous restrictions. If tainted shares are material (i.e. they exceed 10% of the shares to be issued to effect the combination) in relation to the planned combination then pooling accounting is precluded.

(f) Ratio of shareholder interest

The ratio of the interest of an individual common stockholder to those of other common stockholders in a combining company remains the same as a result of the exchange of stock. No premium can be granted to a major shareholder or a control group of the combining company if this criterion is to be met. In other words, all shareholders (including significant shareholders) must receive the same offer in shares.

BUSINESS COMBINATIONS

BUSINESS COMBINATIONS

(g) Contingencies in a pooling

The entire plan of combination must be resolved by the consummation date. This requires that no provisions of the plan relating to the issue of securities or other consideration is pending by that date. This means that the combined entity may not agree to contingently issue additional shares of stock or distribute other consideration at a later date to the former owners of the combining company. For instance, general warranties relating to general contingencies will usually disqualify pooling accounting.

C Absence of planned transactions

After consummation, any transaction (explicitly or implicitly) that is inconsistent with the combining of the interest of the common stockholder groups precludes the use of the pooling-of-interests method for recording the business combination.

APB 16.48

(h) Reacquisition of pooling consideration

Stock issued in a pooling must remain outstanding outside the combined entity without arrangements for any of the entities involved to use their financial resources to buy out former stockholders or induce others to do so.

The SEC concluded that the sale of shares received by a controlling shareholder of either company in the business combination before the financial results covering at least 30 days of post-merger combined operations have been published (i.e. by a Form 10-Q or 8-K filing or any other public announcement giving information about combined sales and net income) would preclude the use of the pooling method since the risk sharing required for pooling would not have taken place.

ASR 135

Similarly, an agreement which requires sale of shares after such a period would preclude pooling treatment.

ASR 130

(i) Other financial arrangements

The combined company may not enter into other financial arrangements for the benefit of the former stockholders of a combining company, such as the guarantee of loans secured by stock issued in the combination, which in effect negates the exchange of equity securities.

APB 16.48

(j) Disposal of assets

The combined company may not intend or plan to dispose of a significant part of the assets of the combining companies within two years after the combination other than disposals in the ordinary course of business of the formerly separate companies and the elimination of duplicate facilities or

BUSINESS COMBINATIONS

2.3.2 *Application of merger accounting*

SSAP 23.18-20   The mechanics of merger accounting are similar to those for pooling of
CA 85 Sch 4A.11   interests in the US except where indicated below.

CA 85 s 131   The carrying value of the investment will normally be recorded at the
nominal value of the shares issued by the holding company to effect the
combination together with any other consideration given (see section 32.2.1).
On consolidation, this amount is set off against the share capital of the
subsidiary. Where the cost of the investment is less than the share capital of
the subsidiary, this difference is generally classified as a capital reserve in
shareholders' funds in the balance sheet (see section 33.7). Where the
reverse situation applies, the net debit has to be eliminated against
consolidated reserves in some way and the normal practice is to apply these
first against the most restricted category of reserves and subsequently, if any
excess remains, against the group's retained earnings.

BUSINESS COMBINATIONS

excess capacity. In the view of the SEC staff, the sale of significant assets by the combining companies prior to consummation would also preclude pooling accounting. Dispositions within up to six months prior to consummation are presumed to be in contemplation of pooling if the registrant cannot substantiate otherwise.

(k) The 10% Catch-All rule

In addition to the 10% tests in (b) and (d) above, a '10% Catch-All' rule is applied whereby transactions that would violate certain criteria (tainted treasury shares, inter-corporate investments etc.) are equated in terms of the number of shares of the isssuing company's stock. The total of all such shares may not exceed 10% of the issuing company's shares needed to acquire 100% of the voting common stock of the combining company.

2.3.2 Application of pooling-of-interests method

When applying the pooling-of-interests method, the recorded assets and liabilities of the separate companies should be combined in the financial statements.

APB 16.51

Adjustments may have to be made to eliminate differences in accounting policies adopted by the separate enterprises if the change in policy could otherwise have been appropriate for the separate company. Such changes in accounting policy should be applied retroactively.

The carrying value of the investment should be recorded in the issuer's accounting records at par value of the capital stock issued to effect the combination. Differences between the carrying value of the investment and the total capital stock of the other separate company should be first adjusted against the combined 'other contributed capital' and then from the combined retained earnings.

APB 16.53

The consolidated financial statements should report results of operations for the period in which the combination occurs as though the companies had been combined as of the beginning of the period.

APB 16.56

BUSINESS COMBINATIONS

CA 85 s 130(2)   Some of the expenses of the merger may qualify to be written off against the share premium account of the issuing company (e.g. expenses of the share issue).

Other expenses which cannot be disposed of in this way are dealt with either in the profit and loss account for the period of the combination or, historically, added to the cost of the investment in the issuing company's books and eliminated through reserves in the set-off exercise described above.

COMMENT

ED 48 proposes that merger expenses should be charged to the profit and loss account, except to the extent they are charged to share premium account (see section 32.5).

SSAP 23.9   The effective date of the merger should be taken as the earlier of:

CA 85 Sch 5.10,29

- the date on which the consideration passes; or

- the date on which the offer becomes or is declared unconditional.

2.3.3 Disclosure

SSAP 23.23   When merger accounting is used the disclosures required are broadly in line

CA 85 Sch 5.10,29 with those required by APB 16 except for the following additional disclosures:

- the fair value of the consideration given by the issuing company;

- an explanation of significant merger adjustments; and

- details of any transaction (including the amount of any profit or loss arising) involving the disposal of shares in or fixed assets of the subsidiary that has been merger accounted which occurs in the year of merger or in the following two financial years.

2.4 ACQUISITION ACCOUNTING

CA 85 Sch 4A.8   Acquisition accounting must be used if the conditions for merger accounting

SSAP 23.15   are not met or when accounting for a business combination where the merger accounting option is available but has not been selected.

2.4.1 The cost of the acquired enterprise

There are no prescribed rules on how to determine the value of the consideration, including contingent, deferred and market price related

BUSINESS COMBINATIONS

Expenses related to effecting the business combination should be charged against net income in the consolidated financial statements for the period in which the expenses are incurred.

APB 16.58

Business combinations accounted for by the pooling-of-interests method should be recorded as of the date the combination is consummated.

APB 16.61

2.3.3 Disclosure
Disclosures in the acquirer's financial statements for the period in which a business combination accounted for by the pooling-of-interests method occurs include, inter alia:

- A reconciliation of the revenue and earnings previously reported by the company issuing the shares with the amounts presented in the financial statements of the combined entity.

  APB 16.63(g)

- Notes to the financial statements should disclose details of the effects of a business combination which is to be accounted for by the pooling method consummated before the issuance of but after the date of the financial statements. The details including revenue, net income and earnings per share should be disclosed as if the consummation had occurred at the date of the financial statements.

  APB 16.65

2.4 THE PURCHASE METHOD
The purchase method follows principles normally applicable under historical cost accounting when recording acquisitions of assets and issuances of stock.

APB 16.66

2.4.1 The cost of the acquired enterprise
Cash and other assets distributed, securities issued unconditionally and amounts of contingent consideration that are determinable (i.e. where the

APB 16.78

BUSINESS COMBINATIONS

conditions (but see comment following section 2.4.2 below).

UK companies tend to use share prices during the period immediately following the announcement of the bid to value such consideration. The price may be at a single point in time, for example the date of acquisition or issue of shares or alternatively, an average for a certain period around these dates.

2.4.2 The fair value exercise

CA 85 Sch 4A.9(2-3)
SSAP 14.29
SSAP 23.16-17

The results of the acquired company should be brought into the group accounts from the date of acquisition only (see 2.4.5 below). The fair values should be based on circumstances existing at that date and should not be affected by matters arising after that date.

COMMENT

The methods proposed by ED 53 are broadly similar to those set out in APB 16 as amended by subsequent statements except in the following areas:

- the 'hindsight period' permitted for the purposes of adjusting fair values originally assigned is normally restricted to the period from the date of acquisition to the date of publication of the first financial statements issued after the acquisition. However, where an acquisition takes place less than six months before the date of board approval of those accounts, adjustments may be made, where necessary, in the financial statements of the following period.

- the fair value of listed securities given as part of the consolidation should be based on the market price of those securities on the date on which the bid becomes unconditional (the 'effective date'). In order to eliminate the effect of general short-term market fluctuations, however, it is suggested that the average price for the ten days up to and including the effective date may be used instead.

BUSINESS COMBINATIONS

outcome of the contingency is determinable beyond reasonable doubt) at the date of acquisition should be included in determining the cost of an acquired enterprise and recorded at that date.

The cost of an acquired company is measured by the fair values of assets distributed (e.g. marketable securities) and of liabilities incurred by an acquiring company. In the case of quoted equity securities, the market price for a reasonable period before and after the date the terms of the acquisition are agreed to and announced should be considered in determining the fair value of securities issued.

APB 16.72-75

Contingent consideration is usually recorded when the contingency is resolved and consideration is issued or becomes issuable.

APB 16.79

The issue of additional securities or other consideration at the resolution of contingencies based on earnings results in an addition to the cost of an acquired company and consequently to the goodwill also. This additional element should be amortised over the remaining life of the goodwill.

Additional securities or other consideration issued at the resolution of contingencies based on security prices do not change the recorded cost of an acquired company.

2.4.2 Purchase price allocation

An acquiring company should allocate the cost of an acquired company to the assets acquired and liabilities assumed, on the basis of their fair values at the date of acquisition. General guidance is given on assigning fair values to the individual assets acquired and liabilities assumed as detailed below.

APB 16.87,88

- If FAS 96 has been adopted, a deferred tax liability or asset should be recognised for differences between the assigned values and the tax bases of the assets and liabilities recognised in a purchase business combination except, inter alia, goodwill.

FAS 96.23

- If FAS 96 has not been adopted, the tax effects of such differences should not be separately recorded as deferred tax but instead be a factor in assigning amounts to identifiable assets and liabilities.

APB 16.89

- Marketable securities at current net realisable values;

APB 16.88

- Receivables at their present values based on appropriate current interest rates and after making provisions for bad debts;

BUSINESS COMBINATIONS

- contingent gains should be treated in the same way as contingent liabilities for the purposes of determining fair value.

BUSINESS COMBINATIONS

COMMENT   *SAB 61*

The SEC staff are likely to raise questions where bad debt provisions raised during the fair value exercise are materially different from those made by the acquired company prior to its acquisition (the same applies to extra provisions that are made against the value of stock).

- Inventories:

  Finished goods at estimated selling price less any future anticipated costs and less a reasonable profit allowance for the selling effort of the acquiring company;

  Work in progress at estimated selling price less any future costs to completion and less a reasonable profit allowance for the completing and selling effort of the acquiring company;

  Raw materials at current replacement costs;

- Plant and equipment:

  If it is to be used, at current replacement cost;

  If it is to be sold, at current net realisable value;

- Identifiable intangible assets (except goodwill) at appraised values;

COMMENT   *SAB 42*

Determination of the values of identifiable intangible assets purchased is often considered impracticable because they are not easily quantified. The SEC staff recognises that this process is often difficult and that little practical guidance exists to facilitate such valuations. Nevertheless, they believe that the allocation of purchase price to all identifiable intangible assets acquired is necessary. If their fair values are not determinable, no recognition is given to such assets and their 'values' should be assigned to goodwill.

- Other assets, such as land and non-marketable securities, at appraised values;

- All liabilities, accruals and commitments at their present value determined at appropriate current interest rates;

- If the acquired company operates a defined benefit pension plan, the   *FAS 87.74* allocation of the cost of the acquired company should include a liability for projected benefit obligations in excess of plan assets, or an asset in the reverse case.

BUSINESS COMBINATIONS

2.4.3 The allocation period

The 'allocation period' is the term used in the US to mean the period of time within which the acquirer can investigate the assets and liabilities which have been acquired and make a reasoned allocation of values to them. The length of this period is not defined in UK GAAP at present. (see comments on ED 53 in section 2.4.2 above.)

2.4.4 Accounting for goodwill

CA 85 Sch 4A.9
SSAP 14.29
SSAP 22.13,36
SSAP 23.16

When acquisition accounting is used, goodwill arising on consolidation is computed by comparing the fair value of the purchase price with the aggregate of the fair values of the separable net assets acquired including identifiable intangibles such as patents, licences etc.

CA 85 Sch 4.21
SSAP 22.41-42

Purchased goodwill (including goodwill on consolidation) should normally be written off immediately to reserves; alternatively it may be amortised through the profit and loss account on a systematic basis over its useful economic life. Either policy may be adopted in respect of goodwill which relates to different acquisitions (see section 27.1.3).

COMMENT

ED 47 seeks to require that goodwill be capitalised and amortised over a period of not more than 20, or in exceptional circumstances, 40 years.

CA 85 Sch 4A.14

The cumulative amount of goodwill written off (net of goodwill relating to undertakings previously disposed of) should be disclosed.

BUSINESS COMBINATIONS

If the tax benefits of an acquired entity's operating loss or tax credit carryforward for financial reporting are not recognised at the acquisition date, subsequent recognition should:

FAS 96.23

(a)   first be applied to eliminate any goodwill and other non current intangible assets related to the acquisition; and

(b)   next be recognised as a reduction of the tax expense.

If FAS 96 has not been adopted, the acquirer should reduce the goodwill arising on the acquisition retroactively for realised tax benefits of loss carryforwards of an acquired company that were not recorded as part of the purchase price allocation.

APB 16.88

2.4.3 The allocation period

The allocation period should usually not exceed one year from the consummation of a business combination.

FAS 38.4-5

All preacquisition contingencies should be included and allocated a portion of the total cost of a purchased company provided certain conditions are met.

2.4.4 Accounting for intangibles (including goodwill)

The excess of the cost of the acquired company over the sum of the amounts assigned to identifiable tangible and intangible assets acquired less liabilities assumed should be recorded as goodwill.

APB 16.90

APB 17.27-30

Intangibles including goodwill should be amortised on a straight line basis over its estimated useful life not exceeding 40 years. 40 years is only used if the useful life is indeterminate. In most cases the useful life will be determinable and so less than 40 years. The amortisation period for each intangible asset (including goodwill) should be determined separately. An accelerated method of amortisation should be used for goodwill when the amount assigned to goodwill includes costs for identifiable intangibles whose fair values are not determinable and the benefits expected to be received from these intangibles decline over the expected life of the factors which are the basis for those intangibles.

APB 17.30

FIN 9.9

BUSINESS COMBINATIONS

SSAP 22.40   If the aggregate of the fair values of the separable net assets acquired other than goodwill exceeds the fair value of the consideration given, the discount (negative goodwill) is set up as a capital reserve on consolidation which would be included as part of shareholders' equity.

> **COMMENT**
>
> ED 47 proposes an amortisation treatment for negative goodwill, equivalent to that proposed for goodwill, that is that it should be amortised as a credit to the profit and loss account.

SSAP 22.18   Where acquisition accounting is applied to a business combination which
CA 85 s 131   qualifies as a merger, the excess of the fair value of any shares included in the consideration over their nominal (or par) value should be credited to a separate merger reserve (see section 33.6). Normally such an excess has to be credited to the share premium account but CA 85 provides for merger relief in the case of shares issued in a transaction satisfying the criteria for 'merger relief' (see section 32.2.1).

2.4.5 Acquisition date

SSAP 14.32   The effective date of acquisition of a subsidiary should be taken as the earlier
SSAP 23.9   of:

- the date on which consideration passes; or

- the date on which the offer becomes or is declared unconditional.

2.4.6 Disclosure

SSAP 17 App   There is no specific requirement to give pro forma information about the effects of acquisitions after the balance sheet date although a material acquisition would be treated as a non-adjusting post balance sheet event and as such, the financial effects would be disclosed.

SSAP 14-30   Sufficient information about the results of the subsidiary acquired should be disclosed to enable shareholders to appreciate the effect on the consolidated results.

CA 85 Sch 4A.13   Where an undertaking is acquired during the financial year which significantly affects the group accounts, disclosure should be made of its profit or loss (after making fair value and other consolidation

BUSINESS COMBINATIONS

An SEC registrant should amortise goodwill arising on acquisition of financial institutions over a maximum period of 25 years. The amortisation of goodwill arising on acquisitions of banking or thrift institutions is addressed by FAS 72.

Negative goodwill should be allocated to reduce proportionately the values assigned to non-current assets in determining their fair values. Any remainder should be classified as a deferred credit and amortised to income over the period estimated to be benefited but not in excess of 40 years. *APB 16.91*

2.4.5 Acquisition date

The effective date for an acquisition is ordinarily the date assets are received and other assets are given up or securities are issued. However, the parties to an acquisition may designate the end of an accounting period between the date of initiation and consummation of the transaction as the effective date. If this is done, interest should be imputed into the value of the consideration. *APB 16.93*

2.4.6 Disclosure

Disclosure in the acquirer's financial statements for the period in which a business combination accounted for by the purchase method occurs includes, inter alia:

The results of the period and of the immediately preceding period should be disclosed on a pro forma basis as though the companies had been combined throughout those periods. In reflecting such pro forma information, adjustments will be required to take account of fair value adjustments. *APB 16.96* *FAS 79*

Non public enterprises are exempt from this requirement. (Non public is defined in FAS 21.13).

BUSINESS COMBINATIONS

adjustments):

* from the beginning of its current financial year to the date of acquisiton; and

* its previous financial year.

CA 85 Sch 4A.13
SSAP 22.44,47
The amount of goodwill arising during the year should be shown separately for each acquisition where material. The fair value of the consideration and the amount of purchased goodwill arising on each acquisition during the period should be separately disclosed. The method of dealing with goodwill arising should be identified.

SSAP 22.50
If the fair value exercise has only been carried out on a provisional basis at the end of the accounting period in which the acquisition took place this should be stated and the reasons given. Disclosure is required of any subsequent material adjustments to such provisional fair values together with explanations.

CA 85 Sch 4.46(1)
CA 85 Sch 4A.13
SSAP 22.48-49
The following should also be disclosed in respect of each material acquisition during the period and in aggregate for other acquisitions which are material in total but not so individually:

* a table showing the book values as recorded in the acquired company's books and the fair values of each major category of assets and liabilities acquired;

* an analysis of the differences between values (with explanations) for each major category of assets and liabilities analysed into amounts attributable to:

    (a) revaluations;

    (b) provisions established in respect of the acquisition including provisions for future trading losses; and

    (c) bringing accounting policies into line with those of the acquiring group; and

* an analysis of movements on provisions related to acquisitions split between amounts used and the amounts released unused or applied for another purpose. Sufficient detail should be given to identify the extent to which the provisions have proved unnecessary.

BUSINESS COMBINATIONS

The SEC also requires pro forma presentation in certain specified situations (e.g. business combinations, disposals, reorganisations, unusual asset exchanges, restructuring of existing indebtedness etc). *S-X 11.01*

3 CAPITALISATION OF BORROWING COSTS

3.1 AUTHORITATIVE PRONOUNCEMENTS

- SSAP 9

- CA 85

- YB

COMMENT

During 1990, the ASC issued ED 51 — Accounting for fixed assets and revaluations. This exposure briefly deals with the subject of capitalisation of interest and its proposals have been summarised below, wherever appropriate. At the time of writing, it is not possible to determine what areas, if any, of the ED will be amended in any subsequent standard.

3.2 GENERAL APPROACH

CA 85 Sch 4.26(2-3)
SSAP 9, App 1.21

Interest capitalisation is not mandatory in the UK. CA 85 permits the capitalisation of interest on capital borrowed to finance the production of an asset to the extent that it accrues in respect of the period of production.

COMMENT

ED 51 proposes that enterprises should be allowed to choose whether or not they capitalise borrowing costs on projects that take a substantial period of time to be brought into use for their intended purpose. The ED states that once a policy to capitalise has been adopted, it should be applied consistently to all eligible assets.

3.3 QUALIFYING ASSETS

CA 85 permits interest to be capitalised as part of the production cost of any fixed and current asset. In practice, capitalisation only takes place where the production period is sufficiently long for borrowing costs to be significant in relation to the total production cost.

COMMENT

ED 51 addresses the subject of capitalisation of borrowing costs in respect of fixed assets only.

3.4 AMOUNT TO BE CAPITALISED

There is no guidance provided as to the amount of interest to be capitalised except for the CA 85 provisions noted in 3.2 above. In practice, companies capitalise interest costs irrespective of whether or not they relate to

INTEREST CAPITALISATION

3.1 AUTHORITATIVE PRONOUNCEMENTS
- FAS 34 (as amended by FAS 42 & FAS 58)

3.2 GENERAL APPROACH

Interest cost should be capitalised as part of the historical cost of acquiring *FAS 34.6-8* certain assets. To qualify for interest capitalisation, assets must require a period of time to get them ready for their intended use (referred to as qualifying assets).

3.3 QUALIFYING ASSETS

Qualifying assets are defined as: *FAS 34.9*

- assets which are constructed or otherwise produced for an enterprise's *FAS 58.5* own use (including assets constructed or produced for the enterprise by *FAS 42.4* others for which deposits or progress payments have been made);

- assets intended for sale or lease that are constructed or otherwise produced as discrete projects (e.g. ships or real estate developments);

- investments accounted for by the equity method while the investee has activities in progress necessary to commence its planned principal operations provided that the investee's activities include the use of funds to acquire qualifying assets for its operation.

3.4 AMOUNT TO BE CAPITALISED

The amount to be capitalised is the interest cost which could theoretically *FAS 34.12-14* have been avoided if the expenditure on the qualifying asset were not made. This is determined by applying an interest rate (based on borrowings

CAPITALISATION OF BORROWING COSTS

incremental or specific borrowings made for the financing of the asset in question.

COMMENT

The proposed requirements in ED 51 are not very detailed. Borrowing costs are defined to include, inter alia, interest and gains or losses on foreign currency differences relating to borrowed funds to the extent that they are regarded as an adjustment to interest costs. The ED proposes that a capitalisation rate should be determined by relating the borrowing costs incurred in financing expenditure on fixed assets during a period to the borrowings outstanding during that period. However where there have been specific borrowings used to finance the production of an asset, the interest capitalised should be based on actual borrowing costs incurred on those borrowings.

The amount of borrowing costs capitalised should not exceed the total amount of borrowing costs incurred by the enterprise in that period.

3.5 CAPITALISATION PERIOD

There is no further guidance on the determination of the capitalisation period other than the CA 85 provisions noted in 3.2 above.

COMMENT

In comparison to FAS 34, ED 51 deals with the commencement and end of the capitalisation period in rather general terms.

3.6 DISCLOSURE

CA 85 Sch 4.26(2-3)   If interest is capitalised as part of the cost of an asset, the amount involved must be disclosed.

YB 2.21(g)   Listed companies must disclose the amount of interest capitalised during the year and also the amount and treatment of any related tax relief.

COMMENT

ED 51 proposes that the amount of borrowing costs capitalised in the period in respect of each class of fixed assets should be disclosed.

INTEREST CAPITALISATION

outstanding during the year to finance the qualifying asset or a weighted average rate of interest) to the average amount of accumulated expenditure for the asset during the period.

Whilst not specifically addressed by FAS 34, in practice foreign currency differences relating to borrowed funds would not be included in the total interest cost incurred available for capitalisation.

The total amount of interest cost capitalised in a financial year should not exceed the total amount of interest cost incurred by the enterprise.   *FAS 34.15*

3.5 CAPITALISATION PERIOD

The capitalisation period should begin when the following three conditions   *FAS 34.17*
are present:

*   expenditures for the asset must have been made;

*   activities that are necessary to get the asset ready for its intended use are in progress;

*   interest cost is being incurred.

Interest should continue to be capitalised as long as these three conditions are   *FAS 34.18*
present. The capitalisation period ends when the asset is substantially complete and ready for use.

3.6 DISCLOSURE

The total amount of interest cost incurred and the amount capitalised during   *FAS 34.21*
the financial year should be disclosed.

COMMITMENTS AND CONTINGENCIES

4.1 AUTHORITATIVE PRONOUNCEMENTS

- SSAP 18

- SSAP 17

- CA 85

4.2 CONTINGENT LOSSES

CA 85 Sch 4.50 (1-2)
SSAP 18.15-16
A contingent loss should be accrued for if it is probable that it will crystallise. Other contingent losses should be disclosed unless they are remote.

4.2.1 Disclosure

SSAP 18.18
The disclosures required are:

- nature of the contingency;

- uncertainties expected to affect the ultimate outcome; and

- the amount involved or a prudent estimate of the financial effect (taking account of taxation) at date of approval of the financial statements by the board of directors (or a statement that it is not practicable to make such an estimate).

The amount to be disclosed should be reduced by any amounts that have been accrued and any element of the contingency considered to be remote.

CA 85 Sch 4.50
Particulars must be given of any charge on the assets of the company to secure the liabilities of any other person showing the amount secured.

COMMITMENTS AND CONTINGENCIES

4.1 AUTHORITATIVE PRONOUNCEMENTS

- FAS 5

- FIN 14

- FAS 47

- FRR 16

4.2 LOSS CONTINGENCIES

Loss contingencies should be accrued for if: *FAS 5.8*

- it is probable, based on information available prior to issuance of the financial statements, that a loss has been incurred at the balance sheet date, and

- the amount of loss can be reasonably estimated.

If the amount of loss is within a range of estimated amounts and no amount   *FIN 14.3*
within the range appears to be a better estimate than any other amount, the
minimum amount in the range should be accrued.

4.2.1 Disclosure

Disclosure of the nature of the accrual, and in some circumstances the   *FAS 5.9-10*
amount accrued, may be necessary for the financial statements not to be
misleading.

If a loss contingency exists but one or both of the above conditions are not
met or an exposure to loss exists in excess of the amount accrued, the
following should be disclosed unless the loss contingency is remote:

- the nature of the contingency;

- the possible loss (or range of loss).

Disclosure of remote contingencies which have the characteristics of   *FAS 5.12*
guarantees. For example, guarantees of indebtedness of others, guarantees to
repurchase receivables that have been sold or assigned, standby letters of
credit, etc.

If information becomes available before an enterprise's financial statements   *FAS 5.11*
are issued indicating that a loss was incurred after the date of the financial
statements, disclosure may be necessary to keep the financial statements
from being misleading. It may be desirable to present pro forma statements
on the face of the balance sheet.

COMMITMENTS AND CONTINGENCIES

4.3 CONTINGENT GAINS

SSAP 18.17   SSAP 18 does not permit such gains to be accrued. A material contingent gain should be disclosed in financial statements only if it is probable that the gain will be realised.

4.4 COMMITMENTS

CA 85 Sch 4.5 (4-5)   Details of pension commitments (whether or not accrued in the accounts) should be given along with any other financial commitments which have not been provided for and are relevant to assessing the company's affairs. Any pension commitments relating to past directors should be separately disclosed.

CA 85 Sch 4.50(3)   Particulars must be given of any capital commitments split between amounts contracted for but not provided and amounts authorised by the directors but not contracted for.

CA 85 Sch 4.59A   Separate details must be given for commitments undertaken on behalf of any parent undertaking or fellow subsidiary undertaking and any subsidiary undertaking of the reporting company.

COMMITMENTS AND CONTINGENCIES

Unused letters of credit, assets pledged as security for loans and commitments such as those for plant acquisition, obligation to reduce debts, etc should be disclosed.

FAS 5.18
S-X 4-08(b)

4.3 CONTINGENT GAINS

Contingent gains are usually not reflected in the accounts. Disclosure should be given but care should be exercised to avoid misleading implications as to the likelihood of realisation.

FAS 5.17

4.4 COMMITMENTS

A purchaser is required to make certain disclosures concerning unconditional purchase obligations that meet certain criteria. An unconditional purchase obligation is an obligation to transfer funds in the future for fixed or minimum amounts/quantities of goods or services at fixed or minimum prices (e.g. take or pay contracts, etc.). The disclosures include:

FAS 47.6-8

- the nature and term of the obligation;

- the amount of the fixed and determinable portions of the obligation as of the date of the latest balance sheet presented and, if determinable, for each of the next five years;

- the nature of any variable components of the obligation;

- the amounts purchased under the obligation for each period for which an income statement is presented.

Disclosure of the amount of imputed interest necessary to reduce the unconditional purchase obligation to present value is encouraged but not required.

Disclosure is required in the notes to the financial statements of the principal condition and events that raise questions about a company's ability to continue as a going concern and also of any mitigating factors including viable plans to overcome these difficulties.

SAS 59.10-11
FRR 16

Separate disclosure of commitments and contingent liabilities should be given in a caption on the face of the balance sheet.

S-X 5-02.25

5 DISCOUNTING AND INTEREST IMPUTATION

Discounting and the imputation of interest are not the subject of an accounting standard and have not become common practice in the UK.

However, there are a number of existing UK accounting pronouncements and practices where costs and revenues are allocated on a time adjusted basis. For example:

- SSAP 21 — *Accounting for leases and hire purchase agreements,* requires an interest charge to be imputed for finance leases for both lessor and lessee accounting.

- By their nature, the use of actuarial valuation methods permitted by SSAP 24 — *Accounting for pension costs,* in determining the annual pension cost makes allowance for interest so that future cash flows are discounted to their present value. The standard adds that if a scheme is unfunded, the provision for pension costs is assessed and reviewed on a discounted basis and adjusted each year to reflect, inter alia, the interest on the unfunded liability.

COMMENT

1. ED 53 — *Fair value in the context of acquisition accounting,* issued by the ASC recommends that discounting should be employed in respect of long-term receivables and payables where their interest rates are significantly different from prevailing rates.

2. There are two technical releases (TR) which address the subject. TRs contain non-mandatory guidance for the benefit of accountants in the UK. They are normally issued by the ICAEW although in the past certain TRs have been issued by the ASC.

- *Accounting for complex capital issues* (TR 677) recommends the use of discounting techniques and imputation of market rates of interest in its guidance. The main principle included in this Release is that an appropriate annual financing charge should be calculated based on the amount of debt which is outstanding.

- The Technical Committee of the ICAEW published a discussion paper, *The use of discounting in financial statements* (TR 773) in December 1989, which considered the possible applications of discounted cash flow techniques and how these could be used in preparing financial statements. The Technical Committee believes that the recognition of the time value of money is required in certain instances in order that the financial statements should give a true and fair view.

INTEREST IMPUTATION

5.1 AUTHORITATIVE PRONOUNCEMENT
- APB 21

5.2 APPLICABILITY

Receivables and payables which represent contractual rights to receive money or contractual obligations to pay money on fixed or determinable dates must be accounted for in accordance with APB 21 except those which arise from

APB 21.2-3

- transactions entered into in the normal course of business where the terms of settlement do not exceed approximately one year;

- intra group transactions; and

- deposits or progress payments on long term contracts.

5.3 IMPUTING INTEREST

If a transaction involves deferred consideration, and

APB 21.12

(a)   the interest rate on the consideration is either nil or is unreasonable, or

(b)   the stated amount (i.e. the nominal value) of the consideration receivable or payable (the note) is materially different from the current cash sales price for the same/similar items or from the market value of the note at the date of the transaction,

it should be recorded at the fair value of the property, goods or services or at the present value of the note using a market rate of interest, whichever is the more clearly determinable.

The difference between the recorded value and the nominal value of the transaction should be treated as discount or premium and amortised as interest expense or income over the life of the note so as to produce a constant rate of interest on the amount outstanding at the beginning of any given period (generally referred to as the interest method).

General guidance is provided on the selection of an appropriate market rate of interest.

APB 21.13-14

5.4 DISCLOSURE

The discount or premium should be reported as a direct deduction from or addition to the nominal amount of the note in the balance sheet. The effective rate of interest and the face amount should also be disclosed.

APB 21.16

6 DIVIDENDS PAYABLE

6.1 AUTHORITATIVE PRONOUNCEMENTS

- CA 85

- SSAP 8

- SSAP 17

6.2 ACCOUNTING FOR DIVIDENDS PAYABLE

SSAP 17.11
CA 85 Sch 4.3(7)
CA 85 s 263(3)

In the UK, dividends are normally regarded as linked to a particular year's earnings, although they are, in strict statutory terms, paid out of cumulative retained earnings. The final dividend for the year will normally be proposed by the directors after the year end for subsequent approval by the shareholders at the annual general meeting. Even though such final dividends are proposed and approved after the year end, the proposed dividend is nevertheless required to be reflected in the related financial statements.

6.2.1 Disclosure

CA 85 Sch 4.7
SSAP 8.24

The aggregate amount of any dividends paid and proposed should be shown separately in the profit and loss account. Such amounts should not include either the related advance corporation tax (ACT) or the attributable tax credit.

CA 85 Sch 4.49

If any fixed cumulative dividends on the company's shares are in arrears, the following should be disclosed:

- the amount of the arrears; and

- the period for which the dividends are in arrears (for each class of share).

SSAP 8.26

Dividends proposed (or declared and not yet payable) should be included in current liabilities without the addition of the related ACT. The ACT on proposed dividends (whether recoverable or irrecoverable) should be included as a current tax liability.

DIVIDENDS PAYABLE

6.1 AUTHORITATIVE PRONOUNCEMENT
- Regulation S-X

6.2 ACCOUNTING FOR DIVIDENDS

Dividends are a charge to retained earnings at the point of time that they are formally declared by the board of directors. Usually, common dividends are declared on a quarterly basis.

The SEC requires a market-rate dividend to be imputed in the case of increasing-rate preferred stock (see section 32.3.4).

6.2.1 Disclosure

The per-share amount and aggregate amount should be disclosed by each class of stock.   *S-X 3-04*

The per-share and aggregate amounts of cumulative preferred dividends in arrears should be disclosed.   *APB 15.50 fn 16*

The income or loss applicable to common stock should be disclosed on the face of the profit and loss account when it is materially different from reported net income or loss. The income or loss applicable to common stock is calculated by deducting the following amounts from net income or loss: *SAB 64*

(i)   dividends on preferred stock (including arrears on cumulative preference stock), and

(ii) periodic increases in the carrying amounts of instruments reported as redeemable preferred stock (see section 32.3.2)

Any restrictions which limit the payment of dividends by the registrant should be disclosed.   *S-X 4.08(e)*
    FAS 5.18

7 EMPLOYEE SHARE OPTION SCHEMES

There is no requirement in the UK to accrue the cost of the benefit in kind received by an employee when an employer grants share options with exercise prices that are lower than the share price at the date of grant. However, primarily due to tax considerations but also because of pressure from institutional investors, most companies in the UK grant options at or near the market price at date of grant thus resulting in a negligible 'compensation cost'.

CA 85 Sch 4.40   CA 85 requires the following disclosures to be made with respect to 'any contingent right to the allotment of shares', including those arising under an employees' share scheme:

• the number, description and the amount of the shares;

• the period during which it is exercisable; and

• the price to be paid.

STOCK COMPENSATION

7.1 AUTHORITATIVE PRONOUNCEMENTS

- ARB 43

- APB 25

- FIN 28

- FIN 38

7.2 GENERAL APPROACH

Typically, non-cash compensatory plans for key employees are linked to the company's stock, for example, a stock option plan or stock appreciation rights (SARs) granted to employees, giving them a right to receive the appreciation in price of a given number of shares over the plan period. The cost of providing benefits under such plans should be recognised as compensation expense over the periods in which the employee performs related services.

7.3 COMPENSATORY AND NON-COMPENSATORY PLANS

A non-compensatory plan should possess at least the following characteristics:

APB 25.7

- substantially all full-time employees meeting limited employment qualifications may participate;

- stock is offered to eligible employees equally or based on a uniform percentage of salary or wages;

- the time permitted for exercise of an option or purchase right is limited to a reasonable period; and

- any discount from the market price is no greater than would be reasonable in an offer of stock to stockholders.

Plans that do not have all the above characteristics are compensatory.

7.4 ACCOUNTING FOR COMPENSATORY PLANS

Total compensation cost is measured by the difference between the quoted market price of the stock (usually at the date of grant or award) and the price, if any, to be paid by an employee and is recognised as expense over the period the employee performs related services (the 'service period').

APB 25.10

EMPLOYEE SHARE OPTION SCHEMES

STOCK COMPENSATION

In the case of SARs and other 'variable' plans (i.e. plans for which either the number of shares of stock that may be acquired by, or awarded, to an employee or the price to be paid by the employee or both are not specified or determinable until after the date of grant or award), estimates of compensation cost based on the quoted market price of the stock at the period end should be used until the first date on which both the factors noted above are known (called the measurement date). Guidance on how to determine this date for certain types of plans is contained in FIN 38. Compensation accrued during the service period should be adjusted in subsequent periods up to the measurement date to reflect changes in the market value of the shares. These adjustments should be reflected in compensation expense of the period in which changes in the market value of the shares occur.

FIN 28.3-4

On the exercise of an option, the sum of cash received and the amount of compensation charged to income shall be accounted for as consideration received on the issue of stock. No compensation expense for services is recognised when accounting for consideration received for stock that is issued through non-compensatory plans.

ARB 43 Chap 13B
APB 25.7

The amounts recorded as deferred compensation should be presented in the balance sheet as a deduction from stockholders' equity.

SAB 40

7.5 EITF ISSUES

The EITF has addressed a number of stock compensation issues in the last few years which are not mentioned here because of their specialised nature.

7.6 DISCLOSURE

Disclosure is required of the status of the option/plan at the end of the period including:

APB 25.19
ARB 43 Chap 13B.15

• the number of shares under option;

• the option price; and

• the number of shares as to which options were exercisable.

In respect of the options exercised during the period, disclosure is required of the number of shares involved and the option price thereof.

8 EQUITY METHOD OF ACCOUNTING FOR INVESTMENTS

8.1 AUTHORITATIVE PRONOUNCEMENT

- SSAP 1

- CA 85

COMMENT

The ASC has issued ED 50 which is intended to replace and update SSAPs 1 and 14 in the light of the changes made to CA 85 by the Companies Act 1989. For the purposes of this section, it has been assumed that SSAP 1 still applies to associated undertakings.

8.2 APPLICABILITY

The equity method of accounting is essentially the adoption in modified form of the consolidation procedures used for subsidiary companies and should be used to account for investments in the following entities in the investing group's consolidated financial statements (see section 13.5):

- associated undertakings; and

- certain unconsolidated subsidiaries.

COMMENT

ED 50 proposes that where an interest in another enterprise has been acquired exclusively with a view to resale or there are severe long-term restrictions which prevent joint control or influence, that enterprise should be accounted for as a current asset investment and should not be equity accounted or proportionally consolidated.

The cost method should be used to account for such investments in the investing company's individual accounts. Certain disclosures should be made in such situations (see section 8.4).

8.3 METHOD OF ACCOUNTING

SSAP 1.18-23

CA 85 Sch 4A.22

The investing group's share of profits less losses of associates should be included in the group's profit and loss account. The share of pre-tax profit should be disclosed as part of the group profit before tax, and similarly the tax attributed to that share of profits and the investing group's share of extraordinary items should be included (and disclosed separately) within the relevant group items. However, the investing group's share of turnover and other profit and loss account items should not be included.

SSAP 1.25-26

CA 85 Sch 4A.22

The amount at which the investing group's interest in associates should be shown in the consolidated balance sheet is the total of:

- the investing group's share of net assets, other than goodwill, after attributing fair values to the net assets at the time of acquisition;

EQUITY METHOD OF ACCOUNTING FOR INVESTMENTS

8.1 AUTHORITATIVE PRONOUNCEMENTS

- APB 18

- AIN-APB 18

8.2 APPLICABILITY

The equity method of accounting for an investment in common stock should be followed by an investor whose investment in voting stock gives it the ability to exercise significant influence over operating and financial policies of an investee even though the investor holds 50% or less of the voting stock.

APB 18.17

The equity method of accounting should be used for such investments where the investing company does not have any subsidiaries and therefore does not prepare consolidated accounts (see section 13.8).

8.3 METHOD OF ACCOUNTING

The investing group's share of after tax profits or losses of the investee company should be included in the group's income statement as a single line item except that, if material, the investing group's share of extraordinary items and prior period adjustments should be classified separately in the group income statement.

APB 18.19(c),(d)

Under the equity method the investment is included in the balance sheet at cost plus share of post-acquisition profits, less dividends received from the investee.

APB 18.19(c)

If cost differs from the amount of underlying equity (fair value) in net assets at the date of acquisition, the difference should be accounted for as if the

APB 18.19(b)

101

EQUITY METHOD OF ACCOUNTING FOR INVESTMENTS

- the investing group's share of any goodwill in the associate's own financial statements; and

- the premium paid (or discount) on the acquisition of the interest. Any such goodwill should be accounted for in the same way as purchased goodwill in subsidiaries (see section 2.4.4).

Separate disclosure is required, in aggregate for all investments in associated undertakings, of each of the above items except that the last two items may be shown as one aggregate amount.

8.3.1 Non-coterminous financial statements

SSAP 1.36-37   The financial statements of the associate used for the purposes of including its results in the consolidated financial statements of the investing group should be either coterminous with those of the investing group or made up to a date which is either not more than six months before, or shortly after, the date of the financial statements of the investing group. If the effect of using 'non-coterminous' financial statements is material, the facts and the dates of year ends should be disclosed.

8.3.2 Deficiency of net assets

SSAP 1.33   Where the associate has a deficiency of net assets but is still regarded as a long-term investment, the investing group should reflect its share of the deficiency of net assets in its consolidated financial statements.

8.4 DISCLOSURE

SSAP 1.49
CA 85 Sch 5.22

For each principal associated undertaking the following should be disclosed in the consolidated financial statements:

- its name;

- its country of incorporation or, if incorporated in Great Britain, registration;

- if unincorporated, its address;

- the proportion of issued shares held by the investing group, distinguishing between those held directly by the parent company and those held by subsidiary undertakings;

EQUITY METHOD OF ACCOUNTING FOR INVESTMENTS

investee were a consolidated subsidiary, namely as goodwill.

8.3.1 Non-coterminous financial statements

If the financial statements of an investee are not sufficiently timely, the investor should normally record its share of the earnings or losses of an investee from the most recent available financial statements, which may be its audited year end accounts. The investor could base its proportionate share of the results of operations of an investee on the investee's unaudited interim financial statements. Where there is a time lag in reporting, this time lag should be consistent from period to period.

APB 18.19(g)

SAS 1(S332)

For SEC registrants, a 93 day rule operates (as for subsidiaries; see section 13.4.1).

8.3.2 Deficiency of net assets

The investor should normally discontinue applying the equity method when the investment accounted for by the equity method plus advances made by the investor is reduced to zero and should not provide for additional losses unless the investor has guaranteed obligations of the investee or is otherwise committed to provide further financial support for the investee.

APB 18.19(i)

8.4 DISCLOSURE

The following should be disclosed, when material, in the financial statements:

APB 18.20 (a),(b)

- name of each investee and percentage of common stock;

- accounting policies of the investor with respect to investments in common stock;

- the difference, if any, between the amount at which an investment is carried and the amount of underlying equity in net assets, as well as the accounting treatment of the difference; and

EQUITY METHOD OF ACCOUNTING FOR INVESTMENTS

- an indication of the nature of its business; and

- the aggregate market value in respect of each amount disclosed as listed investments (see section 28.5).

CA 85 s 231 Where this information would result in disclosures of excessive length, it need only be given in respect of the principal subsidiary undertakings, provided that:

- the fact that advantage has been taken of this exemption is disclosed; and

- the full information is given in an appendix to the company's next annual return.

SSAP 1.31 The investing group's share of the post-acquisition accumulated reserves of associates and movements therein should be disclosed in the consolidated financial statements. If distribution of accumulated reserves of overseas associates would be subject to further tax, this should be made clear.

SSAP 1.23,30 If the results of an associate are very material to the group, details of total turnover, depreciation and profit before tax should be given by separate disclosure in the notes. Similar considerations also apply in relation to the associates' tangible and intangible assets and liabilities.

SSAP 1.24,35 The information to be disclosed in respect of associates when they have been accounted for under the equity method in the investor company's group accounts should be provided by an investing company (other than a wholly owned subsidiary) that does not prepare consolidated financial statements.

> **COMMENT**
> ED 50 proposes not to require such information from companies which are exempt under CA 85 from preparing consolidated financial statements.

CA 85 Sch 5.25
SSAP 1.38 Where an investment in which 20% or more is held is not equity accounted, similar disclosures to those required by APB 18.19 (see opposite) should be made. In addition, details of the accounting treatment adopted and the reason for doing so (except where disclosure of the reason would be harmful to the business) and the total of its capital and reserves and profit or loss for the last financial year should be provided.

EQUITY METHOD OF ACCOUNTING FOR INVESTMENTS

- for quoted investments, the market value of the investment in associates.

The amount of consolidated retained earnings which represents undistributed earnings of 50% or less owned persons accounted for by the equity method should be disclosed.

S-X 4-08(e)(2)

If equity method investees are significant to the financial position of the investor, summarised details of assets, liabilities and results of operations should be disclosed in the notes or separate investee financial statements may be required. Dividends received from such an investee should also be disclosed, as well as other items required under APB 18.

APB 18.20(d)

S-X 5-03.13

S-X-4-08(g)

If a 20% or more investee is not equity accounted, disclosure should be made of the name of the investee and the reasons why the equity method is not considered appropriate. Similar disclosure is required if less than 20% is held but is accounted for under the equity method.

APB 18.19 fn 13

9 EXTINGUISHMENT OF DEBT

Practice in this area is generally similar to that in the US, except an 'in-substance debt defeasance' is not a common occurrence in the UK. In-substance debt defeasance refers to extinguishment of debt in circumstances where the debtor is not legally released from his obligations.

EXTINGUISHMENT OF DEBT

9.1 AUTHORITATIVE PRONOUNCEMENTS

- FAS 76

- APB 26

- TB 84-4

9.2 WHAT IS EXTINGUISHMENT?

Debt is considered extinguished for financial reporting purposes when: *FAS 76.3-4*

- the debtor pays the creditor and is relieved of all its obligations with respect to the debt; or

- the debtor is legally released as the primary obligor under the debt and it is probable that the debtor will not be required to make future payments as guarantor of the debt; or

- the debtor irrevocably places cash or certain other assets (there are restrictions on the nature of assets that may be held by the trust) in a trust solely for the purpose of satisfying scheduled interest and principal payments of a specific obligation and the possibility that the debtor will be required to make further payments with respect to that debt is remote (described as in-substance defeasance).

Debt may not be extinguished where the debtor irrevocably places in trust   *TB 84-4*
assets that were acquired at about the time that the debt was incurred (instantaneous in-substance defeasance).

9.3 ACCOUNTING AND DISCLOSURE

Gains and losses from extinguishments of debt should be recognised in   *APB 26.20*
income of the period of extinguishment and identified as a separate item.   *FAS 4.8*
Such amounts should be aggregated and if material classified as an extraordinary item, net of related income tax effect (this does not apply to gains and losses arising from extinguishments of debt made to satisfy sinking-fund requirements).

Where the extraordinary classification is made, the following information   *FAS 4.9*
should be disclosed as a note, if not disclosed on the face of the income statement:

- description of the extinguishment transactions including the sources of any funds used to extinguish debt, if practicable;

EXTINGUISHMENT OF DEBT

EXTINGUISHMENT OF DEBT

- the income tax effect in the period of extinguishment; and

- the per share amount of the aggregate gain or loss net of related tax effect.

In the case of an in-substance defeasance, a general description of the transaction and the amount of debt considered extinguished should be disclosed so long as the debt remains outstanding.

FAS 76.6

10 FOREIGN CURRENCY TRANSLATION

10.1 AUTHORITATIVE PRONOUNCEMENTS

- SSAP 20

- CA 85

10.2 INDIVIDUAL COMPANIES

10.2.1 Local currency

SSAP 20-39 SSAP 20 uses the term local currency in the same context as the term functional currency is used in FAS 52. It is defined as the currency of the primary economic environment in which the company operates and generates net cash flows.

10.2.2 Basic requirements

SSAP 20.46-50 All foreign currency transactions should be translated into the company's local currency at the exchange rate ruling on the date the transaction occurs. If the rates do not fluctuate significantly, an average rate for the period is acceptable. Where the transaction is to be settled at a contracted rate, that rate may be used.

At the balance sheet date, monetary assets and liabilities denominated in foreign currencies should be translated by using the closing rate or, where appropriate, the rates of exchange fixed under the terms of the relevant transactions. All exchange differences arising on settled transactions during the period and upon retranslation of monetary items at the balance sheet date should be reported as part of the profit or loss for the year on ordinary activities, unless they arise as a result of events which themselves are treated as extraordinary items, in which case they should be included as part of such items. Recognition of exchange gains on long-term monetary items may have to be restricted on the grounds of prudence where there are doubts as to the convertibility or marketability of the currency in question.

Subject to section 10.2.3, non-monetary assets should not be retranslated but should remain translated at the rate ruling when they were originally recorded.

110

FOREIGN CURRENCY TRANSLATION

10.1 AUTHORITATIVE PRONOUNCEMENTS

- FAS 52

- FIN 37

10.2 FOREIGN CURRENCY TRANSACTIONS

10.2.1 Functional currency

Assets, liabilities and operations of a company should be recorded using the functional currency of that entity. This is defined as the currency of the primary economic environment in which the company operates; normally it is the currency of the environment in which it generates and expends cash.

FAS 52.5

The standard provides useful guidance on how to identify the functional currency. If the entity's accounting records have not been maintained in the functional currency, the standard requires the use of the temporal method to translate the entity's financial statements from the currency in which the accounting records are kept into its functional currency.

FAS 52 App A,B

10.2.2   Basic requirements

The requirements are the same as those in the UK.

FAS 52.15

FOREIGN CURRENCY TRANSLATION

10.2.3 Cover method

SSAP 20.51   An exception to the rule that non-monetary assets are not retranslated is where a company has foreign currency borrowings to finance or provide a hedge against its foreign equity investments. In such situations, the equity investments may be denominated in the appropriate foreign currency and retranslated at the closing rates each year in which case the resulting exchange differences should be taken to reserves. The exchange differences arising on the related foreign currency borrowings should also be taken to reserves and not be reported as part of the profit or loss for the period. The standard limits the amount that can be offset in reserves to the gain or loss arising on the hedged assets and requires that the accounting treatment adopted is applied consistently from period to period.

There is no requirement that borrowings be in the same currency as the investment or in a currency which moves in tandem.

10.2.4 Hedging foreign commitments

This is not specifically addressed by the standard. However, the approach required by FAS 52 is often used except that:

- the required accounting treatment can be adopted where a company has a reasonable expectation of entering into the transaction not just when a contractual commitment exists; and

- it is not clear whether the use of foreign currency debtors or creditors may be regarded as a hedge against a foreign currency commitment (for accounting purposes) under SSAP 20.

FOREIGN CURRENCY TRANSLATION

10.2.3 Hedging

FAS 52 requires that transaction gains and losses arising on either foreign *FAS 52.15,20* currency transactions that are economic hedges of a net investment in a foreign entity or intercompany foreign currency transactions that are of a long-term-investment nature should not be included in net income for the period. This is the equivalent of the cover method in SSAP 20 except for the following differences:

- its use is not optional;

- it can only be applied where the investment which is being hedged is consolidated or equity accounted. Therefore, for example, marketable equity securities denominated in a foreign currency that are not consolidated or equity accounted and are carried at cost should be recorded at the historical exchange rate. Exchange differences arising on the related borrowings should be taken to the income statement;

- the hedging transaction is not restricted to being a foreign currency borrowing;

- the transaction should be designated as, and effective as, an economic hedge of the net investment in the foreign enterprise. Ordinarily this means that a transaction that hedges a net investment should be denominated in the same currency as the functional currency of the net investment. However if it is impossible to hedge in that currency, it is permitted to hedge in a currency which moves in tandem with that of the investment. Also when a transaction is designated a hedge, all exchange differences until such time as it is no longer designated must be taken to reserves.

10.2.4 Hedging foreign commitments

Gains or losses arising on foreign currency transactions intended to hedge an *FAS 52.21* identifiable foreign currency commitment (for example, an agreement to purchase or sell equipment) should be deferred and excluded from the financial statements until the related foreign currency transaction (e.g. the purchase or sale of equipment) is recorded in the future period in the following circumstances:

- the foreign currency transaction is designated as, and is effective as, a hedge of the foreign currency commitment

- the foreign currency commitment is firm (i.e. contractual in nature)

FOREIGN CURRENCY TRANSLATION

10.2.5 Forward exchange contracts

SSAP 20.46,48 There are no specific rules on how to account for a forward foreign exchange contract but the standard notes that where there are related or matching forward contracts in respect of trading transactions or monetary assets and liabilities at the balance sheet date, the forward contract rates may be used to record those transactions and related assets and liabilities.

In practice, the FAS 52 approach is adopted by some UK companies.

10.3 CONSOLIDATED ACCOUNTS

The closing rate/net investment method should be used for translating the financial statements of a foreign enterprise which operates as a separate or quasi-independant entity. Under this method, the balance sheet of the foreign enterprise should be translated into the reporting currency of the investing company using the rate of exchange at the balance sheet date.

Where the trade of the foreign enterprise is more dependent on the economic environment of the investing company's currency than on its own reporting currency, the temporal method should be used for translating the financial

FOREIGN CURRENCY TRANSLATION

- in the case of a deferral of a loss, such a deferral is not expected to lead to recognising losses in later periods.

10.2.5 Forward exchange contracts

The gain or loss on a speculative forward contract should be recognised in net income and is computed by multiplying the contracted amount under the forward contract by the difference between the forward rate available for the remaining maturity of the contract and the contracted forward rate.

FAS 52.19

In the case of a non-speculative forward contract (e.g. a hedge of an existing foreign currency asset or liability) separate recognition should be given to the premium/discount on the contract. This is calculated as the difference between the contracted amount translated at the contracted rate and the amount calculated if translated at the spot rate when the contract was taken out. The premium/discount should generally be recognised in net income over the life of the forward contract.

FAS 52.18

The exchange gain or loss arising on the forward contract is calculated as the difference between the contracted amount at the spot rate at the balance sheet date and the spot rate at the date the contract was taken out. The accounting treatment for this amount will depend on whether the contract is a hedge against

- a net investment in a foreign enterprise; or

- a foreign currency commitment; or

- other foreign currency exposures.

Currency swaps should be accounted for in a manner similar to the accounting for forward contracts.

FAS 52.17

10.3 CONSOLIDATED ACCOUNTS

The closing rate/net investment method should be used for translating the results of a foreign enterprise having a functional currency which is different from the reporting currency of the investing enterprise. The rate to be used for translation purposes is generally the rate applicable to conversion of the foreign currency for the purposes of dividend remittances at the foreign entity's balance sheet date.

FAS 52.12,27b

FOREIGN CURRENCY TRANSLATION

statements for the purposes of consolidation. Under this method, the accounts reflect the transactions of the foreign entity as if they had been carried out by the investing entity itself.

10.3.1 Results in foreign enterprises

SSAP 20.54 The profit and loss account of a foreign enterprise that is accounted for under the closing rate/net investment method should be translated at the closing rate or at an average rate for the period.

10.3.2 Hyper-inflation

SSAP 20.26 The local currency financial statements of a foreign enterprise operating in a country where a very high rate of inflation exists should be adjusted where possible to reflect current price levels before the translation process for consolidation purposes is undertaken. Restatement based on specific price changes or general price changes would appear to be acceptable.

10.3.3 Exchange differences transferred to reserves

SSAP 20 does not specify the category of reserves to which exchange differences arising from the translation of the net investment in subsidiaries etc should be taken. Common practice is to take such differences to retained profits (see section 33.2) but this is not universally done.

10.3.4 Treatment of exchange differences on disposal of subsidiary

This is not addressed by the standard. In practice, companies do not include the corresponding cumulative exchange differences in the profit and loss account in the year of disposal.

10.3.5 Cover method applied in consolidated accounts

SSAP 20.57 In the case where companies have a number of investments financed by a number of borrowings, the cover method could be applied on a pooled basis (i.e. by aggregating all the investments and all the borrowings and comparing the net exchange difference on each). Alternatively, they could apply the cover method on an individual basis or a currency by currency pool basis. Whichever method is used, it should be applied consistently from period to period.

FOREIGN CURRENCY TRANSLATION

10.3.1 Results in foreign enterprises

When the closing rate/net investment method is being used, the standard requires the amounts in the income statement of foreign enterprises to be translated at the exchange rates ruling when those elements are recognised or at an appropriate weighted average rate for the period.

FAS 52.12

10.3.2 Entities operating in highly inflationary economics

A highly inflationary economy is defined as one that has cumulative inflation of approximately 100% or more over a three year period. The temporal method should be used to translate the financial statements of subsidiaries and equity accounted investees where they are denominated in currencies of highly-inflationary economies (i.e. remeasurement of the financial statements as if the parent company reporting currency had always been the functional currency).

FAS 52.11

10.3.3 Foreign currency translation reserve

The translation adjustments resulting from translating the foreign enterprise's financial statements should be accumulated in a separate component of equity.

FAS 52.13

10.3.4 Disposal of an investment

Where all or part of an investment in a foreign enterprise is sold, or it is substantially liquidated, the cumulative exchange differences included in the separate component of equity relating to the part which is sold or liquidated should be included in the net profit for the period as part of the gain or loss on sale or liquidation.

FAS 52.14
FIN 37

10.3.5 Hedging

FAS 52 requires the foreign currency transaction to be designated as a hedge as one of the criteria for using the cover method. Hence the 'global approach' allowed under SSAP 20 is inherently not permitted in FAS 52. The application of the cover method in the parent company and the consolidated financial statements is generally identical.

FOREIGN CURRENCY TRANSLATION

10.3.6 Goodwill on consolidation

SSAP 20.43,53   SSAP 20 does not appear to regard goodwill arising on acquisition as a currency asset and therefore amounts attributable to such goodwill will not generally fluctuate with changes in exchange rates that occur subsequent to the acquisition.

10.3.7 Disclosure

SSAP 20.60(a)   The net exchange gain or loss on borrowings less deposits should be disclosed, distinguishing between amounts included in the profit and loss account and amounts taken to reserves.

SSAP 20.60(b)   The movement in reserves for the period arising from exchange differences should be disclosed. However the cumulative exchange differences will not generally be apparent from the financial statements.

CA 85 Sch 4.15   Disclosure of the amount of unrealised exchange gains on unsettled long-term monetary items taken to the profit and loss account should be made, since they represent a departure from the principle of CA 85 Sch 4.12(a) that only realised profits should be included in the profit and loss account.

CA 85 Sch 4.58(1)   The basis for translating foreign currency items should be disclosed.

FOREIGN CURRENCY TRANSLATION

10.3.6 Goodwill on consolidation

Goodwill arising on the purchase of a foreign enterprise is a currency asset *FAS 52.101* which should be translated at closing rates. Exchange differences arising upon retranslation are taken to the foreign currency translation reserve.

10.3.7 Disclosure

Disclosure is required of the net exchange gain or loss included in the net *FAS 52.30-31* profit. Also, the movements in the reserve for cumulative translation adjustments should be provided.

11 FUTURES CONTRACTS

The subject of accounting for futures contracts is not addressed by a specific accounting standard.

FUTURES CONTRACTS

11.1 AUTHORITATIVE PRONOUNCEMENTS

*   FAS 80

*   FAS 52 (for foreign currency futures - see section 10.2.3 to 10.2.5)

11.2 ACCOUNTING PRINCIPLES

11.2.1 Summary

The accounting treatment of futures contracts depends on whether the futures contract qualifies as a hedge (see below).

If a contract does not qualify as a hedge, it should be accounted for at market value with gains and losses as the contract is marked to market being recognised in the income statement.

If the contract qualifies as a hedge, its accounting treatment depends on whether it is a hedge of an asset or liability or a firm commitment, an item reported at fair value, or an anticipated transaction.

11.2.2 Criteria for qualification as a hedge

The following criteria should be met: *FAS 80.4*

*   the item (asset, liability or firm commitment) to be hedged is exposed to price (or interest-rate) risk and is actually contributing to the overall risk of the entity;

*   the futures contract is designated as a hedge of a specific risk exposure and reduces that exposure.

In assessing whether the futures contract reduces the exposure, there should be a clear economic relationship between the subject of the futures contract and the item being hedged. Past experience must indicate that high correlation of price change is probable.

11.2.3 Hedges of existing assets, liabilities and firm commitments

If the item being hedged is accounted for at market value and unrealised   *FAS 80.5*
changes in the fair value of the hedged item are included in the income statement, the related futures contract should be accounted for similarly and marked to market.

If the item hedged is not accounted for at market value, the accounting   *FAS 80.6*
treatment differs.

In the case of a hedge of an existing asset or liability, changes in the market value of the related futures contract should be recognised as an adjustment of

FUTURES CONTRACTS

FUTURES CONTRACTS

the carrying value of the asset or liability. Where the futures contract hedges a specific item that is deliverable and it is probable that the hedged item and the futures contract will be held to the delivery date specified in the contract, the difference between the futures contract price and the fair value of the item hedged (the premium or discount) may be amortised to the income statement over the life of the contract.

In the case of a hedge of a firm commitment, changes in the market value of the related futures contract should be recognised upon the measurement of the transaction that satisfies the commitment.

11.2.4 Hedges of anticipated transactions

Futures contracts that relate to transactions that an enterprise expects but is not obligated to carry out in the normal course of business may be accounted for as hedges (often referred to as anticipatory hedges) if they meet the hedge qualification criteria referred to in section 11.2.2 and if   *FAS 80.9*

- the significant characteristics of the anticipated transaction are identified (e.g. expected dates of transaction, type of commodity or financial investment involved, expected quantity involved and term to maturity in the case of a financial instrument); and

- it is probable that the anticipated transaction will occur as evidenced by such factors as the frequency of similar transactions in the past, the commitment of resources to the activity so that the proposed transactions are in the normal course, etc.

11.3 DISCLOSURE

The following disclosure is required in respect of futures contracts that have been accounted for as hedges: *FAS 80.12*

- nature of the assets, liabilities, firm commitments or anticipated transactions that are hedged; and

- method of accounting for the futures contracts including a description of the events/transactions that result in recognition in income of changes in value of the futures contracts.

12 GOVERNMENT GRANTS

12.1 AUTHORITATIVE PRONOUNCEMENT

- SSAP 4

- CA 85

COMMENT

SSAP 4 was revised by the ASC during 1990. The requirements below are those of the revised SSAP, which is mandatory for accounting periods beginning on or after July 1, 1990. Prior to revision, the SSAP concentrated almost exclusively on capital grants.

12.2 NATURE OF GRANTS

Government grants represent assistance by government usually in the form of cash to an enterprise in return for past or future compliance with certain conditions relating to the operating activities of the enterprise. Grants may be given in respect of capital or revenue costs or in certain situations, for projects which involve both capital and revenue costs.

12.3 ACCOUNTING TREATMENT

The accounting treatment of government grants is contained in SSAP 4. The general theme of the standard is to seek to match the grant with the expenditure to which it relates.

SSAP 4.24 A grant should be recognised in the profit and loss account only when the conditions for its receipt have been complied with and there is reasonable assurance that it will be received. Subject to this proviso, grants should be accounted for as follows:

SSAP 4.23 (a) grants relating to a fixed asset should be recognised in the profit and loss account over the expected useful life of the assets concerned;

(b) grants made to give immediate financial support or to reimburse costs previously incurred should be recognised in the profit and loss account of the period in which they become receivable;

(c) grants made to finance the general activities of an enterprise over a specific period or to compensate for a loss of current or future income should be recognised in the profit and loss account of the period in respect of which they are paid; and

SSAP 4.26 (d) grants relating to leased assets in the accounts of lessors should be dealt with in accordance with SSAP 21 (see section 15).

GOVERNMENT GRANTS

State and local government offer various inducements (e.g. employment related grants, grants for certain specific types of industries etc) to eligible businesses. There are no pronouncements on how to account for these grants. Accounting practice in this area is consistent with SSAP 4 in the UK. The nature of the grant determines the accounting treatment to be adopted. If the grant is revenue in nature, then it is recognised in the income statement in the period when the qualifying expenditure is expensed. If the grant is of capital nature (e.g. relates to capital expenditure), then it is accounted for either as a deferred credit in the balance sheet or set off against the cost of the asset.

GOVERNMENT GRANTS

SSAP 4.25   Where, as a result of applying the above rules, the recognition of any part of a grant is deferred, the amount so deferred should be treated as deferred income.

Where such a deferred amount relates to a fixed asset, it may in principle be deducted from the cost of that asset. However, the CCAB has received legal advice that this treatment is not permitted by CA 85.

SSAP 4.27   Potential liabilities to repay grants in specified circumstances should only be provided for to the extent that payment is probable. The repayment of a grant should be accounted for by setting off the repayment against any unamortised deferred income relating to that grant, with any excess being charged immediately to the profit and loss account.

12.4 DISCLOSURE

SSAP 4.28   The following should be disclosed:

- the accounting policy for government grants;

- the effect of government grants on the results for the period and/or the financial position of the enterprise; and

- where the results for the period have been affected by government assistance other than grants, the nature and effects of such assistance.

SSAP 4.29   Potential liabilities to repay grants should be disclosed in accordance with the principles of SSAP 18 (see section 4).

GOVERNMENT GRANTS

13 GROUP ACCOUNTS

13.1 AUTHORITATIVE PRONOUNCEMENTS

- CA 85

- SSAP 1

- SSAP 14

COMMENT

The ASC has issued ED 50 — *Consolidated accounts*, which is intended to replace SSAPs 1 and 14. However, the changes proposed by ED 50 are nearly all consequential upon recent changes to CA 85.

Accordingly, the following summary is based on (amended) CA 85 and SSAPs 1 and 14, but on the assumption that the scope of these SSAPs were extended to subsidiary and associated undertakings as currently defined.

13.2 DEFINITION OF A SUBSIDIARY UNDERTAKING

CA 85 s 258
Sch 10A

An undertaking[†] is a subsidiary undertaking of another undertaking, the parent undertaking, if the latter:

(1) holds a majority of the voting rights in the undertaking; or

(2) is a member of the undertaking and has the right to appoint/remove board members with the majority of votes at board meetings; or

(3) has the right to exercise a dominant influence[†] over the undertaking by virtue of provisions contained in the undertaking's memorandum or articles or a control contract (regardless of whether any shares are held); or

(4) is a member of the undertaking and controls, pursuant to an agreement with other members, a majority of the voting rights in the undertaking; or

(5) has a participating interest[†] in the undertaking and

    (a) either actually exercises a dominant influence[†] over it, or

    (b) the two undertakings are managed on a unified basis[†].

[†] These terms are discussed further below.

CA 85 s 259

An 'undertaking' is defined as:

- a body corporate or partnership; or

- an unincorporated association carrying on a trade or business with or without a view to profit.

CONSOLIDATED ACCOUNTS

13.1 AUTHORITATIVE PRONOUNCEMENTS

- FAS 94

- ARB 51

- ARB 43, Chapter 12

- Regulation S-X

- APB 18

13.2 DEFINITION OF A SUBSIDIARY

'Subsidiary' refers to a corporation which is controlled, directly or indirectly, by another corporation. The usual condition for control is ownership of a majority (over 50%) of the outstanding voting stock. However, the power to control may also exist with a lesser percentage of ownership, for example, by contract, lease, agreement with other stockholders or by court decree.

APB 18-3(c)

COMMENT

One of the groups of issues that is being tackled by the FASB's project on the Reporting Entity is concerned with developing a concept of reporting entity and related conceptual matters and applying these to reach conclusions on the broad issue of consolidation policy and on specific issues of consolidation techniques. Board members have expressed views that generally support present consolidation procedures and have tentatively agreed to support consolidation policy based on control. No firm conclusions have yet emerged from the Board's deliberations on this subject.

13.2.1 SEC Registrants

The definition of a subsidiary is based on control and risk. Regulation S-X contains the following definitions:

- *Subsidiary* – a subsidiary of a specified person is a person (individual, corporation, partnership, trust or unincorporated organisation) controlled by such person directly, or indirectly through one or more intermediaries.

- *Control* – means the possession, direct or indirect, of the power to direct or cause the direction of management and policies of a person, whether through ownership of voting shares, by contract or otherwise.

- *Voting shares* – means the sum of all rights to vote for the election of directors.

S-X 1-02(g),(w),(y)

GROUP ACCOUNTS

Thus, enterprises other than companies can be subsidiary undertakings.

CA 85 s 260   A 'participating interest' is defined as an interest in the shares of an undertaking which is held on a long-term basis for the purpose of securing a contribution to its activities by the exercise of control or influence arising from or related to that interest.

COMMENT

Holdings of convertible securities and options are considered to be interests in shares for these purposes.

A holding of 20% or more is presumed to be a participating interest in the absence of evidence to the contrary.

CA 85 Sch 10A.4   'Dominant influence' for the purposes of (3) above means a legal right to give directions to the directors of the subsidiary undertaking whether or not they are for the benefit of that undertaking.

For the purposes of definition (5) 'actually exercises a dominant influence' is not defined, and the definition for the purposes of (3) is not be taken into account in construing its meaning. In effect, this leaves it to be construed in accordance with its vernacular meaning.

'Managed on a unified basis' is similarly not defined for the purposes of definition (5).

COMMENT

ED 50 proposes the following interpretations of these terms:

Dominant influence is effective control with or without the legal rights that normally signify control. The result of dominant influence is that major decisions will be taken in accordance with the wishes of the dominant party whether these are expressed or perceived. Actual exercise of dominant influence is not defined in the Act. Actual exercise implies that the dominant influence should have an effect in practice. It includes both active direction of the operating and financial policies of another enterprise, and the passive influence that can derive from the holding of a legal or effective power of veto.

Two or more enterprises should be regarded as managed on a unified basis if the whole of the operations of the enterprises are completely integrated and they are managed as a single unit. Unified management does not arise by virtue of an enterprise (an operator) managing another on behalf of one or more third parties.

CONSOLIDATED ACCOUNTS

The SEC has not developed a list of criteria that provides definitive guidance for determining when an entity should be consolidated. The SEC staff will look to the substance of a parent-subsidiary relationship rather than the legal form of an equity holding. They have cited cases where consolidation of a less-than-majority-owned subsidiary has been required when the parent essentially has the ability to control the subsidiary.

GROUP ACCOUNTS

13.3 PREPARATION OF GROUP ACCOUNTS

CA 85 s 227(1)   Group accounts must generally be prepared by any company which at the
SSAP 14.19   end of its financial year has subsidiary undertakings. Exemptions are
available for a company which:

CA 85 s 228   •   is a subsidiary undertaking of another undertaking established under the
law of a Member State of the EC (subject to satisfaction of various
regulatory requirements); or

CA 85 s 248   •   heads a small or medium-sized group (as defined) which contains no
public company, banking or insurance company, or any company
authorised under the Financial Services Act.

COMMENT
ED 49 — *Accounting for the substance of transactions in assets and liabilities*, also
seeks to require the consolidation of 'quasi-subsidiaries', defined as entities which,
although not subsidiary undertakings as defined by CA 85, confer similar risks and
rewards on the reporting entity as would be conferred by as a subsidiary undertaking.

CA 85 s 227(2)   Group accounts should be prepared in the form of consolidated accounts,
SSAP 14.15,22   unless this format is incompatible with the overriding requirement for the
group accounts to give a true and fair view.

13.3.1 Exclusion of subsidiaries from group accounts
Both SSAP 14 and CA 85 contain a list of circumstances (which partly
overlap with each other) under which it is considered appropriate not to
consolidate particular subsidiaries, but instead to deal with them in some
other manner or to exclude them from the group accounts altogether.

CA 85 s 229(1)   CA 85 permits exclusion of a subsidiary undertaking from group accounts (in
any form) where:

•   significant long-term restrictions substantially hinder the exercise of the
rights of the reporting company over the assets or management of the
undertaking;

•   the information necessary for the preparation of group accounts cannot
be obtained without disproportionate expense or undue delay;

•   the undertaking is held exclusively for resale and has not previously
been consolidated; or

•   the activities of the undertaking are so different from those of the other
undertakings in the group that its inclusion in the consolidation would

CONSOLIDATED ACCOUNTS

13.3 CONSOLIDATION POLICY

There is a presumption that consolidated statements are more meaningful than separate statements and that they are usually necessary for fair presentation when one company has an indirect or direct controlling financial interest in one or more other companies.

ARB 51.1

If an enterprise has one or more subsidiaries, consolidated statements rather than parent company financial statements are the appropriate general-purpose financial statements.

FAS 94.61

The equity method (see section 8) is not a valid substitute for consolidation.

FAS 94.15(c)

In its rules on consolidation policy, the SEC emphasises the need to consider substance over form to determine the appropriate consolidation policy. The SEC notes that there may be situations where consolidation of an entity, notwithstanding the lack of technical majority ownership, is necessary to present fairly the financial position and results of operations of the registrant, because of the existence of a parent/subsidiary relationship by means other than record (i.e. greater than 50%) ownership of voting stock.

S-X 3A-02(a)

13.3.1 Exclusion of subsidiaries from group accounts

Consolidation is required of all majority-owned subsidiaries (i.e. all companies in which a parent has a controlling financial interest directly or indirectly) except:

FAS 94.13

- if control is likely to be temporary or does not rest with the majority owner; or

- if the subsidiary operates under foreign exchange restrictions, controls or other governmental imposed uncertainties which cast significant doubt on the parent's ability to control the subsidiary.

GROUP ACCOUNTS

be incompatible with the overriding requirement to give a true and fair view.

SSAP 14.20 SSAP 14 states that when a company does not prepare group accounts dealing with all its subsidiaries for one of the reasons permitted under CA 85, consideration will need to be given to whether the resulting financial statements give a true and fair view of the position of the group as a whole.

SSAP 14.20-21 SSAP 14 requires a subsidiary undertaking to be excluded from consolidation (but not from group financial statements altogether) if:

- its activities are so dissimilar that consolidation would be misleading;

- the holding company does not have effective control;

- the subsidiary operates under severe restrictions which significantly impair the holding company's control; or

- control is intended to be temporary.

Before subsidiaries can be excluded from consolidation, it is necessary that both SSAP 14 and CA 85 requirements regarding their exclusion are met.

COMMENT

ED 50 repeats all the exclusions allowed by CA 85 except the disproportionate expense or undue delay exclusion which the ASC considered should only be used in the case of immaterial subsidiaries.

The ED seeks to limit the exclusion specified in CA 85 where the investment is held exclusively for resale and has not been previously consolidated to situations where a purchaser has already been identified or has been sought and the investment is expected to be disposed of within one year. It also seeks to make exclusion on these grounds mandatory rather than optional as it is under the CA 85. This also applies to subsidiaries excluded on the grounds of severe long-term restrictions.

As regards the exclusion of subsidiaries from consolidation on the grounds of dissimilar activities , the ED asserts that this will only arise when the subsidiary is a banking or insurance subsidiary and the parent is not (or vice versa).

13.3.2 *Unconsolidated subsidiaries*

CA 85 Sch 5 SSAP 14 specifies the accounting treatment of subsidiaries excluded from
SSAP 14.23-28 consolidation. In addition, there are various additional disclosure requirements of CA 85 and SSAP 14 to be met in respect of such subsidiaries.

SSAP 14.23-24 Where a subsidiary is excluded from consolidation because of lack of effective control or dissimilar activities it should be accounted for under the

CONSOLIDATED ACCOUNTS

13.3.2 Unconsolidated subsidiaries

The equity method should not be used to account for investments in common *APB 18.17* stock when conditions under which a subsidiary would not be consolidated prevail — namely where control is likely to be temporary, the investee is in legal reorganisation, bankruptcy or operates under foreign exchange restrictions etc. The cost method would be appropriate in such cases.

GROUP ACCOUNTS

equity method as long as the investor has significant influence.

SSAP 14.25-26 Where the exclusion is on the grounds of severe long-term restrictions, the treatment required by SSAP 14 is to 'freeze' the carrying value of the subsidiary under equity accounting at the time the restrictions came into force, and not to accrue for any trading results thereafter as long as the restrictions apply. However, a provision for permanent impairment in value of the investment may be needed.

SSAP 14.27 Where the ground for exclusion is that control is intended to be temporary, that investment should be carried in the group balance sheet as a current asset, at the lower of cost and net realisable value.

13.4 CONSOLIDATION PROCEDURES

13.4.1 Intra-group transactions

Practice in this area is generally similar to US accounting practice.

Prior to amendment of CA 85 by CA 89, there were no detailed statutory provisions on the preparation of consolidated accounts. Various requirements
CA 85 Sch 4A are now codified in CA 85 Sch 4A, such as the elimination of intra-group
6(1),(2) transactions and balances.

CA 85 Sch 4A.6(3) However, transactions with group undertakings which are not wholly-owned need only be eliminated in proportion to the group's interest in those undertakings.

COMMENT

ED 50 proposes that transactions of any sort between group enterprises should be eliminated in full. Profit or loss adjustments in relation to such eliminated transactions should be set against both the controlling interest and the minority in proportion to their interests in the enterprise whose individual amounts recorded such profits or losses.

In respect of profits or losses arising on transactions between the group and its associates which would require adjustment as unrealised if that associate or joint venture were a subsidiary, an adjustment should be made for the group's share of that profit or loss.

13.4.2 Different year ends

CA 85 s 223(5) The accounts of a subsidiary undertaking should be prepared to the same
CA 85 Sch 4A.2(2) accounting dates as those of the parent company. If they are not, the group
SSAP 14.17-18 accounts should be made up from:

- accounts of the subsidiary undertaking for its financial year last ending before the end of the parent company's financial year, provided that year ended no more than 3 months before that of the parent; or

CONSOLIDATED ACCOUNTS

13.4 CONSOLIDATION PROCEDURES

13.4.1 Intra-group transactions

These are broadly in line with UK practice with any intercompany profit or   *S-X 3A-04*
loss remaining within the group being eliminated on consolidation. This
applies to investments accounted for under the equity method as well as to
consolidated subsidiaries. If intercompany transactions have not been
eliminated on consolidation, an explanation of the reasons and the treatment
of those transactions should be disclosed.

13.4.2 Different year ends

Financial statements of subsidiaries with accounting periods ending within   *ARB 51.04*
three months of that of the holding company are acceptable for consolidation.
Any material events in the intervening period should be disclosed.

In addition, Regulation S-X requires that recognition should be given by   *S-X 3A-02(b)*
disclosure or otherwise to the effect of intervening events which materially
affect the financial position or results of operations. If a subsidiary's

GROUP ACCOUNTS

* interim accounts prepared to the same date as the parent company's financial year.

In the former case, appropriate adjustments should be made in the consolidated financial statements for any abnormal transactions in the intervening period.

CA 85 Sch 5.19
SSAP 14.18

Also, the fact that the subsidiary undertaking does not have a coterminous year end must be disclosed along with the actual dates involved and the directors' reasons for not having the same accounting dates.

13.4.3 Different accounting policies

CA 85 Sch 4A.3
SSAP 14.16

Subsidiary undertakings should adopt the same accounting policies as the parent company. If it does not, the group accounts should be adjusted to make the policies consistent. If it appears to the directors that there are special reasons for departing from this requirement, disclosure should be made of the amounts of assets and liabilities involved, the effect on results and net assets of using policies different from those of the group and the reasons for the different treatment.

CA 85 Sch 4A.5

CA 85 also requires disclosure of any differences between accounting policies adopted by the parent company and those of the group. However, this requirement, which is derived from the EC Seventh Directive, will very rarely, if ever, apply in the UK, given the requirements of SSAP 14 outlined above.

13.4.4 Shareholdings in the parent company

CA 85 s 23

CA 85 prohibits a subsidiary undertaking which is also a 'subsidiary' as defined in s 736 (basically this means a company which satisfies definitions (1), (2) or (4) in 13.2 above) from holding shares in its parent company, except where the subsidiary had acquired the holding before the date of its acquisition by the parent company. In that situation, such investments would be treated as fixed or current asset investments but on consolidation might be deducted from issued share capital.

13.4.5 Minority interests

There is no specific requirement on how the minority's share of net assets in a subsidiary should be determined for the purposes of presentation in the consolidated accounts.

COMMENT

ED 50 proposes that the minority's proportion should be recorded at their proportionate share of the fair value of the net assets of the acquired entity at the date of acquisition.

CONSOLIDATED ACCOUNTS

financial statements are as of a date more than 3 months from the parent's year end, the parent should use the equity method to account for the investment.

13.4.3 Different accounting policies
Practice is consistent with UK accounting practice.

13.4.4 Shareholdings in the parent company
These should be treated as in a manner similar to treasury stock (see section 32.4.1).   *ARB 51.13*

13.4.5 Minority interests
Minority interests are generally presented in the consolidated balance at an amount equal to the minority's share of the book value of the subsidiary's net assets.   When consolidating the assets and liabilities of an acquired subsidiary that is not wholly-owned, the fair value adjustments are limited to the amount attributable to the parent company's ownership percentage. As a

GROUP ACCOUNTS

CA 85 Sch 4A.17 Minority interests should be separately disclosed on the face of both the profit and loss account and the balance sheet. On the balance sheet they may be shown either as a deduction from net assets or below capital and reserves.

SSAP 14.34-35 Debit balances should be recognised only if there is a binding obligation on minority shareholders to make good losses incurred which they are able to meet.

13.4.6 Accounting for changes of ownership in a subsidiary

There is no specific requirement on this subject.

COMMENT

ED 50 proposes that where a group increases its interest in an enterprise which is already a subsidiary, the difference between the consideration given and the carrying amount of the minority interest acquired should be treated as goodwill in accordance with SSAP 22. Where any of the net identifiable assets are revalued after such an increase in stake, the relevant proportion of such an increase in value should be set off against the goodwill which arose on the increase in stake and only the excess, if any, should be taken to the revaluation reserve.

The ED also provides guidance on the accounting treatment to be followed where a group decreases its stake in a subsidiary but does not address the specific situations dealt with by SAB 51 and SAB 84.

CONSOLIDATED ACCOUNTS

result, the assets and liabilities of the subsidiary are included on a 'mixed' basis in the consolidated accounts.

Minority interests should be disclosed separately in the balance sheet not as part of stockholders' equity. Similarly the minority interest in income of consolidated subsidiaries should be separately disclosed. *S-X 5-02.27* *S-X 5-03.12*

In the unusual case in which losses applicable to the minority interest in a subsidiary exceed the minority interest in the equity capital of the subsidiary, such excess and any further losses applicable to the minority interest should be charged against the majority interest as there is no obligation of the minority interest to make good such losses (unless there is evidence indicating otherwise). These requirements are consistent with practice under SSAP 14. *ARB 51.15*

13.4.6 Accounting for changes in the parent company's interest in a subsidiary's stock

Where the parent company acquires additional stock held by minority stockholders, the acquisition should be accounted for under the purchase method. Goodwill is calculated as the difference between the consideration for the additional stock and proportionate share of the net assets acquired as a result, based on fair values at the date of acquisition. *AIN-APB 16.26*

Changes in ownership interests also arise where the parent sells stock of a subsidiary or when the subsidiary issues additional stock. A gain may be recognised in certain situations (not just on a sale of the shares to an unrelated party) as long the value of the proceeds can be objectively determined. Gains or losses arising from issuances by a subsidiary of its own stock, if recorded in income by the parent, should be presented as a separate line item in the consolidated income statement (unless the amount is trivial) and clearly be designated as non-operating income. However in certain situations, for example: *SAB 51* *SAB 84*

(i)   where subsequent capital transactions are contemplated that raise concerns about the parent company realising the gain that arises; or

(ii)   where the subsidiary is a start-up company, a research and development company or an entity with going concern problems

the change in the parent's proportionate share of a subsidiary's equity should be accounted as an equity transaction (i.e. through reserves).

GROUP ACCOUNTS

13.5 ACCOUNTING FOR 50% OR LESS OWNED INVESTEES

13.5.1 Associated undertakings

CA 85 Sch 4A.22   The equity method of accounting (see section 8.3) should be used to account
SSAP 1.18,26   for associated undertakings.

CA 85 Sch 4A.20(1)   An 'associated undertaking' is defined as an undertaking (see 13.2 above),
not being a subsidiary undertaking or a joint venture (see 13.5.2 below), in
which the reporting group has a participating interest (see 13.2 above) and
over whose operating and financial policy it exercises significant influence.

SSAP 1.13   Significant influence over a company essentially involves participation in the
financial and operating policy decisions of that company (including dividend
policy) but not necessarily control of those policies. Representation on the
board of directors is indicative of such participation, but will neither
necessarily give conclusive evidence of it nor be the only method by which
the investing company may participate in policy decisions.

CA 85 Sch 4A..20   An undertaking in which the investing group holds 20% or more of the
SSAP 1.14   voting rights is presumed to be an associated undertaking unless the contrary
is shown.

SSAP 1.14   Where less than 20% of the votes are held, an undertaking is presumed not to
be an associated undertaking unless the contrary is shown.

13.5.2 Joint ventures

CA 85 Sch 4A.19(1)   A joint venture is an undertaking, not being a subsidiary undertaking, which
the reporting group manages jointly with one or more others. The CA 85 is
silent in relation to corporate joint ventures which means that they fall under
its general provisions for investments (see section 28).

CA 85 Sch 4A.19(1)   Proportional consolidation may be used to account for unincorporated joint
SSAP 1.10   ventures (e.g. as in some oil and gas joint venture accounting).

> **COMMENT**
>
> ED 50 proposes that the equity method should be used for accounting for corporate
> joint ventures, but proportionate consolidation should be used for non-corporate joint
> ventures 'unless it retains profits and deals with the assets of the business as though it
> were incorporated', in which case the equity method again should be used.

13.6 COMBINED STATEMENTS

These are not common in the UK and there is no pronouncement dealing
with their preparation.

CONSOLIDATED ACCOUNTS

13.5 ACCOUNTING FOR 50% OR LESS OWNED INVESTEES

13.5.1 Investments accounted for under the equity method

The equity method of accounting (see section 8.3) for an investment in common stock should be followed by an investor whose investment in voting stock gives it the ability to exercise significant influence over operating and financial policies of an investee even though the investor holds 50% or less of the voting stock.

APB 18.17

An investment of 20% or more of the voting stock should lead to a presumption that, in the absence of evidence to the contrary, the investor has the ability to exercise significant influence over an investee. Conversely, an investment of less than 20% of the voting stock of an investee should lead to a presumption that an investor does not have the ability to exercise significant influence unless such ability can be demonstrated. The presumption stands until overcome by predominant evidence to the contrary.

APB 18.17
FIN 35.3

13.5.2 Joint ventures

Investments in common stock of corporate joint ventures should be accounted for by the equity method in consolidated financial statements.

FAS 94.15(e)

The equity method of accounting will also be appropriate in accounting for investments in unincorporated joint ventures and partnerships, however circumstances and industry practice may determine that the investor accounts on a pro rata basis for his share of the assets, liabilities, revenues and expenses.

AIN-APB 18-2

13.6 COMBINED STATEMENTS

To justify the preparation of consolidated accounts, the controlling financial interest should rest directly or indirectly in one of the entities included in the

ARB 51.21-23

GROUP ACCOUNTS

13.7 HOLDING COMPANY ACCOUNTS

SSAP 1.18,25   The equity method should not be used to account for investments in subsidiary or associated companies in holding company accounts.

CA 85 s 230   When consolidated accounts are presented there is no requirement to present a profit and loss account of the holding company provided that the amount of the consolidated profit or loss dealt with in the accounts of the holding company is disclosed. The fact that the exemption has been relied upon should also be disclosed. The balance sheet of the holding company (and accompanying notes) must however be included in the consolidated accounts.

13.8 DISCLOSURE

The following is a summary of the main disclosure requirements in respect of subsidiary undertakings and joint ventures (see section 8 for the requirements in respect of associated undertakings).

CA 85 Sch 5.15,16   In respect of each subsidiary undertaking the following should be disclosed:
SSAP 14.33

- its name;

- its country of incorporation or, if incorporated in Great Britain, registration;

- if unincorporated, its address;

- the reason by virtue of which it is a subsidiary undertaking (not required

144

CONSOLIDATED ACCOUNTS

consolidation. There are circumstances, however, where combined financialstatements (as distinct from consolidated statements) of commonly controlled enterprises are likely to be more meaningful than their separate statements. For example, in the case where one individual owns a controlling interest in several enterprises that are related in their operations.

In preparing such statements, matters such as minority interests, foreign operations, different accounting periods etc, should be treated as in consolidated accounts.

13.7 PARENT COMPANY STATEMENTS

Because consolidated, rather than parent company, financial statements are regarded as the appropriate general-purpose financial statements of an entity having subsidiaries, there is no requirement to include parent company statements in a set of consolidated accounts. However, condensed parent company statements may be needed in certain cases under the SEC rules (in addition to consolidated statements). The SEC also requires 'condensed financial information' for the parent company where it may not exercise the level of control that consolidated financial statements lead users to presume (e.g. when restrictions exist on the ability of subsidiaries to transfer funds to it through loans, cash dividends etc.).

FAS 94.61
ARB 51.24
S-X 3-10, 4-08

The equity method should be applied to investments in subsidiaries and other entities where the parent company is able to exercise significant influence over operating and financial policies. The stockholders' equity and net income in such parent company statements would generally be the same as in the consolidated statements.

GROUP ACCOUNTS

if by virtue of holding majority of votes and if the immediate parent undertaking holds the same proportion of the shares);

- the proportion of issued shares held by the investing group, distinguishing between those held directly by the parent company and those held by subsidiary undertakings; and

- an indication of the nature of its business.

CA 85 s 231   Where this information would result in disclosures of excessive length, it need only be given in respect of the principal subsidiary undertakings, provided that the following are satisfied:

- the fact that advantage has been taken of this exemption is disclosed;

- the full information is given in an appendix to the company's next annual return.

CA 85 Sch 5.17   Where a subsidiary undertaking has been excluded from the consolidated accounts, the following additional information must be given:

- profit or loss for the year; and

- total amount of its capital and reserves.

The information need not be given by a reporting group if the holding in the undertaking is less than 50% and the undertaking is not required to publish its balance sheet anywhere in the world or if the undertaking is included by way of the equity method of accounting.

CONSOLIDATED ACCOUNTS

14 INTERIM REPORTING

14.1 AUTHORITATIVE PRONOUNCEMENT

- YB

14.2 PREPARATION OF INTERIM FINANCIAL REPORTS

There is no requirement for companies, other than listed companies and those quoted on the Unlisted Securities Market (USM), to produce interim financial information. USM companies generally follow the rules for listed companies.

YB 5.25.4   The Stock Exchange may authorise a company incorporated in a non-EC country to publish the half-yearly report which it published in its own country instead of the half-yearly report described below, provided that the information given is equivalent to that which would otherwise have been required.

14.3 MINIMUM DISCLOSURES TO BE MADE

YB 5.2.24   Listed companies are required to publish half yearly unaudited interim results
TC Rule 28.6   within four months of the end of the interim period concerned. No review is required by the auditors except in certain take-over situations where a report will be required. The directors should ensure that the accounting policies used in the preparation of the statement are consistent with those used in the preparation of the annual financial statements.

The required contents are as follows:

- an explanation of the group's activities and profit or loss for the period;

- net turnover;

- profit or loss before taxation and extraordinary items;

- taxation on profits (UK taxation and, where material, overseas taxation and taxation relating to associated companies to be shown separately);

- minority interests;

INTERIM REPORTING

14.1 AUTHORITATIVE PRONOUNCEMENTS

- APB 28 (as amended by FAS 3) and FIN 18

- FAS 16

- Regulation S-X

14.2 PREPARATION OF INTERIM FINANCIAL REPORTS

Virtually all US publicly traded companies prepare quarterly interim financial statements for each of the first three quarters in the year. Many private companies also prepare interim statements for a variety of reasons, for instance, pursuant to lending agreements.

APB 28

Where interim reports are being prepared, each interim period should be viewed primarily as an integral part of an annual period. The interim results should be based on the same accounting principles and practices that are deployed for annual reporting purposes unless there has been a change in accounting policy during the current year. However certain accounting principles and practices may require modification at interim reporting dates so that the reported results for the interim period may better relate to the results of operations for the annual period (e.g. income tax provisions).

14.3 MINIMUM DISCLOSURES TO BE MADE

Quarterly condensed financial statements must be filed within 45 days after the end of each quarter by all domestic SEC registrants in accordance with the requirements of Form 10-Q and will comply with Rule 10-01 of Regulation S-X.

S-X 10.01

The financial statements to be filed on Form 10-Q comprise an interim balance sheet, income statement, statement of cash flows and include disclosures either on the face of the financial statements or in accompanying footnotes sufficient so as to make the interim information presented not misleading. Other instructions as to content are contained in Article 10-01(b) of Part 210 of Regulation S-X.

APB 28.30 deals with the minimum level of disclosure that should be made which includes:

- sales;

- provision for income taxes;

- extraordinary items;

INTERIM REPORTING

- profit or loss attributable to shareholders before extraordinary items;

- extraordinary items;

- profit or loss attributable to shareholders;

- rates and amounts of dividend(s) paid and proposed;

- EPS (see section 26);

- comparative figures in respect of the above for the corresponding previous period; and

- any other relevant information.

Some larger listed companies prepare quarterly figures and some prepare balance sheets as well as income statements.

INTERIM REPORTING

- cumulative effect of accounting changes;

- net income;

- EPS in accordance with APB 15;

- contingent items;

- seasonal revenue, costs or expenses; and

- disposal of a segment of the business.

14.4 OTHER GUIDANCE

A change in accounting policy during the interim period reported on should be highlighted in the interim report. The change in policy should be reported in accordance with the provisions of APB 20 (see section 1.2). In general, where the change is made after the first interim period and is accounted for by a cumulative catch-up adjustment, the cumulative effect of the change on retained earnings at the beginning of the year should be included in restated net income of the first interim period of which the change is made.

APB 28.23
FAS 3.9-10

Adjustments to information contained in interim reports of prior interim periods of the current year (e.g. settlement of litigation or similar amounts) are permitted in certain circumstances.

FAS 16.13

Companies should make their best estimate of the annual effective tax rate and apply this rate when providing for taxes on a current year-to-date basis. Further guidance on the application of this general guideline is contained in FIN 18. Companies that have adopted FAS 96 will have to consider separately what the current and deferred tax is expected to be when estimating the total tax charge for the year to compute that tax rate.

APB 28.19
FIN 18

If quarterly information is given for the first three quarters and not the fourth, disclosure must be considered of significant year end adjustments and unusual items recognised in the fourth quarter.

APB 28.31

15 LEASING

15.1 AUTHORITATIVE PRONOUNCEMENT

- SSAP 21

15.2 LESSEE ACCOUNTING

A lease should be capitalised if substantially all of the risks and rewards of ownership are passed to the lessee. There is a rebuttable presumption that if the present value of the minimum lease payments (MLPs), discounted at the interest rate implicit in the lease, is greater than 90% of the fair value of the asset at the inception of the lease, then such risks and rewards have passed.

Otherwise, the lease should be classified as an operating lease.

COMMENT

1. The 90% test is not a strict mathematical definition of a finance lease. The test serves as a guide rather than a rule and should be one of a number of other factors which may influence the decision on whether substantially all the risks and rewards of ownership have passed.

2. If the lessee cannot obtain the implicit interest rate, it should be estimated by reference to rates which he would be expected to pay on similar leases.

15.2.1 Finance leases

SSAP 21.32,36 The amount to be capitalised is the present value of the future MLPs. For hire purchase agreements the capitalised amount should be depreciated over the useful life of the asset, and for finance leases over the lease term if that is shorter.

COMMENT

A hire purchase contract is essentially a lease which contains a provision giving the hirer an option to acquire legal title to the asset usually at the end of the hire period upon payment of a specified final rental. The vast majority are of a financing nature. All references to leases include hire purchase contracts of the appropriate type unless otherwise specified.

SSAP 21.35 Rentals should be allocated between repayment of obligation and finance expense at a rate calculated to produce a constant periodic rate of return on the outstanding obligation for each accounting period, or a reasonable approximation thereto. The guidance notes to SSAP 21 include three methods – actuarial, 'sum of the digits' or straight line.

LEASING

15.1 AUTHORITATIVE PRONOUNCEMENTS

Eight statements, six interpretations and several technical bulletins have been issued to date but the basic requirements are embodied in FAS 13.

15.2 LESSEE ACCOUNTING

A lease must be capitalised if any one of the following criteria is met: *FAS 13.7*

FAS 29.10-11

(a)   it transfers ownership to the lessee by the end of the lease term;

(b)   there is a bargain purchase option;

(c)   the lease term is for 75% or more of the asset's estimated economic life; or

(d)   the present value (PV) of the minimum lease payments (MLPs), discounted at the lessee's incremental borrowing rate (or if known the implicit rate in the lease if that is lower) is greater than or equal to 90% of the fair value of the asset to the lessor at the inception of the lease.

Otherwise, it should be classified as an operating lease.

COMMENT

1. The last two criteria are not applicable if the inception of the lease is in the final 25% of the asset's economic life, including earlier years of use.

2. MLPs should not include contingent rentals (e.g. those dependent on the level of use of the equipment).

15.2.1 Capital leases

The amount to be capitalised is the present value of the MLPs or the fair   *FAS 13.10-11* value of the leased asset if that is lower. The asset should be depreciated as for owned assets if it is capitalised under criterion (a) or (b) above or over the lease term for assets capitalised under criterion (c) or (d).

Each lease payment should be split between capital and interest so as to   *FAS 13.12* produce a constant periodic rate of interest on the remaining balance of the obligation (i.e. the actuarial method).

LEASING

A   Disclosure

SSAP 21.57   The policy adopted for finance leases should be disclosed.

SSAP 21.49,50   Disclosure should be made of the gross amount and related accumulated depreciation of leased assets in each category of fixed assets, the total depreciation for the year, and the future minimum lease payments. Alternatively, these details may be integrated with those for owned assets, and disclosure made of the net amount of assets held under finance leases and the related depreciation charge for the year.

SSAP 21.52   The net amounts of obligations under finance leases should be analysed between the amount payable within 1 year, 2-5 years and thereafter. Alternatively this may be shown as gross obligations with future finance charges being deducted from the total.

SSAP 21.53   The aggregate finance charges allocated for the period in respect of finance leases should also be disclosed.

15.2.2 Operating leases

SSAP 21.37   Operating lease rentals should normally be expensed on a straight line basis over the lease term irrespective of when the payments are due.

A   Disclosure

SSAP 21.57   The accounting policy adopted in respect of operating leases should be disclosed.

SSAP 21.56   Disclosure is required of payments under operating leases which the lessee is committed to make during the next year analysed between leases expiring within one year, 2-5 years, and those expiring thereafter showing separately those relating to land and buildings and others.

SSAP 21.55
CA 85 Sch 4.53(6)   Disclosure should be given of total operating rentals charged, analysed between those payable in respect of hire of plant and machinery and other operating leases.

LEASING

A Disclosure

Assets recorded under capital leases and the related accumulated amortisation should be separately identified. The amortisation charge on capitalised leases should be separately disclosed unless this is included in the depreciation charge, in which case this should be stated.

FAS 13.13

The gross amount of assets recorded under capital leases at the balance sheet date must be disclosed by major classes. This information may be combined with comparable information for owned assets.

FAS 13.16(a)

For capital lease obligations, disclosure is required of the MLPs as of the balance sheet date, in aggregate and for each of the succeeding five years. The amounts representing interest should be shown as an adjustment to the aggregate MLPs in reducing them to present value. Additionally, the minimum sublease rentals to be received for the sublease of capital leases should be disclosed.

FAS 13.16(a)

15.2.2 Operating leases

Operating rental expenses should normally be charged to income on a straight line basis. The amount so charged should be disclosed.

FAS 13.15

A Disclosure

For operating leases having a remaining non-cancellable lease term exceeding 1 year, disclosure is required of future minimum rental payments as of the date of the latest balance sheet presented, in aggregate and over each of the next five years. Additionally, the minimum sublease rentals to be received for the sublease of operating leases should be disclosed.

FAS 13.16(b)

A general description of the lessee's leasing arrangements should be given; for example, disclosing the existence and terms of renewal of purchase options, escalation clauses etc.

FAS 13.16(d)

LEASING

15.3 LESSOR ACCOUNTING

15.3.1 Finance leases

SSAP 21.38

If the lease transfers substantially all of the risks and rewards of ownership (defined as for lessees) the lessor should classify it as a finance lease and account for his net investment in the lease as a finance lease receivable rather than as a fixed asset.

COMMENT

1. No distinction is made between sales type leases and direct financing leases. However, in practice, if there can be seen to be two elements within the manufacturer's/dealer's overall profit or loss on the transaction, it would be appropriate to recognise the 'selling' element of the overall profit or loss at the inception of the lease. This profit may be calculated by comparison with 'normal' gross earnings under the finance lease.

2. There is no distinction made between a leveraged lease and a direct financing lease of an asset purchased for cash.

SSAP 21.38,22,28

The lessor's net investment is calculated as his MLPs plus any unguaranteed residual value (URV) less 'gross earnings' (gross earnings is the sum of the MLPs and URV less the cost/carrying value of the asset net of any grants received in connection with its purchase or use).

SSAP 21.39,23

Gross earnings on a finance lease should be allocated to give a constant rate of return on the net cash investment in the lease. The net cash investment is

LEASING

15.3 LESSOR ACCOUNTING

15.3.1 *Sales-type, direct financing and leveraged leases*

If the lease meets any of the capital lease criteria in 15.2 above and   *FAS 13.6-8,17*

(e) the collectability of the minimum lease payments is reasonably predictable; and

(f) no important uncertainties surround the amount of unreimbursable cost yet to be incurred by the lessor under the lease,

the lease should be accounted for as a sales-type or direct financing lease (see below). In either case, the asset should be removed from fixed assets and the lessor should disclose a net investment in the lease (shown as a finance lease receivable).

A Sales-type leases

Sales-type leases arise when the fair value of the leased property is different from the book amount.

The manufacturer's/dealer's profit arising on such leases should be recognised in the income statement. This is calculated as the difference between the PV of the lessor's MLPs and the cost/carrying amount, plus any initial direct costs less the PV of the unguaranteed residual value (URV).

> **COMMENT**
> A lease involving real estate which gives rise to a manufacturer's/dealer's profit should
> be classified as a sales type lease only if it meets criterion (a) in 15.2 above.

The lessor records his net investment in the lease as the difference between his MLPs plus the URV and the unearned income (the unearned income is the difference between the sum of MLPs and the URV and their PV using the interest rate implicit in the lease).

B Direct financing leases

In the case of a direct financing lease, there is no immediate impact on the income statement.

The lessor's net investment in the lease comprises his MLPs plus the URV less the unearned income plus any unamortised initial direct costs (unearned income is the difference between the sum of the MLPs and the URV, and the cost/carrying value of the asset).

Unearned income under sales and direct financing type leases should be   *FAS 13.17-18*
taken to income at a rate calculated to give a constant rate of return on the net

LEASING

the amount of funds invested in a lease by the lessor comprising the cost of the asset plus or minus other related payments or receipts. When assessing this, tax payments associated with the lease should be taken into account.

SSAP 21 GN 92   Gross earnings should be recognised using an acceptable after tax method of allocation such as the actuarial method after tax or the investment period method. These methods are detailed in the guidance notes to SSAP 21.

In the case of a hire purchase contract, allocation of gross earnings based on the net investment may be used as a suitable approximation to allocation based on net cash investment. The two usual methods are actuarial before tax method and the 'sum of the digits'.

LEASING

investment in the lease. No account is taken of the tax flows generated by the lease.

C Leveraged leases

A leveraged lease is defined as having all of the following characteristics: *FAS 13.42*

*   it meets the definition of a direct financing lease;

*   it involves at least three parties: a lessee, a long-term creditor and a lessor;

*   the long-term creditor provides non-recourse financing (although there may be recourse to the specific property and the unremitted rentals relating to it); and

*   once the investment in the lease has been made, the lessor's net investment declines during the early years and rises during the later years of the lease.

FAS 13 prescribes a different accounting treatment for such leases in the lessor's books. However, there is one exception; if the lease also gives rise to a manufacturer's or dealer's profit it should be accounted for as a sales-type lease (see above).

The method of accounting for these leases is not detailed in this book for the   *FAS 13.43-46*
sake of brevity. The important differences from the accounting treatment prescribed for a direct financing lease are:

*   the investment in the leveraged lease is recorded net of the non-recourse debt;

*   as the lessor's net investment in the lease is negative in certain years, the net income arising on the lease should be attributed to those years in which the net investment is positive.

LEASING

A Disclosure

SSAP 21.58-60 Disclosure is required of:

- the policy adopted for accounting for finance leases and in particular for finance lease income;

- aggregate rentals receivable in the period from finance leases;

- net investment in finance leases; and

- cost of assets acquired for purposes of letting under finance leases.

15.3.2 Operating leases

Leases which are not finance leases are classified as operating leases.

SSAP 21.42 Assets held for use in operating leases should be classified as fixed assets.

SSAP 21.43 Income from an operating lease should be recognised on a straight line basis irrespective of when rentals are actually receivable.

A Disclosure

SSAP 21.58-60 Disclosure is required of:

- the gross amount of assets held for use in operating leases and the related accumulated depreciation;

- the policy adopted for accounting for operating leases; and

- aggregate rentals receivable during the period from operating leases.

15.4 LEASES INVOLVING LAND AND BUILDINGS

SSAP 21 GN 139-144 There are no separate rules for leases of land and buildings although they will normally be classified as operating leases.

CA 85 Sch 4.53(5) Lessors are required to disclose the amount, where material, of rents from land (after deduction of ground rents, rates and other outgoings).

LEASING

D Disclosure

Total future minimum lease payments with separate deductions for bad debt allowance, unguaranteed residual value and unearned income and in the case of direct financing leases, initial direct costs should be disclosed.   *FAS 13.23*

Disclosure of future minimum lease rentals due for each of the five years after the balance sheet date is required.

15.3.2 *Operating leases*

Leases which are not sales-type, direct financing or leveraged are operating leases and the related assets should be classified as fixed assets.   *FAS 13.19*

Income under operating leases should be recognised as it becomes receivable according to the provisions of the lease except where the rentals vary from a straight-line basis, in which case income should generally be recognised on a straight-line basis.   *FAS 13.19(b)*

A Disclosure

For assets held for letting under operating leases, the cost, carrying amount and the accumulated depreciation should be disclosed by major class of asset. Minimum future rentals on non-cancellable leases, in aggregate and for each of the five succeeding years should also be disclosed.   *FAS 13.23*

15.4 LEASES INVOLVING REAL ESTATE

The subject of lessee/lessor accounting is addressed by subdividing leases involving real estate into leases involving:

- Land only

- Land and buildings

- Equipment as well as real estate

15.4.1 *Land only*

A Lessee

If either criterion (a) or (b) in 15.2 above is met, the lease should be accounted for as a capital lease. Otherwise, it is an operating lease.   *FAS 13.25*
FAS 98.22(k)

LEASING

LEASING

If the lease gives rise to manufacturer's or dealer's profit (or loss) and criterion (a) in 15.2 above is met, the lease should be classified as a sales-type lease and the extent to which manufacturer's or dealer's profit may be recognised is governed by the provisions of FAS 66 (in the same manner as a seller of the same property - see section 22.6). However, if criterion (a) is not met, the lease is an operating lease.

If the lease does not give rise to manufacturer's or dealer's profit (or loss) and the criterion of either (a) and/or (b) in 15.2 above and both criteria (e) and (f) in 15.3.1 above are met, the lease should be accounted for as a direct financing or leveraged lease. However, if either criterion (e) and (f) in 15.3.1 above is not met, the lease is an operating lease.

15.4.2 Land and buildings

If the lease meets either criterion (a) or (b) in 15.2 above, it should be accounted for as follows: *FAS 13.26*

A Lessee

See treatment noted in the case of the leases involving land only (15.4.1 A above), except that the capitalised value would have to be allocated between the land and buildings in proportion to their fair values at the inception of the lease. The buildings portion would have to be amortised in accordance with the lessee's normal depreciation policy.

B Lessor

See treatment required in the case of the leases involving land only (15.4.1 B above). *FAS 98.22*

If the lease does not meet either criterion (a) or (b) in 15.2 above:

(a) If the land element of the lease is less than 25% of the total by market value, the lessee and the lessor should consider the land and the building as a single unit and apply criterion (c) or (d) in 15.2 above (and in the case of the lessor, (e) and (f) in 15.3.1 above as well) to determine whether it is a capital/direct financing or leveraged or operating lease. Clearly if the lease gives rise to a manufacturer's or dealer's profit, the lessor should treat it as an operating lease (see 15.4.1 B above). *FAS 98.22(m)*

(b) If the land element is greater than 25%, the land and buildings should be considered separately, the land element being treated as an operating *FAS 98.22(m)*

LEASING

15.5 SALES AND LEASEBACKS

15.5.1 *General*

SSAP 21.46-47 The profit or loss on a sale and leaseback of an asset should be accounted for as follows:

- if the leaseback is a finance lease, any apparent profit or loss should be deferred and amortised over the shorter of the lease term and the useful life of the asset; and

- if the leaseback is an operating lease, any profit or loss should normally be recognised immediately provided the transaction is at fair value.

In some sale and leaseback transactions the sales value may not be based on fair values and the leaseback rentals have been adjusted from normal market rents to compensate. In certain situations, it will be necessary to defer an element of profit or loss arising on the sale and amortise this amount evenly, generally over the lease term.

COMMENT

The recently issued ED 49 — *Accounting for the substance of transactions in assets and liabilities*, contains some guidance notes on the related topic of sale and repurchase agreements. It is proposed that where such transactions constitute a secured borrowing arrangement, they should be accounted for accordingly.

LEASING

lease and the buildings element being treated as an operating or capital/direct financing or leveraged lease, depending on whether or not it meets at least one of criteria (c) or (d) in 15.2 above.

For those purposes, the minimum lease payments attributable to each element are found by determining the fair value of the land and applying the lessee's incremental borrowing rate to it. The minimum lease payments applicable to the buildings element are found by deducting those for the land element from the total minimum lease payments. Again, if the lease gives rise to a manufacturer's or dealer's profit, the lessor should treat it as an operating lease (see 15.4.1 B above).

15.4.3 Leases involving equipment as well as real estate

The equipment should be considered separately; the minimum lease *FAS 13.27* payments applicable to the equipment element of the lease should be estimated by whatever means are appropriate in the circumstances.

15.5 SALES AND LEASEBACKS

15.5.1 Sale and leaseback of property other than real estate

Any profit or loss arising on a sale and leaseback transaction other than one *FAS 28.3* involving real estate should be deferred and amortised by the seller-lessee as follows:

- if the leaseback is recorded as a capital lease, in proportion to the amortisation of the leased asset;

- if the leaseback is an operating lease, in proportion to the gross rental charged to expense over the lease term.

The only exceptions are if:

- the fair value of the asset is less than the book value, then a loss should be recognised immediately, up to the extent of that difference;

- the seller-lessee retains more than a minor part but less than substantially all of the use of the property through the leaseback, in which case certain amounts of profit should be recognised immediately. 'Substantially all' is measured by reference to the 90% recovery criterion for a capital lease in 15.2 above;

- the seller-lessee retains the right to only a minor portion of the remaining use of the property sold, in which case the sale and leaseback

LEASING

15.5.2 Sale and leaseback involving land and buildings

There is no pronouncement in the UK that specifically deals with this subject. The provisions in 15.5.1 above therefore apply here as well.

LEASING

should be accounted for as separate transactions based on their respective terms. Potentially, profit on the sale could be recognised in full at the date of sale. However, if the leaseback rentals are not at market value then profit should be deferred or accrued to adjust these to a reasonable level.

15.5.2 Sale and leaseback involving real estate

A seller-lessee should use sale-leaseback accounting (i.e. recognise a sale and treat the profit or loss as required by FAS 28.3) only to those sale-leaseback transactions with payment terms and provisions that:

FAS 98.7

*   provide for a normal leaseback;

*   adequately demonstrate the buyer-lessor's initial and continuing investment in the property; and

*   transfer all of the other risks and rewards of ownership as demonstrated by the absence of any other continuing involvement by the seller-lessee.

COMMENT

The last two provisions noted should be assessed by reference to FAS 66 which deals with accounting for sales of real estate (see section 22.6). Briefly, FAS 98 precludes sale and leaseback accounting where the transaction does not qualify as a sale under FAS 66. Such transactions should be accounted for by the deposit method or as a financing transaction.

A   Normal leaseback

A normal leaseback is one in which the seller-lessee actively uses substantially all of the leased property in its trade or business during the lease term. 'Minor' subleasing is however permitted.

FAS 98.8

B   Continued involvement

In addition to ensuring that there is no other continued involvement of the sort described in FAS 66, terms of the sale-leaseback that are substantially different from those that an independent third party lessor or lessee would accept should also be considered when evaluating the 'continued involvement' condition noted above.

FAS 98.9

As already noted, FAS 66 provides several examples of continued involvement whereby the risks or rewards of ownership do not transfer to the buyer-lessor. Two of these examples frequently found in sale-leaseback transactions are provisions in which:

FAS 98.11-13

*   the seller-lessee has an obligation or an option to repurchase or the

LEASING

15.6 ACCOUNTING FOR SUBLEASES

SSAP 21,
GN 161-169
There is no pronouncement in the UK on treatment of subleases but the non-mandatory guidance notes describe how to account for them.

If the intermediate party's (sub-lessor's) role is in substance that of a broker or an agent for transactions between the original lessor and the ultimate lessee such that there is no recourse to the intermediate party in the event of default, then the intermediate party should not include the asset or obligation in his balance sheet and should account for any income due to him on a systematic and rational basis. For both operating and finance leases, he should treat any contingent loss as required by SSAP 18.

If, on the other hand, the intermediate party is taken to be acting as both lessee and lessor in two independent though related transactions, he should recognise his assets and obligations under finance leases in the normal way.

LEASING

buyer-lessor can compel the seller-lessee to repurchase;

- the seller-lessee is allowed to participate in any future profits of the buyer-lessor or the appreciation of the leased property, for example, where the seller-lessee has an interest in the buyer-lessor.

C Profit to be recognised

If sale-leaseback accounting is permitted, the profit or loss on the sale portion of the sale-leaseback transaction to be deferred and amortised in accordance with FAS 28.3 (i.e. over the leaseback) would be the profit that could otherwise be recognised in accordance with FAS 66. Note that in certain transactions which qualify for sales recognition under FAS 66, the full amount of profit cannot be recognised at the date of sale (see section 22.6).

FAS 28.3 fn*

15.6 ACCOUNTING FOR SUBLEASES

If an item is subleased, the accounting of the original lessee/sublessor will depend on whether the primary obligation under the original lease remains in force or not.

FAS 13.35-40

If the primary obligation under the original lease is cancelled under the second agreement then if the original lease was a capital lease, the sublessor removes the asset and obligation from the balance sheet if applicable and takes any profit or loss.

If the original lease remains in force the sublessor should continue to account for that lease as before and account for the sublease under the lessor accounting rules in FAS 13 (see 15.3 above) except that if the original lease is:

- an operating lease, then the sublease should also be accounted for as an operating lease;

- a capital lease, because it met either criterion (c) or (d) in 15.2 above and not (a) or (b), the sublessor should classify the sublease as a direct financing lease only if it meets criteria (c) in 15.2 above and (e) and (f) in 15.3.1 above. Otherwise the sublease is an operating lease.

The only exception to this rule is where the sublease is an integral part of an overall transaction in which the sublessor is just an intermediary, in which case criterion (d) is also available for classification purposes.

LEASING

15.7   ACCOUNTING FOR LEASE CHANGES

This is not addressed in SSAP 21.

LEASING

15.7 ACCOUNTING FOR LEASE CHANGES

FAS 13 contains specific accounting rules on how a lessee and lessor should recognise the effects of a renewal, extension, termination or change in the provision of a lease.

FAS 13.14

FAS 13.17(f)

16 NON-MONETARY TRANSACTIONS

This is not the subject of a specific accounting standard.

COMMENT

ED 51 — *Accounting for fixed assets and revaluations*, proposes that when a fixed asset is acquired in exchange for a similar fixed asset that has a similar use in the same type of business and which has a similar fair value, the net carrying amount of the fixed asset given up need only be adjusted for any balancing payment or receipt of cash or other consideration in recording the exchange transaction.

In all other circumstances, when a fixed asset is acquired in exchange or part exchange for another fixed asset the cost of the fixed asset acquired should be measured at its fair value. The difference between the net carrying amount of the fixed asset given in the exchange and the fair value of the asset acquired should be accounted for in the profit and loss account of the period in which the exchange took place.

NON-MONETARY TRANSACTIONS

16.1 AUTHORITATIVE PRONOUNCEMENTS

*   APB 29

*   FIN 30

16.2 APPLICABILITY

These provisions do not apply to:

*   business combinations accounted for under APB 16;

*   transfer of non-monetary assets solely between companies under common control;

*   non-monetary consideration received in respect of an issue of capital stock; and

*   stock dividends and splits.

16.3 DEFINITION OF A NON-MONETARY TRANSACTION

Non-monetary transactions are exchanges and non-reciprocal transfers that involve little or no monetary assets or liabilities.

16.4 THE GENERAL RULE OF APB 29

In general, the accounting for a non-monetary transaction is based on the fair values of the assets exchanged. Thus, a non-monetary asset received in exchange for another non-monetary asset ordinarily is recorded at its fair value or at the fair value of the asset given up, whichever is more clearly evident and a gain or loss is recognised if the fair value recorded for the asset received differs from the book value of the asset given up.   *APB 29.18*

16.5 EXCEPTIONS TO THE GENERAL RULE

There are three exceptions to the general rule: *APB 29.20-23*

*   when neither the fair value of the non-monetary asset received nor the fair value of the non-monetary asset given up can be determined within reasonable limits;

*   when the transaction is not essentially the culmination of an earnings process; for instance, the following two types of non-monetary transactions do not culminate an earnings process:

    (a)   an exchange of a product held for sale in the ordinary course of business for a product to be sold in the same line of business to

NON-MONETARY TRANSACTIONS

NON-MONETARY TRANSACTIONS

facilitate sales to customers other than parties to the exchange;

(b) an exchange of a productive asset not held for sale in the ordinary course of business for a similar productive asset or an equivalent interest in the same/similar productive asset;

- when the transaction is a distribution of non-monetary assets, such as capital stock of subsidiaries, to stockholders in corporate liquidations or plans of reorganisation that involve disposing of all or a significant segment of the business (i.e. spin-offs, split-offs).

In each of the three exceptions, the accounting for the transaction is normally based on the book value of the asset given up and there is no gain/loss recognition.

However, there are circumstances in which gain or loss is recognised on a non-monetary transaction even though it does not culminate an earnings process. For instance, if the transaction includes monetary consideration, the recipient recognises a gain to the extent that the amount of the monetary receipt exceeds the proportionate share of the recorded amount of the asset given up. Also if a loss is indicated by the terms of the transaction, such loss on exchange should be recognised.

16.6 DISCLOSURE

Disclosure should be made of the basis of accounting for the assets transferred in non-monetary transactions and gains or losses recognised on transfers.

APB 29.28

17 PENSIONS AND OTHER DEFERRED EMPLOYEE COSTS

17.1 AUTHORITATIVE PRONOUNCEMENTS

- SSAP 24

- CA 85

17.2 GENERAL APPROACH

SSAP 24.77-78 The accounting objective is to recognise the cost of providing pensions on a systematic and rational basis over the period during which the company benefits from the employees' services.

The difference between the cumulative amount:

- charged in the profit and loss account in accordance with SSAP 24 principles; and

- paid in pensions by the company (i.e. directly to the pensioners) or in contributions to a pension fund or insurance company

should be shown as a provision or prepayment in the balance sheet.

17.3 DEFINED CONTRIBUTION SCHEMES

The amount to be charged to the profit and loss account for a given accounting period is the contribution payable in that period.

17.4 DEFINED BENEFIT SCHEMES

17.4.1 Costing method

SSAP 24.79 The standard does not specify a particular actuarial method for the purpose of attributing the expected cost of pension benefits provided to employees to individual years of service. The only requirement is that the method selected should satisfy the accounting objective of the standard and be such that the regular pension cost is a substantially level percentage of the current and expected future pensionable payroll in the light of the current actuarial assumptions.

17.4.2 Assumptions

The actuarial assumptions and method, taken as a whole, should be compatible and lead to the actuary's best estimate of the cost of providing the pension benefit promised.

176

PENSIONS AND OTHER DEFERRED EMPLOYEE COSTS

17.1 AUTHORITATIVE PRONOUNCEMENTS

- FAS 87

- FAS 88

- Guides to Implementation of FAS 87 and FAS 88 - Q&A booklets

- FAS 81 and FTB 87-1

- APB 12

17.2 GENERAL APPROACH

The fundamental objective of FAS 87 is to recognise the cost of an employee's pension over that employee's service period.   *FAS 87.6*

17.3 DEFINED CONTRIBUTION SCHEMES

Like SSAP 24, the net pension cost for a period is the contribution called for in that period.   *FAS 87.64*

17.4 DEFINED BENEFIT SCHEMES

17.4.1 Costing method

The pension cost to be attributed to a period is (with a few exceptions) equal to the cost of the benefits which accrue in respect of the period under the terms of the pension scheme. This means that for final salary schemes or career-average-salary schemes, the attribution of cost to accounting periods should be calculated using the projected unit credit method (in the UK, this is described as the projected unit method).   *FAS 87.40*

17.4.2 Assumptions

Each significant assumption necessary to determine annual pension cost, such as discount rates, return on the scheme's assets, or future salary   *FAS 87.43-45*

PENSIONS AND OTHER DEFERRED EMPLOYEE COSTS

SSAP 24.35   Allowance should be made (within the scope of the actuarial assumptions) for pension increases of all kinds, even where these are not the result of any contractual obligation. A history of past discretionary and ex gratia pension increases may be sufficient grounds for making allowance for such future increases in the actuarial assumptions.

17.4.3 Annual pension cost

SSAP 24.79-80   The pension expense under SSAP 24 comprises:

- regular pension cost; and

- variations.

SSAP 24.72   Regular cost is the consistent ongoing cost recognised under the actuarial method used. It is that amount which the actuary would regard as a sufficient contribution to the scheme to provide the eventual pensions to be paid in respect of future service only (i.e. without regard to any existing surplus or deficiency), provided present actuarial assumptions about the future are borne out in practice and there are no future changes to the terms of the scheme. When determining regular cost, pension liabilities are discounted using an interest rate representing the expected long-term return on scheme assets (i.e. as is normally done in actuarial valuations for funding purposes). The regular cost so determined is the same irrespective of whether the scheme is in surplus or has a deficit.

Regular cost is broadly equivalent to the aggregate of the following three amounts included in the FAS 87 net periodic pension cost: service cost, interest cost and the expected return on an amount equal to the projected benefit obligation (PBO) (i.e. the expected long-term rate of return expected to be earned by scheme assets applied to an amount equal to the PBO). The PBO is the actuarial present value of benefits attributed by the pension benefit formula to employee service rendered up to the date of the valuation. However, regular cost computed for SSAP 24 purposes is unlikely to coincide with the aggregate of these three components of the FAS 87 cost except by chance (even where the projected unit method has been used to calculate regular cost). This is primarily due to the different discount rate that is applied to calculate pension costs and liabilities for FAS 87 purposes and also the absence of a specific requirement in SSAP 24 to account for interest on pension scheme surpluses/deficits.

PENSIONS AND OTHER DEFERRED EMPLOYEE COSTS

increases, reflects best estimates solely with respect to that individual assumption. Where there is a substantial commitment (a history of retroactive scheme amendments is not enough, in isolation, to establish a substantive commitment) to provide pension benefits for employees beyond the written terms of the scheme, allowance should be made for such a commitment in the actuarial valuation. Actions of the employer (e.g. communications with the employees) can demonstrate the existence of a such a commitment.

FAS 87.41

Q&A;Q52

17.4.3 Annual pension cost

FAS 87 identifies six components of net periodic pension cost and specifies how they are to be measured. The six components are :

FAS 87.20

• service cost;

• interest cost; ·

• actual return on scheme assets, if any;

• amortisation of unrecognised prior service cost, if any;

• gain or loss (including the effects of changes in assumptions) to the extent recognised; and

• amortisation of the unrecognised net obligation or unrecognised net asset existing at the date of initial application of the statement.

The pension cost for both interim and annual financial statements can be based on the last actuarial valuation provided that the obligation obtained after rolling it forward to the current measurement date is substantially the same as that based on a new valuation at that date.

Q&A;Q65

The service cost is the actuarial present value of benefits attributed by the projected unit credit method to services rendered by employees during the period. This cost will be the same irrespective of whether the scheme is unfunded, has minimal funding or is well-funded. FAS 87 departs from normal actuarial practice in the way it requires the actuarial present value of pension benefits to.be calculated. The standard requires that the assumed discount rate in that calculation should reflect an assessed cost for the insurance of the liabilities based on either market annuity rates or returns on long dated gilts. This cost is likely to be greater than the eventual cost of providing the benefits through the scheme because of its ability to invest in potentially higher yielding assets such as equities.

PENSIONS AND OTHER DEFERRED EMPLOYEE COSTS

Correspondingly, the FAS 87 cost is unlikely to be acceptable for SSAP 24 purposes. The requirement in FAS 87 for the pension obligation to be revalued each year using a discount rate reflecting current conditions has the potential of introducing greater volatility in the service cost component of the FAS 87 pension cost and this conflicts with the definition of regular cost in SSAP 24 (defined to be the 'consistent ongoing cost').

17.4.4   Variations from regular cost

SSAP 24.21   Variations from regular cost may arise because of:

- experience surpluses or deficiencies (i.e. actual experience differs from previous actuarial assumptions);

- changes in actuarial assumptions or methods;

- retroactive changes in benefits or conditions; or

- increases to pensions in payment or to deferred pensions for which no previous provision has been made (see 17.4.5 below).

SSAP 24.80,82   Variations from the regular cost should, in general, be allocated over the expected remaining service lives of current employees in the scheme. The standard does not specify the precise method by which variations should be amortised. In exceptional cases which have necessitated the payment of significant additional contributions to the scheme, prudence may require that a deficit be recognised over a shorter period.

PENSIONS AND OTHER DEFERRED EMPLOYEE COSTS

The interest cost component is the increase in the projected benefit obligation (PBO) (this is the actuarial present value of all benefits attributed to employee service rendered prior to the actuarial valuation date calculated using assumptions about future salary levels) due to the passage of time.

Although, the standard requires the actual return on scheme assets to be disclosed as a component of the net periodic pension cost, the net periodic pension cost is effectively based on the expected return on scheme assets. The expected return is determined at the beginning of the year by using an expected long-term rate of return expected to be earned by scheme assets, taking into consideration the availability of all scheme assets for investment throughout the year (including the amount and timing of contributions and benefit payments during the year). The expected return will differ from the actual return on scheme assets and the standard provides for that difference to be included as part of the gain or loss component so that the annual pension cost is actually based on the expected return.

17.4.4 Variations from regular cost

Like SSAP 24, FAS 87 does not require immediate recognition of liabilities resulting from scheme amendments and actuarial gains and losses in the period during which they arose. Such amounts may be deferred and amortised over a number of years.

FAS 87.24-34

The standard specifies in detail the methods of amortising any initial surplus or deficiency, the cost of benefit improvements (i.e. prior service cost) and experience gains and losses (the amount of experience gains/losses amortised (if any) together with the difference between the actual and expected return on scheme assets (see above) form the gain or loss component of the net periodic pension cost).

Immediate recognition of prior service cost due to a retroactive scheme amendment is permitted only if the employer does not expect to obtain any future economic benefits from that amendment. Immediate recognition of gains and losses is permitted provided that method is applied consistently and to all gains and losses.

Q&A;Q.19,33

Unlike SSAP 24 (where the effect of variations can be accumulated at successive valuations and amortised on an aggregate basis), FAS 87 requires that the amortisation of the transition asset or liability and the costs of each past service benefit improvement should be separately tracked. Experience gains and losses (excluding those not yet reflected in market-related values — see 17.4.6) are dealt with on an aggregate basis and a de minimis test (the

PENSIONS AND OTHER DEFERRED EMPLOYEE COSTS

A *Exceptions to the spreading rule*

(a) *Settlements* — there is no equivalent in SSAP 24.

SSAP 24.81 (b) *Significant reductions in scheme membership* — variations resulting from a significant reduction in the number of employees should generally be recognised when the normal level of contributions is adjusted to eliminate the surplus or deficiency which arose because of the event in question.

If the variation is associated with an event which gives rise to an extraordinary item (e.g., on the discontinuance of a business segment), it should be aggregated with other financial effects in accordance with SSAP 6 and recognised in the same period.

SSAP 24.83 (c) *Refunds* — A refund from the pension scheme made subject to tax under the UK Finance Act 1986 may be recognised immediately in the profit and loss account of the period in which the refund occurs (the amount of 'unamortised variations' should be adjusted accordingly).

17.4.5 *Discretionary increases to pensions in payment and deferred pensions*

SSAP 24.84-85 The preferred treatment is for allowance to be made in the actuarial assumptions for such discretionary increases if they are likely to be granted on a regular basis. Such increases are treated as variations provided that they were within the scope of the actuarial assumptions.

182

PENSIONS AND OTHER DEFERRED
EMPLOYEE COSTS

10% corridor) is performed at the beginning of the year to assess whether amortisation is necessary.

A   Exceptions to the spreading rule
There are exceptions to the basic rule on spreading the effects of variations forward.

* *Settlements* — If a settlement occurs thereby relieving the employer of
  primary responsibility for a pension obligation (e.g. through a purchase
  of annuities), a proportional part of any unrecognised transitional
  surplus and any subsequent actuarial experience gains or losses that
  have not been recognised should be recognised in the income statement
  unless the cost of the settlement is not material.   *FAS 88.9,11*

* *Curtailments* — In the event of a curtailment where there has been   *FAS 88.12*

  (a)   a significant reduction of expected years of future service of
        present employees covered by a pension scheme, or

  (b)   an elimination of the accrual of pension benefits for some or all
        future services of a significant number of employees covered by a
        pension scheme,

  a proportionate amount of any unrecognised transition obligation and
  other unamortised prior service costs should be recognised
  immediately. Curtailments may affect the projected benefit obligation
  producing a gain or loss that should first be offset against existing
  unrecognised losses or gains (including any transition asset) before
  being recognised in the income statement. Unlike SSAP 24, the
  recognition of surpluses or deficiencies on account of curtailments is
  independent of the effect on funding.

* *Refunds* — Any such refund is accounted for as a reduction of the   *FAS 87.35*
  pension prepayment in the balance sheet and does not directly affect the
  income statement.

17.4.5 *Discretionary increases to pensions in payment or to deferred*
pensions

Discretionary pension increases should be allowed for in calculating the   *FAS 87.41*
pension cost to be attributed to a period if there is a substantive commitment
to grant such increases (see 17.4.1 above).

PENSIONS AND OTHER DEFERRED EMPLOYEE COSTS

Where no such allowance has been made, the capital cost of such discretionary increases actually granted must be recognised in the profit and loss account in the accounting period in which they are granted, to the extent that it is not covered by a surplus.

17.4.6 Asset valuation method
SSAP 24 does not specify a method to be used for valuing the scheme assets. Discounted income asset valuations are acceptable for the purposes of determining actuarial surpluses and deficits.

17.4.7 Additional balance sheet liability
SSAP 24.88(g) SSAP 24 only requires disclosure of a deficiency on a current funding level basis. An indication should also be given of what action is proposed to remedy the deficiency.

17.4.8 Additional disclosures
The CA 85 requires certain disclosures about pension commitments to be given by employer companies in their accounts. The disclosure requirements of SSAP 24 are fairly detailed and in virtually all the cases, will ensure compliance with the CA 85 requirements. The standard requires the following disclosures, inter alia, to be made:

SSAP 24.88(h) • an outline of the results of the most recent formal actuarial valuation including:

    (a) the actuarial method used and a brief description of the main actuarial assumptions;

    (b) the market value (i.e. fair value) of scheme assets at the date of their valuation or review;

PENSIONS AND OTHER DEFERRED EMPLOYEE COSTS

If no allowance is made for such pension increases, their cost is amortised over the remaining life expectancy of the pensioners concerned if all/almost all of the scheme members are inactive. Otherwise that cost is amortised over the remaining service lives of the active members at the date of the award.

FAS 87.25

17.4.6 Asset valuation method

For the purposes of deciding whether an additional balance sheet liability should be recognised (see 17.4.7 above) the scheme assets should be valued at their fair value as of the balance sheet date.

FAS 87.49

For the purposes of determining the expected return on scheme assets and calculating asset gains and losses, the 'market-related value' of scheme assets should be used. This is either fair market value or a calculated value that smoothes the effect of short term market fluctuations over a period of up to 5 years. To the extent that unrecognised gains and losses based on the fair value of the scheme assets are not yet reflected in the market-related value, these may be excluded from unrecognised gain or loss that is subject to amortisation in the future. Although those excluded gains or losses eventually affect net periodic pension cost in future periods, their impact is delayed through the use of market related value of scheme assets.

FAS 87.50

17.4.7 Additional balance sheet liability

If the accumulated benefit obligation (value of accrued benefits without allowance for future salary increases) exceeds the fair value of scheme assets, an additional minimum liability may be required to be shown in the balance sheet.

FAS 87.36-37

17.4.8 Additional disclosures

The standard requires the following disclosures, inter alia, to be made:

- a schedule reconciling the funded status of the scheme with amounts reported in the balance sheet, showing separately:

FAS 87.54(c)

  (a) the fair value of scheme assets;

  (b) the projected benefit obligation, identifying the accumulated benefit obligation and the vested benefit obligation;

  (c) the unrecognised prior service cost;

  (d) the unrecognised net gain or loss; and

  (e) the remaining unrecognised transition asset or liability.

PENSIONS AND OTHER DEFERRED EMPLOYEE COSTS

(c)   the level of funding expressed in percentage terms; and

(d)   comments on any material actuarial surplus or deficiency.

SSAP 24.88(k)   •   details of the expected effects on future costs of any material changes in the group's pension arrangements.

17.4.9 Implementation options

SSAP 24.92   A choice between two methods of implementation was available. Companies could spread the actuarial surplus or deficiency on implementation over the average remaining service lives of the members of the scheme or, alternatively, incorporate the surplus or deficiency in the balance sheet by means of a prior year adjustment.

However, the 'spreading option' was not available for that part (if any) of the surplus or deficiency

• resulting from a significant reduction in the number of employees;

• when prudence required a material deficit to be recognised over a shorter period; or

• relating to unfunded ex gratia pensions in payment.

17.5 DEFERRED COMPENSATION AGREEMENTS OTHER THAN PENSION SCHEMES

Such deferred compensation schemes are not common in the UK.

PENSIONS AND OTHER DEFERRED EMPLOYEE COSTS

- the weighted-average assumed discount rate, the rate of salary increase used to measure the projected benefit obligation and the weighted average expected long-term rate of return on scheme assets.

  FAS 87.54(d)

- the amounts and types of securities of the employer and related parties included in scheme assets, the approximate amount of annual benefits of employees and retirees covered by annuity contracts issued by the employer and related parties and the alternative amortisation methods used to account for variations.

  FAS 87.54(e)

17.4.9 Implementation

For non US schemes, the statement became effective for periods beginning after December 15, 1988. On implementation, the difference between the projected benefit obligation and the fair value of scheme assets as adjusted for previously recorded pension cost accruals or prepayments shown in the balance sheet (this difference is called the transition asset or liability) was generally to be amortised on a straight-line basis over the average remaining service period of the employees. If this period was less than 15 years, the company could elect to use a 15 year period. Restatement of previously issued financial statements was not permitted.

FAS 87.76-77

17.5 DEFERRED COMPENSATION AGREEMENTS OTHER THAN PENSION SCHEMES

Typically, such agreements impose an obligation on the employer to make future payments to an employee provided certain requirements are complied with, such as continued employment for a specified period and availability for consulting services, and agreements not to compete after retirement.

APB 12.6-7

The estimated amount of future payments to be made under those contracts (based on life expectancy of each individual concerned) should be accrued ina systematic and rational manner over the period of active employment from the time the contract is entered into.

PENSIONS AND OTHER DEFERRED EMPLOYEE COSTS

17.6 POST-RETIREMENT HEALTH CARE AND LIFE ASSURANCE BENEFITS

SSAP 24.75
TR 756

The principles of SSAP 24 may also be applied to other post-retirement benefits, such as medical benefits etc, but not to social security contributions or redundancy payments. However, there is no obligation for companies to apply the principles of SSAP 24 to such benefits.

PENSIONS AND OTHER DEFERRED EMPLOYEE COSTS

17.6 POST-RETIREMENT HEALTH CARE AND LIFE INSURANCE BENEFITS

The FASB have issued an exposure draft which would set accounting and reporting standards for all forms of non-pension post-retirement benefits. At present, FAS 81 prescribes the disclosures to be made about the accounting treatment adopted in respect of the costs of such employee benefits.

17.6.1 Disclosures

An employer that provides health care or life insurance benefits to retirees, *FAS 81.6* their dependants or survivors should disclose as a minimum:

•   description of the benefits provided and the employee groups covered;

•   a description of the accounting and funding policies used;

•   the cost of the benefit recognised for the period; and

•   the effect of significant matters affecting the comparability of the costs for all periods presented.

If such cost cannot be readily separated from the cost of providing such *FAS 81.7* benefits for active employees, the following should be disclosed:

•   the total cost of providing those benefits to both active employees and retirees; and

•   the number of active employees and the number of retirees covered by the scheme.

17.6.2 Change in method of accounting for post-retirement health care and life insurance benefits

The change in method of accounting should be accounted for by : *TB 87-1*

•   either recognising the cumulative effect of the change in net income of the period of the change; or

•   accounting for the effect of the change prospectively in the period of change and in future periods (in the same way as when implementing FAS 87, see 17.4.9 above).

18 POST BALANCE SHEET EVENTS

18.1 AUTHORITATIVE PRONOUNCEMENTS

- SSAP 17

- CA 85

18.2 ADJUSTING EVENTS

SSAP 17.19,22
CA 85 Sch 4.12(b)

Events occurring after the balance sheet date but before the approval of the financial statements which provide additional information about conditions existing at the balance sheet date (adjusting events) should be reflected in the financial statements.

Additionally, events in this period indicating that the application of the going concern concept to the whole or a material part of the company is not appropriate will also require the amounts included in the financial statements to be changed.

SSAP 17.26

The date on which the financial statements are approved by the board should be disclosed. This is normally done by dating the signature of the directors on the balance sheet.

18.3 NON-ADJUSTING EVENTS

SSAP 17.23
CA 85 Sch 7.6(a)

Events occurring between the balance sheet date and the date of approval of the financial statements which do not affect conditions in existence at the balance sheet date should not be reflected in the financial statements.

However, the nature and estimate of the financial effect of an event of this type should be disclosed where it is:

- of such materiality that its non-disclosure would affect the ability of the users of financial statements to reach a proper understanding of the financial position; or

- the reversal or maturity after the year end of a transaction entered into before the year end, the substance of which was primarily to alter the appearance of the company's balance sheet.

There is no requirement to reflect post balance sheet changes in capital structure such as a scrip dividend, share split etc in the balance sheet prior to issuance of the financial statements. However, there are certain post balance sheet events which, because of statutory requirements or customary accounting practice, are reflected in financial statements e.g. proposed

POST BALANCE SHEET EVENTS

18.1 AUTHORITATIVE PRONOUNCEMENT
•   SAS 1

SAS 1 follows a similar line to SSAP 17 in that it recognises two categories of 'subsequent events' which require consideration by management.

18.2 ADJUSTING EVENTS
Events occurring after the balance sheet date but prior to the issuance of the financial statements which provide additional evidence with respect to conditions existing at the balance sheet date should be reflected in the financial statements.

SAS 1

18.3 NON-ADJUSTING EVENTS
Events occurring after the balance sheet date but prior to the issuance of financial statements which provide evidence with respect to conditions which did not exist at the balance sheet date but arose subsequent to that date should not require adjustments.

SAS 1

However, some of these events may be of such a nature that disclosure of them is required to prevent the financial statements from being misleading. In some cases the event may be so significant that disclosure can best be made by disclosing pro forma statements giving effect to the event as if it had occurred on the date of the balance sheet. It may be desirable to present these on the face of the historical statements.

SAS 1
FAS 5.11

In the case of an SEC registrant, a change in capital structure due to a stock dividend, stock split or revenue split occurring after the balance sheet date but before the issuance of the financial statements must be given retroactive effect in the balance sheet, and appropriate disclosures made.

SAB 40

POST BALANCE SHEET EVENTS

dividends, amounts appropriated to reserves, the effects of changes in taxation and dividends receivable from subsidiary and associated companies.

18.4 REISSUED FINANCIAL STATEMENTS

Financial statements are rarely 'reissued' in the UK.

COMMENT

New sections 245-245C of CA 85 (not yet in force) will provide a mechanism for the voluntary or compulsory withdrawal of accounts which are found to be defective after they have been filed with the Registrar of Companies.

POST BALANCE SHEET EVENTS

18.4 REISSUED FINANCIAL STATEMENTS

When financial statements are reissued (e.g. in a later filing of financial statements with regulatory authorities), events occurring between the original issuance and the reissuance of the financial statements should not result in adjustment to the financial statements unless the adjustment meets with criteria for the correction of an error or the criteria for prior period adjustments. However additional disclosures may be made, for example in the form of supplementary pro forma information if considered appropriate.

SAS 1

19 RELATED PARTY TRANSACTIONS

19.1 AUTHORITATIVE PRONOUNCEMENTS

*   CA 85

*   YB

COMMENT

There is presently no accounting standard which deals specifically with related parties. The ASC issued an exposure draft ED 46 — *Related party transactions*, in April 1989. For the purposes of this book, a comparison of ED 46 with FAS 57 in the US is provided below.

19.2 ED 46

19.2.1 Identification of related parties

COMMENT

Related parties under ED 46 are effectively related parties under FAS 57. ED 46 defines related parties as those where for all or part of the financial period:

*   one party is able to exercise either direct or indirect control or significant influence over the other party or over the assets or resources of the other party; or

*   such parties are subject to common control or significant influence from the same source.

In deciding whether parties are related, it is necessary to consider the substance of the relationship. For the purposes of this definition, control comprises determination of, or the ability to determine the financial or operating policies of an enterprise. Significant influence involves participation in the financial or operating policy decisions of an enterprise but not necessarily control of them.

Examples of related parties under (a) above include subsidiaries, associated companies, top management (directors etc.), parent company, significant shareholders (a 10% interest is necessary for a shareholder to be presumed to be a related party).

Examples of related parties under (b) above include fellow subsidiaries/associates, other companies with common shareholders who are themselves related parties of the company and control or can significantly influence the other companies, companies controlled or influenced by directors.

19.2.2 Types of transactions requiring disclosure

COMMENT

ED 46 makes a distinction between two types of related party transaction; normal and abnormal. Only abnormal transactions with related parties would be required to be disclosed under any successor standard to ED 46.

A normal transaction is one which is undertaken by the reporting enterprise in the ordinary course of business on normal commercial terms. Transactions entered into in the ordinary course of business are those which are usually, frequently or regularly undertaken by the enterprise.

RELATED PARTY TRANSACTIONS

19.1 AUTHORITATIVE PRONOUNCEMENTS

*   FAS 57

*   Regulation S-K

*   Regulation S-X

19.2 FAS 57

19.2.1 Identification of related parties

The definition of a related party contained in FAS 57 is very similar to that   *FAS 57.24(f)*
contained in ED 46.   Examples of related party transactions include
transactions between:

*   a parent company and its subsidiaries;

*   subsidiaries of a common parent;

*   an enterprise and trusts for the benefit of employees, such as pension
    and profit-sharing trusts that are managed by or under the trusteeship of
    the enterprise's management;

*   an enterprise and its principal owners, management, or members of
    their immediate families; and

*   affiliates (defined as parties that, directly or indirectly through one or
    more intermediaries, control, are controlled by, are under common
    control with an enterprise).

19.2.2 Types of transactions requiring disclosure

FAS 57 requires disclosure of all material transactions with related parties   *FAS 57.2*
irrespective of whether they are normal or abnormal transactions.

No disclosure is required in respect of compensation arrangements, expense
allowances and other similar items in the ordinary course of business
whereas if these were considered 'abnormal' transactions in terms of ED 46,
disclosure would be required.

RELATED PARTY TRANSACTIONS

Abnormal transactions are those transactions other than normal transactions and are generally of the following types:

- transactions which are entered into in the ordinary course of business and are of such size or nature in a particular accounting period that they have a significant impact on the financial statements; or

- transactions which are entered into other than in the ordinary course of business, irrespective of the terms on which they are undertaken.

19.2.3 Information to be disclosed

A Abnormal transactions

COMMENT

ED 46 proposes that the following information should be disclosed about each abnormal transaction with related parties:

- name of the related party;

- the relationship between the parties;

- the extent of any ownership interest (in % terms) in the related party or by it in the reporting enterprise;

- the nature of the transaction;

- the amounts involved;

- the amount due to or from the related party at the balance sheet date;

- the basis on which the transaction price has been determined; and

- any other information necessary for an understanding of the commercial substance of the transaction and of its effects on the financial statements.

B Controlling relationship

COMMENT

Under ED 46, the existence and nature of controlling related party relationships would have to be disclosed whether or not any transactions between the parties have taken place. Disclosure would include the name of the controlling enterprise and, if different, that of the ultimate controlling enterprise. If the latter is incorporated outside the UK or the Republic of Ireland, disclosure of the ultimate controlling enterprise within these two countries would also be required.

C Economic dependence

COMMENT

ED 46 proposes that where transactions between an enterprise and another party have a pervasive influence on it, or other facts arising from the relationship give rise to economic dependence, the identity of that party and a general indication of the nature and extent of the dependence should be disclosed (e.g. major customer, supplier etc.).

RELATED PARTY TRANSACTIONS

19.2.3 *Information to be disclosed*

A   Material transactions

The disclosures to be made include: *FAS 57.2*

- the nature of the relationship(s) involved. There is no specific requirement to disclose the name of the related party and the extent of ownership interest in either party unless disclosure of the name is necessary to the understanding of the relationship;

- a description of the transaction (including those to which no amounts or nominal amounts were ascribed) and such other information necessary to an understanding of the effects of the transactions on the financial statements;

- the monetary amount of the transaction and the effect of any change in the method of establishing the terms from that used in the preceding period; and

- the amounts due to/from the related party and the terms and manner of settlement if not otherwise apparent.

B   Controlling relationship

If the reporting enterprise and one or more other enterprises are under common ownership or management control and the existence of that control could result in operating results/financial position of the reporting enterprise significantly different from those that would have been obtained if the enterprises were autonomous, the nature of the control relationship should be disclosed even though there are no transactions between the enterprises.

C   Economic dependence

No disclosure is required about situations where the reporting enterprise is economically dependent on another unless required by FAS 30.6 (which requires disclosure about major customers; see section 21.5).   *FAS 30.6*

RELATED PARTY TRANSACTIONS

D Exemptions from reporting

COMMENT

Under ED 46, disclosures would not be required:

- in the parent company's own accounts where consolidated financial statements are presented at the same time; or

- in the financial statements of wholly-owned subsidiaries of transactions with other group companies if the identity of the ultimate parent company is disclosed.

19.3 REQUIREMENTS OF THE COMPANIES ACT AND STOCK EXCHANGE

19.3.1 Directors

The following information should be disclosed in respect of directors of a company.

A Identity

The following information should be given:

CA 85 s 234(2)
- names of directors who have served during the year (in the directors' report); and

YB 5.2.21(t)
- identity of independent non-executive directors together with a short biographical note on each (listed companies only).

B Remuneration

CA 85 Sch 6.1-14
Information about directors' emoluments must be disclosed, distinguishing between:

- fees as directors;

- other emoluments (including payments by any persons in respect of services as a director or otherwise in the management of the company and any of its subsidiaries);

- pensions (paid other than from schemes maintained by contributions);

- amounts paid in anticipation of taking office as director; and

- compensation for loss of office.

In each case, amounts paid to persons connected with, or bodies corporate controlled by, a director are treated as direct payments to him.

RELATED PARTY TRANSACTIONS

D Exemptions from reporting

Disclosure of all material related party transactions in the financial statements of wholly-owned subsidiaries is required if such statements are produced.

The exemption from reporting in the holding company's own accounts where consolidated financial statements are presented at the same time is also available under FAS 57.

19.3 OTHER DISCLOSURE REQUIREMENTS

The SEC's proxy rules (which detail the information required to be given to shareholders by those soliciting shareholder proxies) and the annual report (Form 10-K) rules contain, inter alia, specific disclosure requirements for certain relationships and related transactions, some of which may be considered as related party transactions. The disclosures required are extensive and include disclosures about directors, executive officers (including the remuneration of the five highest paid persons by name and by amount) and certain significant employees, substantial holdings of the company's shares, contracts with corporate substantial shareholders, interests of management in certain transactions etc. Such disclosures do not form part of the general purpose financial statements in the US and the accountant is not usually directly involved in ensuring compliance with those disclosure requirements. Moreover, as foreign private issuer registrants are not subject to the proxy rules or required to file Form 10-K, such information has not been discussed any further in this book. Form 20-F does, however, require foreign private issuers to make certain disclosures regarding the directors and executive officers and their aggregate remuneration as well as, in certain cases, the aggregate pension or similar contributions made on their behalf but these disclosures are considerably less than the proxy/Form 10-K requirements.

RELATED PARTY TRANSACTIONS

CA 85 Sch 6. 9   Disclosure is required of the aggregate amount and nature of consideration paid to third parties (i.e. persons other than the directors or persons connected with them) in respect of directors' services.

The emoluments of the chairman and the highest paid director (if in excess of those of the chairman) and the number of directors in each ascending £5,000 band of emoluments should be disclosed (such disclosures need not be given in respect of any individual whose duties are wholly or mainly discharged outside the UK).

CA 85 Sch 7.5A   Where during the year a company has purchased or maintained insurance on behalf of directors or officers of the company, that fact shall be stated in the directors' report.

In the case of a listed company, disclosure is required of:

YB 5.2.21(n)   •   particulars of any arrangement under which a director has waived or agreed to waive any current or future emoluments; and

YB 5.2.43(c)   •   the period unexpired of any service contract of any director proposed for re-election at the forthcoming general meeting unless the director does not have a service contract of more than one year's duration, in which case an appropriate negative statement should be given.

C   Interests in the company's share capital

CA 85 Sch 7.2-2A   The interests of each director in the share capital or debentures of the company or any other group company (including options to acquire and to subscribe) should be disclosed.

YB 5.2.21(h)   In the case of a listed company, beneficial and non-beneficial interests should be separately distinguished and changes in interests between the balance sheet date and a date not more than one month before the date of the notice of the annual general meeting (AGM).

D   Loans and other transactions

CA 85 Sch 6.15,16   Details should be given of loans and other transactions with directors or persons connected with them. Certain aggregate disclosures are required in respect of loans to officers that would be disclosed if given to a director.

CA 85 Sch 6.15,16
YB 5.2.21(k)   Particulars should be also given of any transaction with the company in which a director has a material interest and in the case of a listed company, of any contract of significance subsisting during or at the end of the financial year in which a director is or was materially interested. In the latter case, if there are no such contracts, a negative statement should be included.

RELATED PARTY TRANSACTIONS

RELATED PARTY TRANSACTIONS

19.3.2 Shareholders

The following information should be given with respect to the shareholders of the company.

A Substantial holdings of the company's shares

YB 5.2.2(i) Listed companies are required to disclose, as at a date not more than one month prior to the date of the notice of the AGM, the interest of any person in any substantial part of the share capital of the company (a substantial holding is one which amounts to 3% or more of the nominal value of any class of capital carrying rights to vote at general meetings).

CA 85 Sch 5.12,31 If at the year end a company is a subsidiary undertaking of another, the name of the company's ultimate parent company and its country of incorporation (or, if incorporated in Great Britain, registration) should be disclosed.

CA 85 Sch 6.11,30 If the company is a subsidiary undertaking, disclosure is required of the name and place of incorporation (or, if incorporated in Great Britain, registration; if unincorporated, the address of its principal place of business) of that parent undertaking which heads:

- the largest group of undertakings for which group accounts are drawn up and of which that company is a member, and

- the smallest such group of undertakings.

If copies of group accounts referred to above are available to the public, the addresses from which copies of the accounts can be obtained should be disclosed.

B Close company status

YB 5.2.21(j) A listed company is required to state whether or not it is a close company for tax purposes. Such disclosure gives information about the concentration of shareholdings and hence possible existence of related parties.

C Contracts with a corporate substantial shareholder

YB 5.2.21(l) Listed companies are required to disclose particulars of:

- any contract of significance between the company or one of its subsidiaries and a 'corporate substantial shareholder' (any company which is entitled to exercise or control the exercise of 30% or more of the voting power at general meetings or one which is in a position to control the composition of a majority of the board); and

YB 5.2.21(m) - any contract for the provision of services to the company or any of its subsidiaries by a corporate substantial shareholder.

RELATED PARTY TRANSACTIONS

RELATED PARTY TRANSACTIONS

D Other disclosures

YB 5.2.21(o)

A listed company is required to disclose any arrangement under which a shareholder has waived or agreed to waive any current or future dividends.

19.3.3. Other disclosures required by CA 85

A Transactions with subsidiary and related companies

CA 85 Sch 4.8,59

Separate disclosure should be given of:

- loans to;

- other amounts owing from; and

- amounts owing to

group undertakings and undertakings in which the company has a participating interest.

The amounts involving group companies should be split into amounts relating to subsidiary undertakings of the company and amounts relating to any parent undertaking or fellow subsidiary undertaking.

Separate disclosure is required in the profit and loss account of;

- income from shares in group undertakings;

CA 85 Sch 4A.21(3)

- income from participating interests (analysed in group accounts between income from associated undertakings and that from other participating interests); and

- interest receivable from, and payable to, group undertakings.

CA 85 Sch 4.59A

Also, details of guarantees or commitments undertaken on behalf of, or for the benefit of, group companies should be separately disclosed from other guarantees and financial commitments that are disclosed.

B Information about subsidiary and other undertakings

Certain information is required to be disclosed if at the year end a company has subsidiary or associated undertakings or other undertakings in which it holds more than 10% (see sections 8.4, 13.8 and 28.5).

RELATED PARTY TRANSACTIONS

RELATED PARTY TRANSACTIONS

19.4 ACCOUNTING FOR RELATED PARTY TRANSACTIONS

There is no specific pronouncement dealing with this subject.

RELATED PARTY TRANSACTIONS

19.4 ACCOUNTING FOR RELATED PARTY TRANSACTIONS

In the absence of any authoritative literature on this subject, the views of the staff of the SEC will influence/direct accounting practice in this area. As a general guideline, the SEC consider the substance of a transaction when evaluating the accounting for a related party transaction. It has issued several SABs which deal with specific related party transactions (e.g. SAB 48 on transfers of non-monetary assets to a company by its promoters in exchange for shares or SAB 79 on expenses or liabilities paid by a principal stockholder). Therefore, whenever the terms of a related party transaction are unusual or the substance of the transaction is different from its form, it is expected that accounting based on the substance of the transaction should be considered unless there is a specific accounting standard which is relevant, in which case the transaction ought to be accounted for in accordance with that standard.

20 RESEARCH AND DEVELOPMENT

20.1 AUTHORITATIVE PRONOUNCEMENTS
- SSAP 13

- CA 85

20.2 ACCOUNTING TREATMENT

SSAP 13.6 SSAP 13 lists examples of activities that would normally be included in research and development (R&D) but does not give guidance on the types of costs which can be included within the category of R&D. However, practice is similar to that recommended in FAS 2.

SSAP 13.7 Market research is normally to be excluded from research and development costs.

SSAP 13.16 The costs of fixed assets (including intangibles) acquired or constructed in order to provide facilities for R&D activities over a number of years should be depreciated over their useful lives in accordance with SSAP 12 (see section 27).

CA 85 Sch 4.3(2)
SSAP 13.24 All types of research costs should be written off as they are incurred.

SSAP 13.9,25 Development costs must be written off too unless certain conditions are met
CA 85 Sch 4.20(1) in which case the expenditure may be deferred to the extent that its recovery can reasonably be assured. The conditions attempt to ensure that:

- an asset, and its cost can be identified; and

- the asset can be shown to be recoverable with sufficient certainty (taking into account such factors as technical feasibility, marketability, and costs to completion).

SSAP 13.28-29 Where a policy of deferral is adopted, the development costs should be amortised from the date of commercial production or application of the product, service or process on a systematic basis, usually by reference to the sale or use of the product, service or process. Deferred development expenditure should be reviewed annually and be written down to its recoverable amount.

208

RESEARCH AND DEVELOPMENT

20.1 AUTHORITATIVE PRONOUNCEMENTS

*   FAS 2 and FIN 6

*   FAS 68

*   FAS 86

20.2 ACCOUNTING TREATMENT

FAS 2 provides examples of activities that typically would be included in research and development (R&D) and also describes what elements of costs should be identified with R&D activities. The costs of R&D are determined by approaches that are generally similar to those used in costing inventory — including allocation of overheads etc.

FAS 2.9-11

Expenditure on market research is not an R&D cost.

FAS 2.8

The costs of materials, equipment and facilities that are acquired or constructed for R&D activities and that have alternative future uses (in other R&D projects or otherwise) should be capitalised and the cost/depreciation of such material, equipment or facilities used in those activities accounted for as R&D costs. However, if the materials, equipment, facilities or intangibles acquired for a specific R&D project have no alternative future use beyond the project for which they were acquired, their cost should be classified as R&D upon acquisition.

FAS 2.11

All R&D costs should be written off at the time they are incurred.

FAS 2.12

All costs incurred to establish the technological feasibility of a computer software product which is to be sold, leased or otherwise marketed are R&D costs. These costs should be charged as incurred as required by FAS 2. Technological feasibility is established upon completion of a detailed program design or, in its absence, completion of a working model (see section 27.1.2 C).

FAS 86.3

RESEARCH AND DEVELOPMENT

SSAP 13.17   Where companies enter into a firm contract:

- to carry out development work on behalf of third parties on such terms that the related expenditure is to be fully reimbursed, or

- to develop and manufacture at an agreed price calculated to reimburse expenditure on development as well as on manufacture,

any such expenditure which has not been reimbursed at the balance sheet date should be dealt with as contract work-in-progress.

20.3 DISCLOSURE

SSAP 13.30   The accounting policy on R&D expenditure should be explained.

CA 84 Sch 4.20(2)   Where development costs have been capitalised, the reasons for so doing and the period over which they are being amortised should be disclosed.

SSAP 13.31   The amount of R&D charged to the profit and loss account should be disclosed, analysed between current year's expenditure and amounts amortised from deferred expenditure. This disclosure need only be given by companies which are, or which have subsidiary undertakings which are, public companies, banking and insurance companies. Certain very large private companies must also make the disclosure.

SSAP 13.32   The movements on the deferred development expenditure capitalised in the balance sheet should be given. Such expenditure should be disclosed under intangible fixed assets in the balance sheet.

RESEARCH AND DEVELOPMENT

If an enterprise enters into an arrangement with other parties for the funding of its R&D, it must determine whether it is obligated only to perform contractual R&D for others (i.e. treat R&D costs incurred as part of cost of sales), or is otherwise obligated. FAS 68 provides guidance in determining the nature of the obligation in such arrangements and states that: *FAS 68.4-6*

(a) if the enterprise is obligated to repay any of the funds provided, it should estimate and recognise that liability and charge the R&D costs to expense as incurred

(b) a critical factor when determining whether a liability exists or not is whether the financial risks involved in the R&D arrangement have been substantively and genuinely transferred to the other parties.

20.3 DISCLOSURE

The total R&D costs charged to expense in each period should be disclosed. *FAS 2.13*

Where an enterprise has entered into a contract to perform R&D for others on the basis that repayment of any of the funds provided by the other parties depends solely on the outcome of the R&D having economic benefit, the following disclosures should be made: *FAS 68.14*

• the terms of significant agreements relating to the R&D arrangement including purchase provisions, licence agreements, royalty arrangements and commitments to provide additional funds; and

• the amount of R&D costs incurred and compensation earned during the period for such R&D arrangements.

21 SEGMENTAL REPORTING

21.1 AUTHORITATIVE PRONOUNCEMENTS

- CA 85

- SSAP 25

- YB

21.2 SCOPE

The CA 85 requirements on segmental disclosures apply to any company with substantially differing classes of business or geographical markets.

SSAP 25.41 SSAP 25 applies only to:

- companies which are, or which have subsidiary undertakings which are, public companies;

- banking and insurance companies; and

- large private companies.

Companies that are listed on the ISE are also required to provide additional segmental disclosures though derogations from these requirements may be obtained on application.

The SSAP 25 requirements are mandatory for accounting periods beginning on or after July 1, 1990. Some of its requirements overlap with those of CA 85. The disclosure requirements of SSAP 25 that go beyond CA 85 requirements are indicated by [†] in the text below.

CA 85 Sch 4.55
SSAP 25.43
Where the directors consider that disclosure of any information required to be disclosed by CA 85 or SSAP 25 would be seriously prejudicial to the interests of the company, it may be omitted, provided that it is stated that certain information has not been been disclosed on these grounds.

21.3 SEGMENT INFORMATION TO BE PRESENTED

SSAP 25.34 SSAP 25 takes a similar approach to FAS 14. Information should be segmented by class of business and geographically.

21.3.1 Business segments

SSAP 25.8 Like FAS 14, SSAP 25 leaves the determination of the different business segments of an enterprise to the directors. However, it provides guidance on factors which should influence the definition of segments.

SEGMENTAL REPORTING

21.1 AUTHORITATIVE PRONOUNCEMENTS

- FAS 14

- FAS 30

21.2 SCOPE

FAS 14 applies to all enterprises:

(a) whose debt or equity securities are traded in a public market on a foreign or domestic stock exchange or on the Over-the-counter (OTC) market, or

(b) which are required to file financial statements with the SEC.

There is no exemption in FAS 14 to allow companies not to disclose segmental information on the grounds that disclosure would be seriously prejudicial to the interests of the company.

21.3 SEGMENT INFORMATION TO BE PRESENTED

Segment information is required to be reported :

- by industry segment; and

- by geographical area.

21.3.1 Reportable industry segments

Reportable industry segments should be determined by: *FAS 14.11*

- identifying the individual products and services from which the enterprise derives its revenue;

SEGMENTAL REPORTING

In particular the directors are to have regard to the overall purpose of presenting segmental information as outlined in SSAP 25, and the extent to which the reporting entity operates in business or geographical segments which:

- earn a return out of line with the remainder of the business;

- are subject to different degrees of risk;

- have experienced different rates of growth; or

- have different potentials for future development.

SSAP 25.9   A business or geographical segment should normally be regarded as significant (and therefore separately reportable) if it accounts for 10% or more of:

- third party turnover;

- total of segments in profit or total of segments in loss (whichever is the greater); or

- net assets

of the reporting entity.

21.3.2 Geographical segments
See 21.3.1 above.

SEGMENTAL REPORTING

- grouping those products and services by industry lines into industry segments. The determination of different industry segments is left to the judgment of management;

- selecting those industry segments that are significant with respect to the enterprise as a whole. For this purpose, significance is established if one or more of the following criteria are met:

    (a) its revenue from both external customers and other customers is 10% or more of the total revenue of all the enterprise's segments;   *FAS 14.15-16*

    (b) its operating profit or loss (see below) is 10% or more of the greater of the following two amounts:

        - the combined operating profit of all industry segments that did not incur an operating loss, and

        - the combined operating loss of all industry segments that did incur an operating loss;

    (c) its identifiable assets are 10% or more of the combined identifiable assets of all industry segments.

A further test should be applied once the reportable segments are identified.   *FAS 14.17*
The total revenue from sales to unaffiliated customers of all reportable segments must constitute at least 75% of total revenue from sales to unaffiliated customers of all industry segments. If this test is not met, additional industry segments must be identified as reportable until the 75% test is met. Though a limit is not set, ten reportable segments is given as an indication of a practical maximum.

21.3.2 Reportable geographical segments
If an enterprise's foreign operations are conducted in two or more   *FAS 14.33-34*
geographical areas, information about those operations is to be presented for each significant foreign geographical area and in aggregate for all foreign geographical areas not deemed significant.

Foreign operations are defined as those revenue producing operations that are:

- located outside the enterprise's home country; and

- generating revenue either from sales to unaffiliated customers or from intra-enterprise sales or transfers between geographical areas.

SEGMENTAL REPORTING

21.4 SEGMENT INFORMATION TO BE DISCLOSED

CA 85 Sch 4.55
YB 5.2.21(c)
SSAP 25.24

The following information should be disclosed by geographical and business segment:

- turnover (analysed between third party and inter-segmental turnover[†]). The geographical analysis should be made by source and destination[†];

- result before taxation, minority interests and extraordinary items ([†]for geographical analysis). This will normally be disclosed before interest. However, where interest income or expense forms a significant part of the reporting entity's business, interest should be included in segmental results; and

- net assets[†].

SSAP 25.36

The above information should also be given in respect of associated undertakings if these account for 20% or more of the reporting entity's result or net assets[†].

SEGMENTAL REPORTING

Foreign geographical areas are individual countries or groups of countries as may be determined to be appropriate in an enterprise's particular circumstances. Management is given discretion over the appropriate choice of the different geographical segments of an enterprise.

A foreign geographical area is deemed to be significant if its sales revenue to unaffiliated customers or its identifiable assets are at least 10% of related consolidated amounts.

21.4 SEGMENT INFORMATION TO BE DISCLOSED

The following information is required for each reportable segment (industry or geographical, unless otherwise specified) identified:

FAS 14.22-26

FAS 14.35,36

- *Revenue* — both sales to unaffiliated customers and sales or transfers to other segments should be separately identified. The basis of accounting for inter-segment sales should be that used for pricing purposes and should be disclosed.

  A geographical analysis of turnover by destination is not required except for export sales to unaffiliated customers made by an enterprise's domestic operations. Where the amount of export sales revenue is at least 10% of total sales revenue to unaffiliated customers that amount should be reported, in aggregate, and by such geographical areas as are considered appropriate in the circumstances.

- *Profitability* — operating profit or loss of each reportable segment derived from continuing operations should be presented before tax and interest expense (except in the case of industry segments whose operations are principally of a financial nature). It should also exclude the group's share of income in equity accounted investees. Disclosure is also required of the nature and amount of any unusual or infrequently occurring item which has been added or deducted in computing operating profit or loss of a reportable segment.

  In the case of geographical segment information, alternative measures of profitability may be disclosed instead – i.e. net income or some other measure between operating profit or loss and net income

- *Identifiable assets* — comprising those tangible and intangible assets (i.e. without deduction of operating liabilities) used exclusively by that segment and one or more other segments.

SEGMENTAL REPORTING

21.4.1 Exemptions from the disclosure requirements

The only exemptions available have been noted in 21.2 above.

21.5 INFORMATION ABOUT MAJOR CUSTOMERS

SSAP 25 does not require such disclosure to be made.

SEGMENTAL REPORTING

- FAS 14 requires disclosure of information which is additional to that   *FAS 14.27*
  required by SSAP 25. In the case of each reportable industry segment
  (by class of business):

  - the types of products and services supplied;

  - the aggregate amount of depreciation, depletion and amortisation;

  - the amount of capital expenditure; and

  - the enterprise's equity in the net income from and investment in
    the net assets of equity method investees whose operations are
    vertically integrated with the operations of that segment.

The information about revenue, profitability, and identifiable assets should
be reconciled to related amounts in the group financial statements.

21.4.1 Exemptions from the disclosure requirements

In circumstances where an enterprise has one industry segment or a dominant   *FAS 14.20*
segment (i.e. revenue, operating profit or loss and identifiable assets each
constitute more than 90% of the total for all industry segments), disclosures
required for reportable segments do not need to be made except that the
industry must be identified.

Geographical segment information is not required if both the following   *FAS 14.32*
conditions are met:

- sales revenue generated by the enterprise's foreign operations is less
  than 10% of consolidated revenue as reported in the enterprise's income
  statement; and

- identifiable assets of the enterprise's foreign operations are less than
  10% of consolidated total assets as reported in the enterprise's balance
  sheet.

21.5 INFORMATION ABOUT MAJOR CUSTOMERS

If an enterprise's sales to one customer (or a group of entities under common   *FAS 30.6*
control) are 10% or more of its total revenue, that fact and the amount of
revenue from each such customer must be disclosed. The industry segment
making the sales should be disclosed.

22 REVENUE RECOGNITION

22.1 AUTHORITATIVE PRONOUNCEMENTS

* CA 85

* SSAP 2

In comparison to the US, however, there is hardly any accounting literature on the subject.

REVENUE RECOGNITION

22.1 AUTHORITATIVE PRONOUNCEMENTS

There is a considerable amount of accounting literature dealing with the subject of revenue recognition which collectively constitutes generally accepted accounting practice in this area. The principal pronouncements include the following:

- APB 4

- SFAC 5

- ARB 43

- ARB 45

- FAS 45

- FAS 48

- FAS 49

- FAS 50

- FAS 53

- FAS 66

- FAS 91

Generally, most of the literature either relates solely to a particular industry or deals with the recognition of certain forms of revenue. In addition:

- the SEC has issued several Accounting and Auditing enforcement releases addressing specific revenue recognition issues faced by registrants, detailing why in their opinion the issue had not been accounted for properly and citing their preferred accounting treatment;

- there are several AICPA Industry Audit and Accounting Guides and Statements of Position that deal with revenue recognition;

- the EITF has released several consensuses on a number of revenue recognition issues.

This section provides a brief summary of the general principles that are applied in practice for the recognition of revenue earned from operations. Pronouncements dealing with special industry situations or other very specific issues are outside the scope of this book.

REVENUE RECOGNITION

22.2 THE GENERAL RULE

CA 85 Sch 4.12(a)
CA 85 s 262(3)

Only profits realised at the balance sheet date should be included in the profit and loss account; in establishing whether or not profits of a company should be treated as 'realised', reference should be made to principles generally accepted with respect to the determination for accounting purposes of realised profits.

Existing practice is based on the following accounting concepts:

SSAP 2.14

- *Prudence*

  Revenue and profits are not anticipated but are recognised by inclusion in the profit and loss account only when realised in the form either of cash or of other assets the ultimate cash realisation of which can be assessed with reasonable certainty.

- *Accruals or matching*

  Revenue and costs are accrued, matched with one another so far as their relationship can be established or justifiably assumed and dealt with in the P&L account of the period to which they relate; where the accruals concept is inconsistent with the prudence concept, the latter prevails.

Existing practice indicates that a wider interpretation is placed on the concept of 'realisation' than permitted prima facie by the prudence concept as outlined in SSAP 2. For example, despite the emphasis on 'cash' and 'ultimate cash realisation', in practice companies do recognise the profit effects of barter transactions.

REVENUE RECOGNITION

22.2 THE GENERAL RULE

22.2.1 Basic criteria

Revenue recognition involves consideration of two factors: *CON 5.83*

- being realised or realisable, and

- being earned

with sometimes one and sometimes the other being the more important consideration.

Revenues generally are not recognised until realised or realisable. Revenues are realised 'when products (goods or services), merchandise or other assets are exchanged for cash or claims to cash' and are realisable 'when related assets received or held are readily convertible to known amounts of cash or claims to cash'.

Revenues are not recognised until earned. They are considered to have been 'earned' when the entity 'has substantially accomplished what it must do to be entitled to the benefits represented by the revenues'.

22.2.2 Broad principles

- The two factors mentioned above are usually met by the time the product is delivered or the services rendered to customers and revenues from manufacturing and selling activities are commonly recognised at time of sale (usually meaning delivery). *CON 5.84*

- If sale or cash receipt (or both) precedes production and delivery (e.g. magazine subscriptions), revenues may be recognised as earned by production and delivery.

- If a product is contracted for before production, revenues may be recognised by a percentage-of-completion method as earned (i.e. as production occurs) provided reasonable estimates of results at completion and reliable measures of progress are available (see section 29.3).

- If services are rendered or rights to use assets extend continuously over time (e.g. interest or rent), reliable measures based on contractual prices established in advance are commonly available, and revenues may be recognised as earned as time passes.

- If products are readily realisable because they can be sold at reliablydeterminable prices without significant effort (e.g. marketable

REVENUE RECOGNITION

22.3 REVENUE RECOGNITION WHEN RIGHT OF RETURN EXISTS

There is no specific pronouncement on the subject. Practice in the UK would involve, inter alia, consideration of the factors noted in FAS 48 but generally with more flexibility than allowed by FAS 48.

22.4 PRODUCT FINANCING ARRANGEMENTS

There is no specific pronouncement on this subject. Following the publication of ED 49 — *Accounting for the substance of transactions in assets and liabilities*, and its emphasis on the concept of substance over form, practice in the UK may in the future reflect the requirements of FAS 49. Appendix A to ED 49 deals specifically with consignment stock, and proposes that such stock should be included in the balance sheet of whichever party to the consignment arrangement bears the slow-moving stock risk.

224

REVENUE RECOGNITION

securities, precious metals etc), revenues may be recognised at completion of production or when prices of the assets change.

- If products or services are exchanged for non-monetary assets that are not readily convertible into cash, revenues may be recognised on the basis that they are earned. Recognition depends on the provision that the fair values involved can be determined within reasonable limits.

- If collectability of assets received for products or services is doubtful, revenues may be recognised on the basis of cash received.

22.3 REVENUE RECOGNITION WHEN RIGHT OF RETURN EXISTS

If the buyer has the right to return the product, revenue should be recognised at time of sale only if all of the following conditions are met:

- the seller's price is substantially fixed or determinable at the date of sale;

- the buyer has paid the seller or is obligated to pay and the obligation is not contingent on resale of the product or would not be changed in the event of theft, physical destruction or damage of the product;

  FAS 48.6

- the seller does not have significant obligations for future performance to directly bring about resale of the product by the buyer;

- the buyer acquiring the products for resale has independent economic substance apart from the seller; and

- the amount of future returns can be reasonably estimated.

Reported income should be reduced to reflect estimated returns.

FAS 48.7

22.4 PRODUCT FINANCING ARRANGEMENTS

Product financing arrangements, in which a company sells and agrees to repurchase inventory at a repurchase price to cover substantially all fluctuations in costs incurred by the other entity in purchasing and holding the product (i.e. interest costs etc.) or other similar transactions, should be accounted for as a borrowing rather than a sale.

FAS 49.8

The financing and holding costs should be accounted for by the vendor company as they are incurred by the other entity in accordance with its accounting policies for such costs.

FAS 49.9

REVENUE RECOGNITION

22.5 INITIAL FEES
22.5.1 Franchising
There is no specific pronouncement on the subject.

22.5.2 Non-refundable loan fees and costs
There are no corresponding requirements in the UK. However in practice:

•   recognition of non-refundable arrangement fees on receipt is acceptable;

•   the ICAEW Industry Accounting and Auditing Guide on Banks states that commitment fees should usually be accounted for on a time apportionment basis (over the facility period); and

•   credit card fees may be recognised upon receipt.

REVENUE RECOGNITION

22.5 INITIAL FEES

22.5.1 Franchising

Initial franchise fee revenue should be recognised, with an appropriate provision for estimated uncollectable amounts, when: *FAS 45.5*

- all material services or conditions relating to the franchise sale have been substantially performed or satisfied by the franchisor; and

- any obligation to refund cash or forgive receivables has expired; and

- no other conditions or obligations exist.

An appropriate portion of the initial fee should be deferred and amortised over the life of the franchise if it is probable that the continuing fee will not cover the cost (with a reasonable profit allowance thereon) of continuing services to be provided by the franchisor. *FAS 45.7*

The relationship between the franchisor and the franchisee may affect recognition of franchise fee revenue. For example, if the franchisor has an option to purchase a franchisee business and there is an understanding that he will do so, initial franchise fee revenue should be completely deferred and applied against the franchisor's investment in the outlet when the option is exercised. *FAS 45.10-11*

Where the initial franchise fee incorporates not only the consideration for the franchise rights and the initial services to be provided by the franchisor but also tangible assets such as equipment, signs, etc. that part of the fee relating to the tangible assets should be separated out and treated as revenue from the sale of assets. *FAS 45.12*

22.5.2 Non-refundable loan fees and costs

The provisions that follow apply to all lending activities and purchases of loans and other debt securities whether or not fees are involved. Hence, for example, loans which may not have fees but do have costs associated with their origination fall within the scope of these provisions. These provisions do not apply to non refundable fees and costs associated with originating or acquiring loans carried at market value.

Loan origination fees should be deferred and recognised over the life of the loan as an adjustment of yield. Direct loan origination costs should generally be deferred and recognised as a reduction in the yield of the loan. *FAS 91.15*

REVENUE RECOGNITION

22.6 DISPOSAL OF LAND AND BUILDINGS

In practice, recognition of the proceeds on disposal of land and buildings
takes place either upon the date of exchange of contracts or on completion of
the contract. Although legal title and beneficial ownership do not pass until
the contract is completed and the transfer registered, usually there are no
significant uncertainties as to eventual completion of the sale by the date of
exchange of contracts. The vendor and purchaser are both bound by a legally
enforceable contract of sale. However, if significant uncertainties still exist
by that date, recognition of the sale should be delayed until completion.

REVENUE RECOGNITION

Commitment fees and direct costs incurred to make a commitment to originate (or purchase) a loan should be offset and the net amount should generally be deferred and

FAS 91.8-9

* if the commitment is exercised, recognised over the life of the loan as an adjustment of yield; or

* if the commitment expires unexercised, recognised in income upon expiration of the commitment.

Credit card fees should be deferred and recognised on a straight-line basis over the period the fee entitles the cardholder to use the card.

FAS 91.10

Loan syndication fees should be recognised when the syndication is complete unless a portion of the syndication loan is retained and the yield on that portion is less than the average yield to the other syndication participants (taking into account the syndication fees paid), in which case a portion of the fee should be deferred so as to produce a yield on the portion of the loan retained that is not less than the average yield on the loans held by the other syndication participants.

FAS 91.11

The net fees or costs that are required to be deferred and amortised as an adjustment of yield over the life of the loan generally should be amortised using the interest method. Variations of the interest method are to be used when the stated interest rate is not constant over the life of the loan.

FAS 91.18

A Disclosure

The unamortised balance of loan origination, commitment, and other fees and costs should be disclosed in the balance sheet as part of the related loan balance. The amounts which are recognised as an adjustment of yield should be reported as part of interest income in the income statement. Amortisation of other fees such as commitment fees included in income when the commitment expires should be reported as service fee income.

FAS 91.21-22

22.6 SALE OF REAL ESTATE

The recognition of profit and real estate transactions is dealt with in FAS 66. FAS 66 provides separate guidance on revenue recognition issues relating to 'retail land sales' and 'real estate sales other than retail land sales'. 'Retail land sales' refer to transactions of the sort entered into by property companies and are not dealt with in this publication. The provisions relating to real estate sales other than retail land sales (e.g. sales of houses, buildings, factories, parcels of land etc.) apply to any type of company and are highlighted below.

REVENUE RECOGNITION

REVENUE RECOGNITION

22.6.1 Basic criteria

Profit should be recognised in full (the 'full accrual' method) when real estate is sold provided *FAS 66.3*

- · the profit is determinable (i.e. collectability of sales price is reasonably assured or the amount that will not be collectable can be estimated); and

- the earnings process is virtually complete (i.e. seller is not obliged to perform significant activities after the sale to earn the profit).

Recognition of all of the profit arising on a real estate sales transaction is precluded until all of the following criteria are met: *FAS 66.5*

- a sale is consummated;

- the buyer's initial and continuing investments are adequate to demonstrate a commitment to pay for the property;

- the seller's receivable is not subject to future subordination; and

- the seller has transferred to the buyer the usual risks and rewards of ownership and does not have a substantial continuing involvement with the property.

A When is a sale consummated?

There are four criteria that must be met for a sale of real estate to be considered 'consummated': *FAS 66.6*

- the parties are bound by the terms of a contract;

- all consideration has been exchanged;

- any permanent financing for which the seller is responsible has been arranged; and

- all conditions precedent to closing have been performed.

The above criteria are rarely met prior to the date of completion.

B Adequacy of the buyer's initial and continuing investments

The standard provides guidance on how to assess the adequacy of the buyer's initial and continuing investments for the purposes of revenue recognition. Essentially, this assessment involves both a review of the composition of the investments and a size test. *FAS 66.8-12*

REVENUE RECOGNITION

REVENUE RECOGNITION

C Substantial continuing involvement

Several examples are provided of continuing involvement without transfer of risks and rewards. These include, inter alia, transactions where the seller

FAS 66.18

- · has an obligation or an option to repurchase the property; or

- guarantees the return of the buyer's investment.

If the buyer is not independent of the seller (e.g. where the seller has an equity interest in the buyer), only the part of the profit proportionate to the outside interests in the buyer may be recognised at the date of sale.

FAS 66.34

22.6.2 *Revenue recognition where the basic criteria are not met*

When a sale does not meet all of the above criteria, an alternative method of recognising profits must be applied. The standard does prescribe appropriate accounting for a few specific situations. The alternative methods of profit recognition noted include:

FAS 66.19-43

- the deposit method;

- the cost recovery method;

- the instalment sales method;

- the reduced profit method.

In certain situations, usually where the seller has a continuing involvement without transferring substantially all of the risks and rewards of ownership, the transaction may have to be accounted for as a financing arrangement rather than a sale.

23 EXCEPTIONAL ITEMS

23.1 AUTHORITATIVE PRONOUNCEMENTS
- SSAP 6

- CA 85

23.2 ACCOUNTING TREATMENT

SSAP 6.29,36 These are material items which derive from events or transactions that fall within the ordinary activities of the company.

SSAP 6.36
CA 85 Sch 4.57(3) Such items should be credited or charged in arriving at the profit/loss on ordinary activities and separately disclosed by way of note. Where it is necessary in order that the accounts show a true and fair view, the profit before exceptional items and the exceptional items should be shown separately on the face of the profit and loss account.

An adequate description of each exceptional item should be given to enable its nature to be understood. Exceptional amounts written off current assets should be disclosed separately.

UNUSUAL OR INFREQUENT ITEMS

23.1 AUTHORITATIVE PRONOUNCEMENT

- APB 30

23.2 ACCOUNTING TREATMENT

A material event or transaction that is unusual in nature or occurs infrequently, but not both, should be reported as a separate component of income from continuing operations.

APB 30.26

The nature and financial effects of each event or transaction should be disclosed on the face of the income statement or alternatively in the notes. The earnings per share effects of such items should not be disclosed on the face of the income statement.

24 EXTRAORDINARY ITEMS

24.1 AUTHORITATIVE PRONOUNCEMENTS

- SSAP 6

- CA 85

24.2 DEFINITION

SSAP 6.30   Extraordinary items are material items which derive from events or transactions that fall outside the ordinary activities of the company and which are therefore expected not to recur frequently or regularly.

SSAP 6.28   Ordinary activities are defined as any activities which are usually, frequently or regularly undertaken by the company and any related activities in which the company engages in furtherance of, incidental to, or arising from, those activities.

The standard provides examples of items which might be treated as extraordinary. Whilst the above definition appears to be similar to the US definition, in practice it is less rigidly applied and, consequently, often gives rise to a difference with APB 30.

EXTRAORDINARY ITEMS

24.1 AUTHORITATIVE PRONOUNCEMENTS

- APB 30 (and AIN-APB 30)

- APB 16

- APB 11

- FAS 4 (as amended by FAS 64)

24.2 DEFINITION

Extraordinary items are events and transactions that are distinguished by their unusual nature and by the infrequency of their occurrence. They should possess both of the following criteria :

APB 30.20

- a high degree of abnormality, being of a type clearly unrelated to, or only incidentally related to, the ordinary and typical activities of the enterprise;

- being of a type that would not reasonably be expected to recur in the foreseeable future.

24.2.1 Exceptions to the definition

Material gains or losses from extinguishment of debt (except those from extinguishments of debt made to satisfy sinking-fund requirements that a company must meet within one year of the date of extinguishment) should be reported as extraordinary items even though they do not meet the above criteria.

FAS 4.8

FAS 64.4

Material profits or losses resulting from the disposal of a significant part of the assets or a separable segment of previously separate enterprises which are now combined should be disclosed as extraordinary if:

APB 16.60

- the combination was accounted for as a pooling of interests, and

- the disposition is within two years after the combination is consummated.

If FAS 96 has not been adopted, the tax benefits on loss carry forwards recognised in subsequent periods (which had not been previously recognised in the loss period) should be reported as extraordinary.

APB 11.61

EXTRAORDINARY ITEMS

24.3 DISCLOSURE

SSAP 6.37

CA 85 Sch 4.8,54(3)

The following should be disclosed separately, if material, after the profit or loss on ordinary activities after taxation:

- extraordinary income;

- extraordinary charges; and

SSAP 15.34

- taxation on extraordinary profit or loss (split between UK corporation tax, income tax, overseas tax and double tax relief and deferred tax relating to the extraordinary item)

In practice a single figure is usually shown on the face of the profit and loss account with the analysis given in a note.

SSAP 6. 37

CA 85 Sch 4.57(2)

The amount of each extraordinary item should be shown individually and an adequate description of each item given to enable its nature to be understood.

EXTRAORDINARY ITEMS

24.3 DISCLOSURE

The disclosures required are broadly similar to those made in the UK.   *APB 30.11*
Extraordinary items should be disclosed after the results from operations.
Descriptive captions and the amounts for individual extraordinary events or
transactions should be disclosed, preferably on the face of the income
statement.

Taxes applicable to extraordinary items should be disclosed on the face of
the income statement if practicable, and otherwise in the notes.

25 DISCONTINUED OPERATIONS OF A BUSINESS SEGMENT

25.1 AUTHORITATIVE PRONOUNCEMENTS

- SSAP 6

- SSAP 22

25.2 DEFINITION OF A BUSINESS SEGMENT

SSAP 6.32

A business segment is a separately identifiable component of a company whose activities, assets and results can be clearly distinguished from the remainder of the company's activities. A business segment will normally have its own separate product lines or markets.

25.3 GAIN OR LOSS FROM THE DISPOSAL OF A SEGMENT

SSAP 6.11

Once a decision has been made to discontinue a business segment, a provision should be made for the net costs relating to the disposal or closure arising from decisions taken up to the balance sheet date, after taking account of trading results expected to arise after the implementation date.

25.3.1 Decision and implementation dates

The decision date is equivalent to the measurement date APB 30.

The implementation date is the date on which the implementation of the scheme commences.

25.3.2 Disposal of goodwill

When calculating the profit or loss on disposal of a previously acquired business segment, there is no requirement to take account of the goodwill

DISCONTINUED OPERATIONS OF A BUSINESS SEGMENT

25.1 AUTHORITATIVE PRONOUNCEMENTS

* APB 30

* AIN-APB 30

25.2 DEFINITION OF A BUSINESS SEGMENT

A business segment is a component of an entity whose activities represent a separate major line of business or class of customer. A segment may be in the form of a subsidiary, a division or a department.

APB 30.13

The disposal of a subsidiary is not necessarily the disposal of a segment of a business (see 25.5 below). Also, the inability to identify the results of operations of the part of the business being disposed of would clearly suggest that the definition of a segment has not been met.

25.3 GAIN OR LOSS FROM THE DISPOSAL OF A SEGMENT

If a loss is expected from the discontinuance of a business segment, the estimated loss shall be provided for as of the measurement date (see section 25.3.1 below). The computation of the estimated loss on disposal should take into account the estimated results from the discontinued operation between the measurement date and the expected disposal date.

APB 30.15

25.3.1 Measurement date

The standard defines the measurement date as the date on which the management having authority to approve the action commits itself to a formal plan to dispose of a segment of the business. The plan of disposal should include as a minimum:

APB 30.14

* identification of the major assets to be disposed of;

* the expected method of disposal;

* the period expected to be required for completion of the disposal;

* an active programme to find a buyer if disposal is to be by sale;

* the estimated results of operations of the segment from the measurement date to the disposal date; and

* the estimated proceeds or salvage to be realised by disposal.

25.3.2 Disposal of goodwill

If a large segment, separable group of assets of an acquired company or the entire acquired company is sold, all or a portion of the unamortised cost of

APB 17.32

DISCONTINUED OPERATIONS OF A BUSINESS SEGMENT

SSAP 22.52(b) attributable to the business segment disposed of which has previously been written off against reserves but the amount of goodwill in question and its treatment must be disclosed.

25.4 PRESENTATION IN FINANCIAL STATEMENTS

SSAP 6.11,13 In the UK, there is no requirement to distinguish between the results of continuing and discontinued operations except that a provision for the effect of a decision made prior to the balance sheet date to discontinue an entire business segment could be treated as an extraordinary item. Once implementation of a scheme for discontinuing the segment has commenced, all trading results thereafter relating to the discontinued activities should be included within the extraordinary item.

Trading results for the period before the implementation date (see definition above) are part of the trading results for the year and should not be included in the extraordinary item.

25.4.1 Other disclosures

SSAP 6.13 Separate disclosure of the trading results of the discontinued operations before the commencement of implementation may be required to enable the results of continuing operations to be ascertained.

SSAP 22.52 The following should be disclosed in respect of each material disposal of a previously acquired business or business segment:

- the profit or loss on disposal;

- the amount of purchased goodwill attributable to the business segment disposed of and how it has been treated in determining the profit or loss on disposal; and

- the accounting treatment adopted and the amount of the proceeds in situations where no profit or loss is recorded on a disposal because the proceeds have been accounted for as a reduction in the cost of the acquisition.

SSAP 14.30 For material disposals from the group, the consolidated accounts should contain sufficient information about the results of the subsidiaries sold to enable shareholders to appreciate the effect on the consolidated results.

CA 85 Sch 4A.15-16 In the case of material disposals of subsidiary and associated undertakings, the amount of the group result attributable to these undertakings should be disclosed in a note to the accounts. If such disclosure is thought to be prejudicial, an exemption is available if the undertaking is incorporated outside the UK or carries on business outside the UK.

DISCONTINUED OPERATIONS OF A BUSINESS SEGMENT

the goodwill recognised in the acquisition should be included in the cost of the assets sold.

25.4 PRESENTATION IN FINANCIAL STATEMENTS

Where there is a disposal of a business segment, the following should be disclosed separately from income from continuing operations but not as an extraordinary item:

APB 30.8

- the income (loss) from the operations of the discontinued business segment (both current and prior periods); and

- the gain (loss) resulting from the disposal of the business segment.

25.4.1 Other disclosures

The notes to the financial statements should also disclose:

APB 30.18

- the identity of the segment;

- the expected disposal date;

- the expected manner of disposal;

- a description of the remaining assets and liabilities of the segment at the balance sheet date; and

- the income or loss from operations and any proceeds from disposal of the segment during the period from the measurement date to the date of the balance sheet.

DISCONTINUED OPERATIONS OF A BUSINESS SEGMENT

25.5 DISPOSAL OF A PORTION OF A BUSINESS SEGMENT

The gain or loss arising from a disposal of a part of a continuing business segment (whether a subsidiary or associated undertaking or a business) should be reported as part of the profit or loss on ordinary activities. There is no specific guidance on the computation of the gain or loss arising on such a disposal; in practice, the gain or loss on the sale is computed as the difference between the proceeds of the sale and the holding company's share of the net assets of the disposed entity. The turnover and cost of sales of the part sold in respect of the period prior to disposal is not segregated on the face of the profit and loss account but usually aggregated with the results of all the continuing business segments.

Such a disposal may need to be reported as an exceptional item (see section 23) if material and the disclosures noted in 25.4 above may be required as well.

DISCONTINUED OPERATIONS OF A BUSINESS SEGMENT

25.5 DISPOSAL OF A PORTION OF A BUSINESS SEGMENT

The gain or loss on a sale of a portion of a line of business that is not a *AIN-APB 30.1* segment (as defined in 25.2 above), should be calculated in the same manner as if it were a segment of the business. However, whilst such an item may have to be reported as a separate component of income from continuing operations (by virtue of being an unusual of infrequent item (see section 23)), it should not be reported on the face of the income statement in a manner that would suggest that it is a disposal of a business segment. The notes to the financial statements should contain the disclosures notes in 25.4.1 above if the information is known.

26 EARNINGS PER SHARE

26.1 AUTHORITATIVE PRONOUNCEMENT

- SSAP 3

26.2 APPLICABILITY

SSAP 3.13   Applies only to listed companies. Companies whose shares are traded on the USM would also be expected to comply.

26.3 BASIC EARNINGS PER SHARE (EPS)

SSAP 3.10   The basic EPS is based on profits after tax but before extraordinary items less preference dividends and minority interests divided by the weighted average number of equity shares in issue and ranking for dividend in respect of the period.

26.4 FULLY DILUTED EPS

SSAP 3.16   In addition, a fully diluted EPS figure must be calculated and disclosed on the face of the profit and loss account (with equal prominence to the basic EPS) if any of the following are in existence:

- equity shares which do not at present rank for dividend but will do so in the future;

- convertible debentures, loan stock or preference shares; or

- share options or warrants.

EARNINGS PER SHARE

26.1 AUTHORITATIVE PRONOUNCEMENTS

- APB 15

- AIN-APB 15

- FAS 21

- FAS 85

- APB 30

26.2 APPLICABILITY

Applies to enterprises whose securities (debt or equity) are publicly traded.   *FAS 21.12*

26.3 PRIMARY EPS

Companies should present primary earnings per share calculated on a basis   *APB 15.24*
similar to the computation of the basic EPS under SSAP 3 except that it is
based not only upon outstanding shares of common stock but also other
securities which are in substance 'common stock equivalents' and which
dilute earnings per common share by more than 3%. Common stock
equivalents include options, warrants and certain convertible securities.
FAS 85 contains guidance for determining whether convertible securities are
'common stock equivalents' in the primary earnings per share computation.

The 'treasury stock' method should be used to reflect the use of the proceeds   *APB 15.36*
of options or warrants etc. when computing the dilution in earnings per share
data due to common stock equivalents. Under this method, shares of
common stock are assumed to be issued, and the proceeds received on the
exercise of the option or warrant are assumed to be used to purchase the
company's own shares at the 'exercise' date using an average price for the
period.

26.4 FULLY DILUTED EPS

If common shares are contingently issuable at the end of any period   *APB 15.41*
presented or if common shares were issued during the period presented due
to conversions, exercise etc., then the fully diluted EPS amounts must also be
disclosed on the face of the income statement.

EARNINGS PER SHARE

SSAP 3 App 1.31   For the purposes of calculating the fully diluted EPS, it should be assumed that any proceeds receivable when options or warrants are taken up are invested in $2^1/_2\%$ Consolidated Stock (a UK Government loan stock).

SSAP 3.16   The fully diluted EPS need not be shown unless the dilution is in excess of 5% of the basic figure.

26.5 DISCLOSURE

SSAP 3.15   The basis of calculating EPS and fully diluted EPS must be disclosed. In particular the amount of earnings and the number of shares used in the EPS calculations must be shown.

SSAP 3.9,14   Disclosure of a nil-distribution EPS (which is based on a post-tax earnings figure that recognises only those components of the tax charge that are unaffected by a dividend distribution) is recommended where materially different from the basic EPS.

EARNINGS PER SHARE

The fully diluted EPS need not be disclosed if the dilution is less than 3% of earnings per common share.

AIN-APB 15.11

26.5 DISCLOSURE

Earnings per share amounts should be presented on the face of the income statement for:

APB 15.12-13
APB 30.9

- income from continuing operations;

- income before extraordinary items;

- the cumulative effect of a change in accounting principle; and

APB 20.20

- net income.

It may be desirable to present EPS amounts for:

- extraordinary items;

- results of discontinued operations; and

- the gain or loss on disposal of a business segment.

Consideration should be given to disclosing details of the computation including all assumptions and any resulting adjustments in order to facilitate understanding of how the per share amounts were arrived at. Such disclosure should include, inter alia, the identification of common stock equivalents.

APB 15.20-21

Supplementary EPS data should be provided where changes occur in the capital structure of a company after the balance sheet date but before completion of the financial report or where conversions have taken place during the current period which would have affected primary EPS had they taken place at the beginning of the period.

APB 15.22-23

27 FIXED ASSETS

CA 85 s 262(1) Fixed assets are defined as assets intended for use on a continuing basis in the company's activities and any assets not intended for such use are taken to be current assets. They comprise:

- intangible assets including development costs and goodwill;

- tangible assets; and

- investments held for the long term e.g. shares in subsidiary and associated undertakings. These are addressed in section 28.4.

COMMENT

During 1990 the ASC issued ED 47 — *Accounting for goodwill*, ED 51 — *Accounting for fixed assets and revaluations* and ED 52 — *Accounting for intangible fixed assets*. The more important changes proposed by these EDs are noted at appropriate points in this section.

27.1 INTANGIBLE ASSETS

27.1.1 Authoritative pronouncements

- CA 85

- SSAP 12

- SSAP 13

- SSAP 22

27.1.2 Recording intangible assets

A General

CA 85 Sch 4.17 Intangible assets should be recorded at cost.

CA 85 Sch 4.31(1) The Alternative Accounting Rules in Part C of Schedule 4 to CA 85 permit intangible assets (other than goodwill) to be included at their current cost (see 27.2).

SSAP 22.13,37 Purchase costs of identifiable intangibles that can be separated from the business as a whole should be capitalised and, if material, included under the appropriate heading within intangible fixed assets in the balance sheet.

NON-CURRENT ASSETS

Under US GAAP a distinction is made between current and non-current assets. The term 'current assets' is used to designate cash and other assets or resources which are reasonably expected to be realised in cash or sold or consumed during the normal operating cycle of the business. The average time intervening between the acquisition of materials or services and the final cash realisation upon sale of the products to which such costs attach constitutes an operating cycle. A one year period is to be used as a basis for segregation of current assets in cases where there are several operating cycles occurring within a year.

Non-current assets, which comprise non-current investments, property, plant and equipment and intangible assets, are presented in the balance sheet below current assets. Each category is presented as a separate line item on the face of the balance sheet in the aforementioned order.

27.1 INTANGIBLE ASSETS

27.1.1 Authoritative pronouncements

- APB 17

- FAS 72

- FAS 86

27.1.2 Recording intangible assets

A   General

Identifiable intangible assets should be recorded at cost at the date of acquisition. Cost is measured by the amount of cash disbursed, the fair value of other assets distributed or the present value of amounts to be paid for liabilities incurred.

APB 17.24-25

Where the consideration for the asset is in the form of shares or stock of the company, cost may be determined either by the fair value of the consideration given or by the fair value of the property acquired, whichever is the more clearly evident.

A company should record as assets the costs of intangible assets acquired from other enterprises or individuals. However, costs of developing, maintaining or restoring intangible assets that:

- are not specifically identifiable;

- have an indeterminate life; or

FIXED ASSETS

However, internal costs to produce a similar specific intangible are unlikely to be capitalised unless they satisfy the criteria for capitalisation as development costs (see section 20.2).

COMMENT

ED 52 proposes that an intangible asset should be recognised only if the historical cost of creating it is known, its characteristics can be clearly distinguished from goodwill and other assets, and its cost can be measured independently of that of goodwill and other assets.

B Goodwill

CA 85 Sch 4.8,31(1)
SSAP 22.35,37,41

No amount should be attributed to non-purchased goodwill in the balance sheet. The amount attributed to purchased goodwill should not include any value for separable intangibles. Purchased goodwill should not be revalued.

C Computer software costs

This is not addressed by any specific accounting standard in the UK. However, to the extent that such costs are research and development costs, the provisions of SSAP 13 would apply (see section 20.2).

27.1.3 Amortisation of intangible assets

CA 85 Sch 4.18
SSAP 12.15

Any fixed asset which has a limited useful life must be depreciated. However, in practice, some companies which capitalise their intangible assets (e.g. brands) take the view that such assets do not have a finite life, and therefore do not have to be depreciated.

The requirements of the CA 85 and SSAP 12 relating to depreciation have been summarised in 27.2.2 below and are equally applicable to intangible and tangible assets.

SSAP 22.38,39,41
CA 85 Sch 4.21

Purchased goodwill should not be carried in the balance sheet of a company or a group as a permanent item. It should normally be eliminated from the accounts immediately on acquisition, by write-off to reserves. If purchased goodwill is not eliminated from the accounts immediately on acquisition, it should be amortised through the profit and loss account on a systematic basis over its useful life.

NON-CURRENT ASSETS

- are inherent in a continuing business and related to an enterprise as a whole (i.e. inseparable), e.g. goodwill

should be deducted from income when incurred.

Costs incurred to develop identifiable intangible assets through internal research efforts should be written off as incurred under the application of the R&D standard (see section 20.2).

APB 17.6

B   Goodwill

Goodwill is recorded only when purchased as part of the assets of a business acquired and effectively is the cost of unidentifiable intangible assets purchased (see section 2.4.4).

APB 17.26

C   Computer software costs

The majority of US companies expense all costs of developing software for internal use. Costs incurred internally in creating a computer software product to be sold, leased or otherwise marketed should be charged to expense when incurred as R&D until technological feasibility has been established upon completion of detail program design or, in its absence, completion of a working model.

FAS 86.3-4

After technological feasibility is deemed established, costs of producing the software documentation and training materials should be capitalised until such time as the product is available for general release to customers.

FAS 86.5-6

27.1.3 Amortisation of intangible assets

The cost of each type of intangible asset should be amortised over the estimated life of that specific asset. The period of amortisation of the intangible asset should be determined after an analysis of all the pertinent factors. The standard lists some of the factors which should be taken into consideration. However, the period of amortisation should not exceed forty years. The straight-line method of amortisation should be applied unless another systematic method is more appropriate.

APB 17.28-30

Goodwill should be amortised over its estimated useful life. See section 2.4.4 for further detail.

APB 17.30

FIXED ASSETS

When the latter treatment is selected:

*   if there is a permanent diminution in the value of the purchased goodwill, it should be written down immediately through the profit and loss account to its recoverable amount (see 27.2.2 E below)

*   the useful economic life should be estimated at the time of the acquisition and should not include any allowance for the effects of subsequent expenditure.

COMMENT
ED 47 proposes that purchased goodwill should always be recorded as an asset and amortised over a period not exceeding 20, or in exceptional circumstances 40 years. The amortisation charge should be calculated using the straight line basis or any other systematic basis which is more conservative and considered to give a more realistic allocation. ED 52 makes a similar proposal with regard to the amortisation of other intangibles.

SSAP 22.41(c)   See 27.2.2 C below. However, the estimated useful economic life over which purchased goodwill is being amortised may be shortened but may not be increased as a result of this review.

27.1.4 Disposal of goodwill
SSAP 22.52   When calculating the profit or loss on disposal of a previously acquired business segment, there is no requirement to take account of the goodwill attributable to the business segment disposed of which had previously been written off against reserves, although the accounting treatment adopted must be disclosed (see section 25.4.1).

27.1.5 Disclosure
The note disclosures to be made are based on the requirements of CA 85 and SSAP 12. These are detailed in 27.2.3 below. The following additional disclosures are required to be made concerning goodwill:

SSAP 22.43   •   the accounting policy followed in respect of goodwill should be explained in the notes.

NON-CURRENT ASSETS

In the case of capitalised software costs, amortisation for a period should be based upon the ratio of current revenue from the product to the total of current and anticipated future revenue. However, this figure of amortisation should not be less than a figure arrived at by spreading the unamortised balance equally over the estimated remaining life of the products including the period reported on.   *FAS 86.8*

The periods of amortisation should be continually reviewed and the unamortised cost should be allocated to the increased or reduced number of remaining periods in the revised useful life (not exceeding 40 years from the date of acquisition).   *APB 17.31*

27.1.4 Disposal of goodwill

If a large segment, separable group of assets of an acquired company or the entire acquired company is sold, all or a portion of the unamortised cost of the goodwill recognised in the acquisition should be included in the cost of the assets sold.   *APB 17.32*

27.1.5 Disclosure

Disclosure is required of each class of intangible assets which is in excess of 5% of total assets, the carrying basis and any significant additions or deletions.   *S-X 5-02.15*

The method and period of amortisation of intangible assets should be disclosed.   *APB 17.30*

FIXED ASSETS

SSAP 22.45

CA 85 Sch 4.8,21(4)

- where the amortisation treatment is selected, a number of additional disclosures should be made:

  (i) goodwill as a separate item under intangible fixed assets in the balance sheet until fully written off;

  (ii) movement on the goodwill account during the year and the amount amortised during the year; and

  (iii) the period selected for amortising the goodwill relating to each major acquisition and the reason for choosing that period.

CA 85 Sch 4A.14

The cumulative amount of goodwill written off (net of amounts relating to undertakings disposed of) should be disclosed.

Other disclosures concerning goodwill are detailed in section 2.4.6 and section 25.4.1.

27.2 TANGIBLE FIXED ASSETS

27.2.1 Authoritative pronouncements

- CA 85

- SSAP 12

- SSAP 19

27.2.2 Accounting for tangible fixed assets

A   Recording fixed assets

CA 85 Sch 4.17, 31(2),34(1)

Tangible fixed assets should be included at their purchase price or production cost less any provision for depreciation or diminution in value. Revaluations are permitted.

> **COMMENT**
> ED 51 proposes various rules regarding the determination of the purchase price or production cost of a fixed asset. These specify that costs arising from inefficiencies should not be included in the production cost of a fixed asset and also sets out limits to the period during which costs can be accumulated in respect of a fixed asset under construction. The ED also addresses the subject of capitalisation of borrowing costs incurred in financing the production of fixed assets — see section 3.

The Alternative Accounting Rules in Part C of Schedule 4 to the CA 85 give the statutory bases and rules regarding revaluations. There are two permitted bases for the valuation of tangible fixed assets; such assets may be included at market value or current cost. Valuations are permitted on an asset-by-asset basis and need not cover all of the assets in a particular class. When an

NON-CURRENT ASSETS

The amortisation and accumulated amortisation should be disclosed.   *S-X 5-02.16*

Unamortised capitalised computer software costs and the amounts charged to   *FAS 86.11*
income in respect of amortisation and write down of capitalised software
costs must be disclosed.

27.2 PROPERTY, PLANT AND EQUIPMENT (PPE)
27.2.1 Authoritative pronouncements
*   ARB 43, Chapter 9A-9C

*   APB 6

*   APB 12

27.2.2 Accounting for PPE
A Recording PPE

PPE are reported at their historical cost. PPE should not be written up to   *CON 5.67*
reflect appraisal at market or current values which are above cost to the   *APB 6.17*
entity except in certain specific cases, for example in quasi- reorganisations
or push down accounting.

FIXED ASSETS

asset is revalued, the gain or loss on revaluation must go to a separate reserve, the revaluation reserve (see section 33.5).

> **COMMENT**
>
> ED 51 proposes that valuations must cover all assets in a particular class, and must be updated at least every 5 years or more frequently if the value changes materially.

B Depreciation

CA 85 Sch 4.18,32
SSAP 12.15

Any fixed asset that has a limited useful economic life should be depreciated over that life, on a systematic basis down to its residual value (if any). Asset lives should be estimated on a realistic basis and reviewed regularly (see C below).

Under the historical cost rules, depreciation should be based on the purchase price or production cost. If the alternative accounting rules are being followed, depreciation should be based on the revalued amounts and the remaining life of the asset at the time of the valuation.

SSAP 12.21

A change from one method of providing depreciation to another is only permitted if this results in a fairer presentation of an enterprise's results and financial position. Such a change does not constitute a change in accounting policy.

C Asset lives

SSAP 12.18

If there is a revision of life of an asset, the unamortised cost has to be charged to revenue over the remaining life of the asset. Where, however, future results would be materially distorted the adjustment to accumulated depreciation may be made through the profit and loss account in the form of a cumulative catch up adjustment. This would be dealt with in arriving at profit on ordinary activities, unless it were to arise from an extraordinary event and should be separately disclosed.

D Depreciation of land and buildings

CA 85 Sch 4.18
SSAP 12.23-24

Freehold land does not normally require to be depreciated unless it is subject to depletion. Buildings are assets with a finite life and therefore should be subject to depreciation, except in the case of investment properties (see below). In practice, some companies do not provide depreciation either because it is not material or because the residual value is estimated to equal or exceed cost (e.g. because the buildings are kept in a high state of maintenance).

NON-CURRENT ASSETS

B Depreciation

Generally accepted accounting principles require the cost of a productive facility (less any salvage value) to be spread over its expected useful life in such a way as to allocate it as equitably as possible to the periods during which services are obtained from the use of the facility.

ARB 43 Chap 9C.5

A change in amortisation method for a class of identifiable assets is a change in accounting principle and requires an adjustment for the cumulative effect of the change in the income statement of the period of the change (see section 1.2.2).

C Asset lives

There is no pronouncement dealing with asset lives.

D Depreciation of land and buildings

Buildings must be depreciated. In most cases, land is not depreciated.

FIXED ASSETS

SSAP 19.7 Investment properties are completed properties which are held for their investment potential with any rentals being negotiated at arm's length. They do not include properties owned and occupied by the reporting company for its own purposes or those let to other group companies.

SSAP 19.10-11 Investment properties should not be subject to depreciation (except for properties held on lease, which should be depreciated at least over the last 20 years of the lease term) and should be included in the balance sheet at their open market value.

E Permanent diminution

CA 85 Sch 4.19 Provisions for diminution in value should be made on an asset by asset basis
SSAP 12.19-20 in respect of fixed assets if the reduction in value is expected to be permanent. Such provisions should be made through the profit and loss account and if no longer required are to be written back again through the profit and loss account. In the case of a permanent diminution of a revalued asset, the amount of the permanent diminution may be split, with previous valuations being reversed while the deficit below depreciated historical cost is charged to the profit and loss account.

COMMENT

ED 51 proposes that the full amount of any permanent diminution should be recognised in the profit and loss account.

27.2.3 Disclosure

SSAP 12.25 Disclosure is required for each specified class of asset of:

CA 85 Sch 4.42
- method used in computing depreciation and the rate or useful economic life used;

- cost or valuation amount at the start and end of the year;

NON-CURRENT ASSETS

E Permanent diminution

There is no specific standard that addresses this issue. However, basic accounting concepts would suggest recognition of impairments in value where economic impairment (loss of economic value) has occurred.

APB Stat No.4

When discussing what generally acceptable accounting principles should be used for determining whether a write-down would be required, the EITF failed to reach a consensus on the subject. It made the following observations:

EITF 84-28

- recognition of only permanent impairments continues to be the dominant practice;

- assets are not written down below a break-even point, based on future cash flows measured either on a gross basis or on a discounted basis; and

- once written down, the assets are not subsequently written back up even if circumstances change.

The SEC believes that a write-down is necessary in the current period if it is probable that estimated, undiscounted future cash flows will be less than the net book value of an asset. It will accept but not require discounting in estimating future cash flows.

The FASB has set up a Task Force to research this topic and address the issues involved.

27.2.3 Disclosure

Disclosure should be made of:

S-X 5-02.13(a),14
S-X 12-06,-07
APB 12.4-5

- the method or methods used in computing depreciation for major classes of depreciable assets;

- cost of major classes of depreciable assets;

FIXED ASSETS

- additions and disposals during the year;

- revaluations during the year;

- accumulated depreciation at start and end of the year; and

- depreciation expense for the period.

CA 85 Sch 4.44, Land and buildings should be analysed between freehold and long and short
83(1) leaseholds. Long leases are those with 50 years or more unexpired at the
balance sheet date.

CA 85 Sch 4.33 Where assets are included at valuation, the effect of the revaluation should be
disclosed, i.e. it must be possible to ascertain what the historical cost figures
would have been for both cost and accumulated depreciation.

CA 85 Sch 4.43 It is necessary to disclose the carrying basis and if held at valuation, the year
and amount of valuation. If valued during the year, the names or
qualifications of the valuers and the bases used must be disclosed. Also the
SSAP 12.27 effect on the depreciation charge for the year should be disclosed if material.
SSAP 19.12 In the case of an investment property, if the person making the valuation is
an employee or officer of the company or group, this should be disclosed.

NON-CURRENT ASSETS

- accumulated depreciation either by major class of depreciable asset or in total; and

- depreciation expense for the period.

The PPE disclosures are not required to be given by SEC registrants whose PPE (net of accumulated depreciation) is less than 25% of total assets at both the beginning and end of the current accounting period.

28 INVESTMENTS

28.1 AUTHORITATIVE PRONOUNCEMENTS

*   CA 85

*   YB

COMMENT
During 1990, the ASC issued ED 55 — *Accounting for investments*. The proposals in
the ED are intended to apply to all enterprises, although it recognises that particular
industry sectors may require to develop more detailed guidance for their own
circumstances.

28.2 BALANCE SHEET CLASSIFICATION
Classification between current and non-current depends on management's
intentions with regard to holding the investment.

COMMENT
ED 55 defines a fixed asset investment as one which is intended to be held for use on a
continuing basis in the activities of the enterprise. Classification as a fixed asset should
only be made where an intention to hold the investment for the long term can clearly be
demonstrated or where there are restrictions as to the investor's ability to dispose of the
investment. Current asset investments are defined as investments other than fixed asset
investments.

28.3 CURRENT ASSET INVESTMENTS
CA 85 Sch 4.22-23   Current asset investments (of all types) will normally be stated at the lower
of cost and net realisable value.

CA 85 Sch 4.31(4)   However, under the Alternative Accounting Rules in CA 85, current asset
investments may be included at their current cost.

COMMENT
ED 55 proposes that current asset investments that are readily marketable should be
marked to market with all gains and losses dealt with in the profit and loss account.
This proposal conflicts with the CA 85 valuation rules and so in order to adopt such a
policy it would be necessary to invoke the true and fair override (see Chapter 2.2.1).
The ED's proposals in respect of all other current asset investments follow the CA 85
rules.

Transfers between current and non-current investments are generally made at
the lower of cost or net realisable value of the investment at the date of
transfer.

COMMENT
ED 55 proposes that transfers of readily marketable investments between fixed and
current asset categories should be effected at market value. Any gain or loss arising
should be reported in the profit and loss account and be separately disclosed. Transfers
of other investments should be recorded at their carrying values.

INVESTMENTS

28.1 AUTHORITATIVE PRONOUNCEMENTS
- FAS 12

- ARB 43

Certain industries, e.g. investment companies, brokers and dealers in securities etc. apply specialised industry accounting practices (e.g. marking to market) with respect to marketable securities; a discussion of such practices is outside the scope of this book.

28.2 BALANCE SHEET CLASSIFICATION
In the case of a classified balance sheet, classification between current and non-current depends upon whether or not the investment is reasonably expected to be realised in cash during the normal operating cycle of the business.

ARB 43
Chap 3A.4

28.3 CURRENT ASSET INVESTMENTS
Investments in non-marketable or non-equity securities should be stated at the lower of cost and net realisable value.

Investments in marketable equity securities should be segregated into current and non-current portfolios. The current portfolio is carried at the lower of aggregate cost or market value at the balance sheet date. The amount by which aggregate cost of the portfolio exceeds market value is called the valuation allowance and shown as a deduction from aggregate cost. Changes in the valuation allowance are included in net income of the period in which they occur.

FAS 12.8,11

If there is a change in the classification of a marketable equity security between current and non-current, the security should be transferred at the lower of its cost or market value at date of transfer. If market value is less than cost, the market value becomes the new cost basis and the difference is included in net income.

FAS 12.10

INVESTMENTS

28.4 FIXED ASSET INVESTMENTS

These usually comprise investments in subsidiary and associated undertakings. Other items such as loans to subsidiary and associated undertakings are also included in this category. Such investments should be included at cost or alternatively, under the Alternative Accounting Rules in CA 85, at market value or at directors' valuation.

CA 85 requires provisions for diminution in value to be made if the reduction in value is expected to be permanent. The accounting treatment noted in section 27.2.2 E is equally applicable to fixed asset investments.

Unrealised gains arising from stating investments at market value should not be dealt with in the profit and loss account but credited directly to a revaluation reserve (see section 33.5) which forms part of shareholders' funds.

COMMENT

The ED largely repeats the CA 85 rules for accounting for fixed asset investments. However the ED proposes that where the directors adopt a policy of valuation for a class of investments they should apply it consistently to all the investments (rather than on a selective basis) and the investments should be revalued annually. In the case of redeemable interest-bearing securities which are not marked to market, the ED proposes that the discount or premium should be amortised over the period to redemption so as to reflect a constant yield on the investment in the profit and loss account.

28.5 DISCLOSURE

CA 85 Sch 4.45   Disclosure is required of:

•   the aggregate amounts of:

(a)   investments listed on a recognised Stock Exchange;

(b)   other listed investments; and

(c)   unlisted investments.

266

INVESTMENTS

28.4 FIXED ASSET INVESTMENTS

Investments in non-marketable or non-equity securities are stated at the lower of cost and net realisable value. The carrying value should be written down in the event of a permanent decline in value.

The non-current portfolio of marketable equity securities (other than investments accounted for by the equity method) should also be carried at the lower of its aggregate cost or market value at the balance sheet date. However, accumulated changes in the valuation allowance (reflecting the net unrealised losses on the portfolio of non-current marketable equity securities) are included in the stockholders' equity section of the balance sheet and disclosed separately.   *FAS 12.11*

If a decline in market value of a non-current marketable equity security is judged to be 'other than temporary', the cost basis of the individual security should be written down and the amount of the write down accounted for as a realised loss. Once written down, the new cost basis should not be changed for subsequent recoveries in market value.   *FAS 12.21*
    SAB 40.59

Note that the phrase 'other than temporary' is not necessarily confined to situations where there is 'permanent impairment'. The SEC Staff have cited a number factors in evaluating the realisable value of an investment:

*   the length of time and the extent to which the market value has been below cost;

*   the financial condition and short-term prospects of the investee, including any specific events that may influence its operations (e.g. a change in technology that may affect the earnings potential of the investment etc.);

*   the intent and ability of the investor to retain its investment for a sufficient time to allow for any anticipated recovery in market value.

28.5 DISCLOSURE

The following should be disclosed with respect to marketable equity securities owned at each balance sheet date: *FAS 12.12-13*
    S-X 5-02.2,12

*   the aggregate cost and market value of the current and non-current portfolios identifying which is the carrying value;

*   the gross unrealised gains and gross unrealised losses for the current and non-current portfolios;

INVESTMENTS

- for each amount disclosed as listed investments, the aggregate market value if different from book value. If the market value of any listed investment disclosed is greater than its Stock Exchange value, the latter must also be disclosed.

The same disclosure is required of movements during the year and of certain details in respect of items carried at valuation (other than for listed investments) as noted in section 27.2.3 for other tangible fixed assets.

CA 85 Sch 5 7-8, 23-4, 26-7

Where a company holds shares in another undertaking (other than a subsidiary, associated or joint venture undertaking — see sections 8 and 13) which:

- represent more than 10% of the nominal value of any class of the share capital of the investee undertaking (where group accounts are prepared, the interests of all undertakings in the group are combined in calculating the 10%); or

- have a total book value in excess of 10% of the reporting company's own assets,

the following should be disclosed in respect of the investee undertaking:

- its name;

- its country of incorporation or, if incorporated in Great Britain; registration;

- if unincorporated, its address; and

- a description and proportion of the nominal value of the allotted shares of each class held.

CA 85 Sch 5.9,25,28

Where the interest held amounts to 20% or more of the nominal value of the shares of the undertaking (where group accounts are prepared, the interests of all undertakings in the group are combined in calculating the 20%), the following additional information should be disclosed in respect of the investee undertaking:

- profit or loss for the year; and

- total amount of its capital and reserves.

INVESTMENTS

- the net realised gain or loss included in the income statement;

- the basis on which cost was determined in computing realised gain or loss;

- the change in the valuation allowances for both the current and non-current portfolios; and

- significant net realised and net unrealised gains and losses arising after the balance sheet date.

Disclosure of material changes in market value which have occurred during the year should be made on the face of the balance sheet and income statement. *ASR 166*

With respect to all other current and non-current marketable securities, the basis of determining the aggregate amount shown in the balance sheet along with the alternatives of the aggregate cost or aggregate market value at the balance sheet date should be disclosed. *S-X 5-02.2,12*

If the carrying value of marketable securities is material in the context of the balance sheet (see S-X 5-04 Schedule I), certain additional disclosures are required in a separate schedule or in a note to the financial statements. *S-X 12-02*

INVESTMENTS

The information required by the previous paragraph need not be given:

- by a reporting company which is not required to prepare group accounts or which equity accounts for all such investments; or

- by a reporting company or group if the holding in the investee is less than 50% and the investee is not required to publish the information anywhere in the world.

CA 85 s 231 Where the above disclosure would be of excessive length, it need only be given in respect of the principal undertakings, provided that:

- the fact that advantage has been taken of this exemption is disclosed; and

- the full information is given in an appendix to the company's next annual return.

YB 5.2.21(e) A listed company is required to give the following additional information in respect of each company (not being a subsidiary) in which the reporting company has an interest (calculated on a group basis) of 20% or more in the equity share capital:

- its principal country of operation;

- particulars of its issued capital and debt securities and unless the company is equity accounted for, the total amount of its reserves; and

- the percentage of each class of debt securities attributable to the company's interest.

INVESTMENTS

29 STOCKS AND LONG-TERM CONTRACTS

29.1 AUTHORITATIVE PRONOUNCEMENTS

- SSAP 9

- CA 85

29.2 ACCOUNTING FOR STOCKS

29.2.1 Definition

SSAP 9.16   Stocks comprise:

- goods or other assets purchased for resale;

- consumable stores;

- raw materials and components purchased for incorporation into products for sale;

- products and services in intermediate stages of completion; and

- finished goods.

29.2.2 Determining the cost of stock

SSAP 9.17-20
CA 85 Sch 4.26

Cost is defined in relation to the different categories of stocks as being that expenditure which has been incurred in the normal course of business in bringing the product or service to its present location and condition. This expenditure should include in addition to cost of purchase, such costs of conversion as are appropriate to that location and condition.

Cost of purchase comprises purchase price inclusive of import duties, transport and handling costs and any other directly attributable costs, less discounts, rebates and subsidies.

Costs of conversion include production overheads incurred in respect of materials, labour or services for production based on the normal level of activity, taking one year with another, and other overheads attributable in the particular circumstances of the business to bringing the product or service to its present location and condition.

INVENTORIES AND LONG-TERM CONTRACTS

29.1 AUTHORITATIVE PRONOUNCEMENTS

* ARB 43

* ARB 45

* AICPA Issues Paper, *Identification and discussion of certain financial accounting and reporting issues concerning LIFO inventories*

* AICPA Industry and Accounting Guide, *Construction contractors*

29.2 ACCOUNTING FOR STOCKS

29.2.1 Definition

The definition is consistent with the SSAP 9 definition. The term inventory refers to those items of tangible personal property which:

ARB 43
Chap 4.3

* are held for sale in the ordinary course of business;

* are in process of production for such sale; or

* are to be currently consumed in the production of goods or services to be available for sale.

29.2.2 Determining the cost of stock

Cost has been defined generally as the price paid or consideration given to acquire an asset. In the context of inventories, cost means the sum of the applicable expenditures and charges directly or indirectly incurred in bringing an article to its existing condition and location. It includes that portion of general and administrative expenses which may be clearly related to production.

ARB 43
Chap 4.5

While there is no explicit reference to 'production overheads . . . based on the normal level of activity', the standard states that items such as idle facility expense, excessive spoilage, double freight costs etc. may be so abnormal as to require treatment as current period charges rather than as a portion of the inventory cost.

A change in composition of the elements of cost included in inventory is also an accounting change.

FIN 1

STOCKS AND LONG-TERM CONTRACTS

29.2.3 Costing method

SSAP 9.4
SSAP 9 App 1.11
CA 85 Sch 4.27

It is not normally possible/practicable to attach a specific cost to each individual item of stock that is sold (referred to as the actual cost method of calculating cost of goods sold). In practice, various methods have been developed for the measurement of the cost to be matched against revenue from a sale. The methods used in allocating costs to stocks should be selected so as to provide the fairest possible approximation to the expenditure actually incurred in bringing the product to its present location and condition.

SSAP 9 App 1.11-12
CA 85 Sch 4.27

Stocks may be stated using FIFO, weighted average or any other method which provides the fairest practicable approximation to the expenditure actually incurred. LIFO and base stock are valuation methods permitted by CA 85. However, these methods are ordinarily not appropriate under SSAP 9 because they often result in stocks being stated in the balance sheet at amounts that bear little relationship to recent cost levels.

LIFO is very rarely used in the UK, principally because the Inland Revenue have never permitted its use for tax purposes.

29.2.4 Lower of cost and net realisable value

CA 85 Sch 4.22-23
SSAP 9.26

Stocks should be recorded in the balance sheet at the total of the lower of cost and net realisable value (NRV) of the separate items of stock. Where this is impracticable, the comparison of cost and NRV may be done by groups of similar items.

SSAP 9.21

NRV is the actual or estimated selling price less all further costs to completion and all costs to be incurred in marketing, selling and distributing.

INVENTORIES AND LONG-TERM CONTRACTS

29.2.3 *Costing method*

FIFO, Average and LIFO are all acceptable methods of determining the cost of goods sold. Companies should choose the method which, under the circumstances, most clearly reflects the periodic income. The AICPA Issues paper referred to above provides the accounting profession's guidance on what constitutes acceptable LIFO accounting practice.

ARB 43

Chap 4.6

Unlike the UK tax authorities, the Internal Revenue Service in the US officially recognises LIFO as an acceptable method for the computation of tax provided that it is used consistently for tax and financial reporting purposes. This has led to its widespread use in the US.

29.2.4 *Lower of cost or market*

Inventories should be recorded at the lower of cost or market. Market means current replacement cost of the inventory item (by purchase or by reproduction, as the case may be) except that:

ARB 43

Chap 4.8-10

- market should not exceed the NRV (defined as in SSAP 9), and

- market should not be less than NRV reduced by an allowance for an approximately normal margin.

The rule of pricing of inventories at the lower of cost or market is intended as a guide. It should be applied realistically in the light of the objectives of accounting for inventories (i.e. the proper determination of income through the process of matching appropriate costs against revenues) and with due regard to the form, content and composition of the inventory. For instance, in the retail trade, the use of the retail inventory method, if adequate markdowns are taken, is an acceptable method of inventory pricing.

The most common practice is to apply the lower of cost or market rule separately to each item of the inventory. However, if there is only one end-product category, the rule of cost or market, whichever is lower may properly

ARB 43

Chap 4.11

STOCKS AND LONG-TERM CONTRACTS

Practice has developed, principally among commodity dealing companies, of stating stock at market value and also taking into account accounting profits and losses arising on the valuation of forward contracts. Such practice is generally justified as being necessary in order to show a true and fair view.

29.2.5 Disclosure

SSAP 9.27
CA 85 Sch 4.8
Stocks should be sub-classified on the face of the balance sheet or in the notes thereto as follows:

- raw materials and consumables;

- work in progress;

- finished goods and goods for resale; and

- payments on account.

SSAP 9.32
The accounting policy that has been applied to stocks should be stated and applied consistently within the business and from year to year.

INVENTORIES AND LONG-TERM CONTRACTS

be applied to the total of the inventory (since the reduction of individual items to market may not always lead to the most useful result if the utility of the total inventory of the business is not below its cost). Similarly, where more than one major product or operational category exists, application of the rule to the total of the items included in such major categories may result in the most useful determination of income.

In exceptional circumstances (and also where it is accepted industry practice, for example, investment companies reporting their investment securities at market/fair value, the practice used by broker dealers of marking stocks to market etc.), inventories may be stated above cost. For example, precious metals having a fixed monetary value with no substantial cost of marketing may be stated at such monetary value. Where goods are stated above cost, the facts should be fully disclosed.

ARB 43

Chap 4.16

29.2.5 *Disclosure*
Disclosure is required separately in the balance sheet or in a note thereto of the amounts of major classes of inventory such as:

S-X 5-02.6(a)

- finished goods;

- costs relating to long-term contracts/programs;

- work-in-progress;

- raw materials; and

- supplies.

The basis of determining amounts should be disclosed and consistently applied. If inventory amounts are included at cost, a description of the nature of the elements of cost included in inventory should be given.

ARB 43

Chap 4.15

S-X 5-02.6(b)

The method by which amounts are removed from inventory (LIFO, FIFO etc.) should be described.

The aggregate amount of the general and administrative costs incurred in each period and the actual or estimated amount remaining in inventory at the balance sheet date should be disclosed.

If an SEC registrant on the LIFO basis of accounting liquidates a substantial portion of its LIFO inventory, disclosure is required of the amount of income recognised in its income statement (which would not have been recorded had the inventory liquidation not occurred), if material.

SAB 40

STOCKS AND LONG-TERM CONTRACTS

CA 85 Sch 4.27   The difference between the amount at which stock is recorded in the balance sheet and its replacement cost or most recent actual purchase price or production cost should be disclosed if material unless stocks are included at actual purchase price.

29.3 LONG-TERM CONTRACTS

29.3.1 Definition

SSAP 9.22   A long-term contract is a contract entered into for the design, manufacture or construction of a single substantial asset or the provision of a service (or of a combination of assets or services which together constitute a single project) where the time taken substantially to complete the contract is such that the contract activity falls into different accounting periods. A contract that is required to to be accounted for as long-term will usually extend for a period exceeding one year. However, a duration exceeding one year is not an essential feature of a long-term contract.

29.3.2 Accounting for long-term contracts

SSAP 9.28-29   Long-term contracts should be assessed on a contract by contract basis and reflected in the profit and loss account by recording turnover and related costs as contract activity progresses (percentage-of-completion method). If the outcome of the contract can be assessed with reasonable certainty before its conclusion, the prudently calculated attributable profit should be recognised (as part of the reported turnover for that contract).

SSAP 9.23,28   The standard does not specify a method for determining turnover or related costs but instead states that:

- turnover should be ascertained in a manner appropriate to the stage of completion of the contract, the business and the industry in which its operates;

- attributable profit is that part of the total profit currently estimated to arise over the duration of the contract, after allowing for estimated remedial and maintenance costs and increases in costs so far as not recoverable under the terms of the contract, that fairly reflects the profit attributable to that part of the work performed at the accounting date.

278

INVENTORIES AND LONG-TERM CONTRACTS

Substantial and unusual losses resulting from the application of the lower of cost or market rule should be separately disclosed from the 'cost of goods sold' in the income statement. Similarly accrued net losses on firm purchase commitments for inventory should, if material, be separately identified in the income statement.

ARB 43
Chap 4.14,17

If the LIFO method is used, the excess of replacement or current cost over stated LIFO value should, if material, be disclosed either parenthetically on the balance sheet or in the notes.

S-X 5-02.6(c)

29.3 LONG-TERM CONSTRUCTION-TYPE CONTRACTS
29.3.1 Definition
There is no specific definition of a long-term contract. The accounting rules contained in ARB 45 apply to contracts for construction of a specific project which are long-term as compared with those requiring relatively short periods for completion.

The SEC regards long-term contracts or programmes to be those which have been or are expected to be performed over a period of more than twelve months.

S-X 5-02.6(d)

29.3.2 Accounting for long-term contracts
The percentage-of-completion method and the completed-contract method are acceptable methods of accounting.

ARB 45.3

The percentage-of-completion method is preferable when estimates of costs to complete and extent of progress toward completion of long-term contracts are reasonably dependable.

ARB 45.15

The completed-contract method is preferable when lack of dependable estimates or inherent hazards cause forecasts to be doubtful. Under this method, income should be recognised only if the contract is completed or substantially so.

Special rules apply when accounting for cost-plus contracts (i.e. where the contractor is reimbursed for all costs plus a fixed fee) which have not been addressed here.

ARB 43
Chap 11

STOCKS AND LONG-TERM CONTRACTS

29.3.3 Disclosure

SSAP 9.32 The accounting policies should disclose the method of ascertaining both turnover and attributable profit and be applied consistently within the business and from year to year.

SSAP 9.30 Long-term contracts should be disclosed in the financial statements as follows.

The amount by which recorded turnover is in excess of payments on account should be classified as 'amounts recoverable on contracts' and separately disclosed within debtors.

The balance of payments on account (in excess of amounts (i) matched with turnover and (ii) offset against long-term contract balances) should be classified as payments on account and separately disclosed within creditors.

The amount of long-term contracts, at costs incurred, net of amounts transferred to cost of sales, after deducting foreseeable losses and payments on account not matched with turnover, should be classified as 'long-term contract balances' and separately disclosed within the balance sheet heading 'stocks'. The balance sheet note should disclose separately the balance of:

•   net cost less foreseeable losses; and

•   applicable payments on account.

The amount by which the provision or accrual for foreseeable losses exceeds the costs incurred (after transfers to cost of sales) should be included within either provisions for liabilities and charges or creditors as appropriate.

INVENTORIES AND LONG-TERM CONTRACTS

29.3.3 Disclosure

The method of recognising profits under long-term contracts should be disclosed.   *ARB 45.15*

Where the percentage-of-completion method is used, it is necessary to disclose the methods used in measuring the extent of progress toward completion.   *SOP 81-1.21*

Under this method, current assets may include costs and recognised income not yet billed with respect to certain contracts; and liabilities (mainly current) may include billings in excess of costs and recognised income with respect to other contracts.

Where the completed-contract method of accounting is followed, the excess of accumulated costs over related billings should be designated as 'costs of uncompleted contracts in excess of related billings' rather than as inventory or work in process and classified in current assets if collectable within one year or within an operating cycle if longer. The excess of accumulated billings over related costs should be designated as 'billings on uncompleted contracts in excess of related costs' in current liabilities.   *ARB 45.12*

In respect of amounts due under long-term contracts, the following disclosures should be made in the balance sheet or in a note: *S-X 5-02.3(c)*

- balances billed but not paid under retention provisions in contracts, stating by year, if practicable, when such amounts are expected to be collected;

- amounts representing the recognised sales value of performance and such amounts that had not been billed and were not billable at the balance sheet date;

- billed or unbilled amounts representing claims or other similar items subject to uncertainty concerning their determination or ultimate realisation. A description of the nature and status of the principal items comprising such amount is included.

With respect to each of these items, the amounts included therein which are expected to be collected after one year should be disclosed.

The amount of progress payments netted against inventory at the balance sheet date should be separately disclosed in a note.   *S-X 5-02.6(d)*

Claims in excess of the agreed contract price should be disclosed.   *SOP 81-1*

30 CREDITORS

30.1 AUTHORITATIVE PRONOUNCEMENTS

- CA 85

- YB

30.2 CREDITORS: AMOUNTS FALLING DUE WITHIN ONE YEAR

CA 85 Sch 4 Amounts falling due within one year of the balance sheet date are classified in this category.

There is no pronouncement dealing specifically with the classification of short-term obligations.

CA 85 Sch 4.85 In general, a loan is treated as falling due for repayment on the earliest date on which the lender could require repayment or (as the case may be) payment, if he exercised all the options and rights available to him.

CA 85 Sch 4.8 The following items should be disclosed separately within 'Creditors: amounts falling due within one year', if material, either on the face of the balance sheet, or in the notes:

- debenture loans (the amount of convertible loans should be disclosed separately);

CURRENT LIABILITIES AND LONG-TERM DEBT

30.1 AUTHORITATIVE PRONOUNCEMENTS

There are several pronouncements dealing with accounting and disclosure of liabilities which are referred to below where appropriate.

30.2 DEBT, ACCOUNTS PAYABLE AND ACCRUALS

Current liabilities are obligations whose liquidation is reasonably expected to require the use of existing resources classified as current assets or the creation of other current liabilities.

ARB 43
Chap 3A.7-9

Short-term obligations (e.g. commercial paper, current portion of long-term debt etc.) that are scheduled to mature within one year after the balance sheet date (or within the enterprise's operating cycle) should be classified as current liabilities. Such obligations should be excluded from current liabilities only if:

FAS 6.8-11

- the enterprise intends to refinance the obligation on a long-term basis, and

- the enterprise's ability to consummate the refinancing is demonstrated by either a post balance sheet date issue of a long-term obligation or equity securities, or the execution of a financing agreement which permits the refinancing of the short-term obligation on a long-term basis prior to the issuance of the financial statements.

A long-term obligation that becomes callable by the creditor because of a violation of the debt agreement which is not cured within the period of grace, if any, allowed should be classified as a current liability.

FAS 78.5
S-X 4-08(c)

If a violation exists but a waiver has been obtained for a stated period of time, the amount of the obligation and the period of the waiver should be disclosed.

Details of all breaches/defaults in debt agreements, sinking fund or redemption provisions at the date of the latest balance sheet should be stated in the notes.

It is necessary to disclose separately amounts payable to:

S-X 5-02.19-20

- banks for borrowings;

- factors or other financial institutions for borrowings;

CREDITORS

- bank loans and overdrafts;

- payments received on account;

- trade creditors;

- bills of exchange payable;

- amounts owed to group undertakings;

- amounts owed to undertakings in which the company has a participating interest;

- taxation and social security;

- other creditors; and

- accruals and deferred income.

The total of 'Creditors: amounts falling due within one year' must be shown on the face of the balance sheet.

CA 85 Sch 4.48(4)   In respect of each item shown under 'creditors' in the balance sheet (long-term and short-term), the amount of debt which is secured and the nature of the security given should be disclosed.

CURRENT LIABILITIES AND LONG-TERM DEBT

- holders of commercial paper;

- trade creditors;

- related parties; and

- any other current liability in excess of 5% of total current liabilities.

The total of current liabilities should be shown on the balance sheet.   *FAS 6.15*

If short-term obligations are excluded from current liabilities because they   *FAS 6.15*
are expected to be refinanced, a general description should be given of the
financing agreement and the terms of any new obligation incurred or equity
securities issued (or expected to be incurred/issued) as a result of a
refinancing.

It is necessary to disclose current liabilities guaranteed by others.   *FRR 23*

Compensating balance arrangements (a compensating balance is a demand   *ASR 148*
deposit that is maintained as support for existing borrowing arrangements
with a lending institution) that are sufficiently material should be disclosed.

If the aggregate amount of compensating balances exceeds 15% of liquid
assets (current cash balances plus marketable securities), this would
generally be considered material.

If such balances are maintained under an agreement which legally restricts
the use of such funds, they should be segregated on the face of the balance
sheet. Otherwise, footnote disclosure is appropriate.

Additional disclosures are required where compensating balances were
materially greater during the period than at the end of the period.

For each category of short-term borrowings, the following disclosures should   *S-X 12-10*
be given, in aggregate:

- the balance at the end of the period;

- the maximum amount outstanding at any month end during the period;

- the weighted average interest rate both during and at the end of the
  period; and

- the average amount outstanding during the period.

The amount and terms of unused lines of credit for short-term financing   *S-X 5-02.19(b)*
should be disclosed if significant.

CREDITORS

30.3 CREDITORS: AMOUNTS FALLING DUE AFTER MORE THAN ONE YEAR

The aggregate amount of such liabilities should be disclosed on the face of the balance sheet. An identical analysis to that required for 'Creditors: amounts falling due within one year' (see 30.2 above) is required on the face of the balance sheet or in the notes.

30.3.1 Long-term debt

CA 85 Sch 4.48 The following disclosures should be given:

- the aggregate amount due after 5 years otherwise than by instalments;

- the aggregate amount due by instalments any of which fall due after 5 years. In this case, the aggregate amount of instalments falling due after 5 years should also be disclosed; and

- the terms of repayment and rate of interest.

These disclosures are required in respect of each item included under 'Creditors: amounts falling due after more than one year' and not just for long-term debt.

CA 85 Sch 4.85 A loan is treated as falling due for repayment on the earliest date on which the lender would require repayment, if he exercised all options and rights available to him.

YB 5.21(f) An analysis of bank loans and overdrafts and other borrowings is required, showing the aggregate amounts repayable:

- in one year or less;

- between one and two years;

- between two and five years; and

- in five years or more.

CA 85 Sch 4.41 Particulars should be given of any redeemed debentures capable of reissue. Details of debentures held for the company by a nominee should also be disclosed.

If the company has issued any debentures during the year, the following information should be given:

- the reason for the issue;

CURRENT LIABILITIES AND
LONG-TERM DEBT

30.3 LONG-TERM LIABILITIES

30.3.1 Long-term debt

For long-term debt such as bonds, mortgages etc., the following disclosures   *S-X 5-02.22*
should be given for each issue or type of obligation:

- the general character of each type of debt including rate of interest;

- the date of maturity or, if maturing serially, a brief indication of the serial maturities;

- if the payment of principal or interest is contingent, an indication of such contingency;

- a brief indication of priority (i.e. subordinated); and

- if convertible, the basis.

For recorded obligations and redeemable stock, the following should be   *FAS 47.10*
disclosed for each of the 5 years following the date of the latest balance
sheet:

- the combined aggregate amount of maturities and sinking fund requirements for all long-term borrowings; and

- the amount of redemption requirements for all issues of capital stock that are redeemable at fixed or determinable prices on fixed or determinable dates, separately by issue or in aggregate.

Any significant changes in the authorised or issued amounts of bonds,   *S-X 4-08(f)*
mortgages and similar debt since the balance sheet date should be disclosed.   *SAS 1*

Outstanding debt securities of the company that have been repurchased (e.g.   *S-X 4-06*
under sinking fund requirements) should be deducted from the corresponding
liability. However disclosures of such amounts and the purpose for which
they are acquired should be given.

The presentation of the unamortised discount or premium relating to long-   *APB 21.16*
term debt is addressed in section 5.4.

CREDITORS

- the classes of debentures issued; and

- as respects each class of debentures, the amount issued and the consideration received by the company for the issue.

CA 85 Sch 4.48(4) In respect of each item shown under 'creditors' in the balance sheet (long-term and short-term), the amount of debt which is secured and the nature of the security given should be disclosed.

30.3.2 *Other liabilities*

CA 85 Sch 4.46 Provisions for liabilities and charges (e.g. provisions, deferred tax etc.) should not be included within creditors but shown separately on the face of the balance sheet and described as such. Provisions in respect of pensions and deferred taxation should be shown separately.

Particulars of each provision included as 'other provisions' should be given in a note where these are material.

Any transfers to or from a provision account (except transfers made for the purpose for which they were originally established) must be disclosed together with the amounts of the provisions at the start and end of the year and the source and application of any such transfers.

30.3.3 *Convertible debt*

There is no specific requirement prescribing the presentation of convertible bonds on the balance sheet. However, practice has historically been to disclose convertible bonds as a long-term liability rather than equity. Increasingly, however, issuing companies are including convertible bonds, whose ultimate conversion into equity is virtually assured, in the capital 'half' of the balance sheet, below the total of shareholders' funds.

CA 85 Sch 4.40(1) The following particulars are required to be given with respect to any contingent right to the allotment of shares in the company:

- the number, description and amount of the shares that may be issued;

- the period during which the rights are exercisable; and

- the price to be paid.

There is no pronouncement or generally accepted practice for those cases where terms of convertible debt have been altered for a limited period so as to induce holders to convert.

CURRENT LIABILITIES AND
LONG-TERM DEBT

The amount and terms (including commitment fees) of unused commitments for long-term financing arrangements should be disclosed if significant.

S-X 5-02.22(b)

The approximate amounts of assets mortgaged or pledged as collateral and the obligations collateralised should be disclosed.

S-X 4-08(b)
FAS 5.18

30.3.2 Other liabilities

Any liability which is not included in one of the other categories of non-current liabilities requiring separate disclosure (i.e. other than a bond, mortgage, other long-term debt or non-current indebtedness to related parties) and is in excess of 5% of total liabilities should be disclosed separately in the balance sheet or in a note thereto (e.g. deferred tax, provision for liabilities).

S-X 5-02.24

Liabilities of a related stock ownership plan that are guaranteed by the company should be reflected in the balance sheet of that company.

SOP 76-3

Disclosure should be given of any non-current liabilities guaranteed by others.

FRR 23

30.3.3 Convertible debt

The proceeds received from an issue of convertible debt should all be credited to a liability account. An allocation of the proceeds to the conversion option is not permitted due to the inseparability of the debt and the conversion option.

APB 14.12

The rights and privileges of the convertible securities outstanding should be disclosed including conversion prices or rates, dates etc.

APB 15.19

Where the terms of conversion of convertible debt have been altered for a limited period of time so as to induce holders to convert, an expense equal to the fair value of the additional securities or other consideration issued to induce the conversion should be recorded. This expense is measured to the

FAS 84.3-4

CREDITORS

There is no pronouncement on how to account for the proceeds of debt securities issued with detachable warrants. TR 677, which provides non-mandatory guidance on accounting for complex capital issues, would suggest a similar approach to that required by APB 14.

30.3.4 Convertible bonds issued with redemption premium option

There is no pronouncement dealing with how to account for this type of bond, which are generally classified as a liability rather than equity. TR 677 recommends that the redemption premium should be accrued for over the period from the date of issue of the bond to the date when the put may be exercised.

In addition to the accounting treatment required in the US, the following treatments are also used in practice:

- the potential redemption premium is noted as a contingent liability but not accrued; or

- accrual is only made if subsequent changes in the value of the debt or equity make exercise of the put likely.

CA 85 s 130(2)   Under CA 85, the premium payable on the redemption of debentures may be charged to the share premium account (see section 32.5).

CURRENT LIABILITIES AND LONG-TERM DEBT

date the inducement offer is accepted by the convertible debt holder and should not be reported as an extraordinary item.

The portion of the proceeds of debt securities issued with detachable stock purchase warrants which is allocable to the warrants should be accounted for as paid-in capital. The allocation should be based on the fair values of the two elements of the security at the date of issue.

APB 14.16

30.3.4 Convertible bonds with a 'Premium Put'

The EITF has considered the accounting issues arising when convertible bonds are issued at par with a 'premium put'. Such instruments allow the investor to redeem the bonds for cash at a multiple of the bond's par value at a date or dates prior to maturity; if the premium put is not exercised, the put expires.

EITF 85-29

The EITF reached a consensus that the issuer should accrue a liability for the put premium over the period from the date of debt issuance to the initial put date. Accrual should continue regardless of changes in the market value of the debt or underlying common stock.

If the put expires unexercised and at that time, the market value of the common stock under conversion exceeds the put price, the put premium should be credited to additional paid-in capital. In the reverse case, the put premium should be amortised as a yield adjustment over the remaining term of the debt.

Such bonds should not be included in equity.

31a TAXATION

31a.1 AUTHORITATIVE PRONOUNCEMENTS

- SSAP 8

- SSAP 15

- SSAP 1

- CA 85

31a.2 ALLOCATING TAX BETWEEN PERIODS

SSAP 15 is concerned with accounting for the tax on profits and surpluses which are recognised in the financial statements in one period but assessed in another (i.e. deferred tax). The standard requires the use of the liability method when computing tax deferred/accelerated due to the effects of timing differences and chooses the partial provision approach as its general approach.

31a.2.1 Timing differences

SSAP 15.18-21   Timing differences are differences between profits or losses as computed for tax purposes and results as stated in financial statements, which arise from the inclusion of items of income and expenditure in tax computations in periods different from those in which they are included in financial statements. Timing differences originate in one period and are capable of reversal in one or more subsequent periods.

Some specific timing differences are discussed, as follows.

A loss for tax purposes which is available to relieve future profits from tax constitutes a timing difference.

The revaluation of an asset (including an investment in an associated or subsidiary company) will create a timing difference when it is incorporated

292

INCOME TAXES - PRE FAS 96

31a.1 AUTHORITATIVE PRONOUNCEMENTS

In December 1987, the FASB issued FAS 96 'Accounting for Income taxes' to supersede APB 11 'Accounting for Income taxes'. Its effective date has been delayed to periods beginning after December 15, 1991 by FAS 103. Because of the delayed effective date, companies have the option in respect of accounting periods beginning before that date, of either:

* continuing to apply the provisions of APB 11; or

* adopting FAS 96 early.

In view of this, this book covers both standards.

Under both standards, taxation is dealt with as an expense of the business and the accounting rules that have been developed are based on that premise. However, their approach to accounting for taxation is very different. APB 11 focuses on the matching concept and requires tax expense to be matched with the corresponding income in the profit and loss account. FAS 96 is a balance sheet approach and focuses on the balance sheet amounts in order to allocate tax between different accounting periods.

31a.2 INTER-PERIOD TAX ALLOCATION UNDER APB 11

Deferred tax should be provided on all timing differences using the deferral method (except in certain special situations covered by APB 23 and APB 24 e.g. undistributed earnings of subsidiaries, investments (other than subsidiaries and corporate joint ventures) accounted for under the equity method). *APB 11.35-37* *APB 23* *APB 24*

31a.2.1 Timing differences

The definition is very similar to that contained in SSAP 15. These are differences between the periods in which transactions affect taxable income and the periods in which they enter into the determination of pretax accounting income. Timing differences originate in one period and reverse or 'turn around' in one or more subsequent periods. *APB 11.13(e)*

TAXATION

into the balance sheet, insofar as the profit or loss that would result from realisation at the revalued amount is taxable, unless disposal of the revalued asset and of any subsequent replacement assets would not result in a tax liability, after taking account of any excepted rollover relief.

Retention of earnings overseas creates a timing difference only if:

• there is an intention or obligation to remit them; and

• remittance would result in a tax liability after taking account of any related double tax relief.

31a.2.2 Method of computation
Deferred tax should be accounted for under the liability method.

SSAP 15.24-26
SSAP 15 App Para 4

Tax deferred or accelerated by the effect of timing differences should be accounted for to the extent that it is probable that a liability or asset will crystallise. Tax deferred or accelerated by the effect of timing differences should not be accounted for to the extent that it is probable that a liability or asset will not crystallise. For this purpose, the combined effect of all timing differences should be considered rather than looking at individual categories in isolation.

SSAP 15.27-28

The assessment of whether deferred tax liabilities or assets will or will not crystallise should be based upon reasonable assumptions which take into account all relevant information available up to the date on which the financial statements are approved by the board, and also the intentions of management. Such information will usually include financial plans or projections covering a period of years sufficient to enable an assessment to be made of the likely pattern of future tax liabilities. A prudent view should be taken in the assessment of whether a tax liability will crystallise, particularly where the financial plans or projections are susceptible to a high degree of uncertainty or are not fully developed for the appropriate period.

SSAP 15.29

The provision for deferred tax liabilities should be made after taking account of any deferred tax debit balances arising from separate categories of timing differences and any advance corporation tax (ACT) which is available for offset against those liabilities. Best estimates of the tax rates that will be payable on the taxable profits when the timing differences reverse should be used. This need not be the enacted tax rates. For example, if a change of rate is announced after the year end but before the financial statements are finalised, the effect will be reflected in the year which has just ended.

INCOME TAXES - PRE FAS 96

Deferred tax must be provided on the unremitted earnings of foreign subsidiaries unless the presumption that these earnings will be remitted can be overcome. Deferred tax must be provided on the unremitted earnings of investments accounted for by the equity method.

APB 23.9,12

APB 24.7

31a.2.2 *Method of computation*

Having identified timing differences, their tax effects should be measured by the difference between income taxes computed with and without inclusion of the transaction creating the timing difference (the 'with and without' method). Timing differences may be considered individually or similar timing differences may be grouped for this purpose.

APB 11.36-37

Reversals of timing differences are calculated using either the 'net change' method (i.e. current tax rates are applied to the net of the originating and reversing timing differences for the period) or the 'gross change' method (i.e. the rates at which the originating timing difference was initially recorded).

The APB 11 approach is based on the matching concept and attempts to reflect the tax effects of all transactions entering into the determination of the results of operations for the period in the tax charge for that period. The resulting deferred tax amounts in the balance sheet reflect the tax effects of timing differences which will reverse in future periods.

Enacted rates should be used when making provisions for deferred taxes under APB 11.

TAXATION

The difference in the total deferred tax calculated at consecutive year ends gives the deferred tax in respect of the intervening year.

31a.2.3 Deferred tax assets

SSAP 15.30 Deferred tax net debit balances should not be carried forward as assets, except to the extent that they are expected to be recoverable without replacement by equivalent debit balances. This is simply the obverse of the same rule for liabilities. Under SSAP 15, a liability is not provided where there is a 'hard core' of timing differences which represent a postponement of tax; correspondingly, a hard core of timing differences which represents a permanent acceleration of the tax liability should not be regarded as an asset.

SSAP 15 App 14-15 Tax losses may be regarded as recoverable assets if the following conditions are satisfied:

- the loss has resulted from an identifiable and non-recurring cause;

- the enterprise, or predecessor enterprise has been consistently profitable over a considerable period, with any past losses being more than offset by income in subsequent periods; and

- it is assured beyond reasonable doubt that future taxable profits will be sufficient to offset the current loss during the carry-forward period prescribed by tax legislation.

There are corresponding rules and conditions relating to capital losses.

SSAP 15.31-32 Debit balances arising in respect of ACT on dividends payable or proposed at the balance sheet date should be carried forward to the extent that it is foreseen that sufficient corporation tax will be assessed on the profits or income of the succeeding accounting period, against which ACT is available for offset.

Debit balances arising in respect of ACT other than on dividends payable or proposed at the balance sheet should be written off unless their recovery is assured beyond reasonable doubt.

31a.3 DISCLOSURE

31a.3.1 Balance sheet

No classification is required between current and non-current deferred tax.

CA 85 Sch 4.47 The amount of the provisions for deferred taxation must be shown separately from any other provisions for taxation.

INCOME TAXES - PRE FAS 96

31a.2.3 Deferred tax assets

Deferred tax assets relating to loss carry-forwards or to other unused deductions and credits for tax purposes can only be carried if realisation is assured beyond reasonable doubt (similar criteria to those specified in SSAP 15).

APB 11.45,53

The following illustrative criteria are included in APB 11:

APB 11.47-48

- certainty of future taxable income - the loss results from an identifiable, isolated and non-recurring event (the company having been profitable over a long period of time) and future taxable income is virtually certain to be large enough to offset the loss carry-forward;

- if future taxable profits cannot be assumed and deferred tax credits from previous years remain in the books, then it is appropriate to draw down from the recorded deferred tax credit amounts to the extent of the loss carry-forward.

Similar criteria apply when determining whether deferred tax debits can be recorded as assets. The tax effects of such 'book operating losses' may be recognised in the accounts either where realisation is assured beyond reasonable doubt or when there are existing deferred tax credits from prior years which are expected to reverse and offset the debits in future periods.

Tax benefits of loss carry-forwards that have not been recognised previously should be reported as an extraordinary item in the period in which they are realised. The amounts of unused carry-forwards and significant unused deductions or credits for both financial reporting and tax purposes and their expiry dates should be disclosed.

APB 11.61,63

31a.3 DISCLOSURE

31a.3.1 Balance sheet

The deferred tax amount must be split between current and non-current according to whether the asset or liability to which the provision relates is a current or non-current item or if not related to a particular asset or liability, in accordance with the expected reversal date of the timing difference. In the

APB 11.57; FAS 37

TAXATION

SSAP 15.37   The deferred tax balance, analysed into its major components should be disclosed in the balance sheet or in the notes to the accounts.

SSAP 15.40,41   The total amount of unprovided deferred tax should also be disclosed in the notes, analysed into its major components. Where no information on unprovided deferred tax in respect of a revalued asset is given on the grounds that it is argued not to be a timing difference because it will never crystallise, the fact that the potential liability has not been quantified should be stated.

SSAP 15.38   Transfers to and from the deferred tax balance should be disclosed.

SSAP 15.39   Movements in reserves (e.g. revaluation reserve) which relate to deferred tax should be disclosed.

SSAP 15.42   Where the value of an asset is disclosed by way of note because it differs materially from its book value, the tax effect of disposing of it at that value should be disclosed.

SSAP 15.43   Any assumptions regarding the availability of group relief and the payment therefor which are relevant to an understanding of the company's deferred tax position should be disclosed.

SSAP 15.44   Where deferred tax is not provided on earnings retained overseas, this should be stated.

31a.3.2 Profit and loss account

CA 85 Sch 4.54   The charge for taxation should be split between UK tax and overseas tax
SSAP 8.22   with the items below separately disclosed:
SSAP 15.33-34

- the basis on which the tax charged has been computed;

- any special circumstances affecting the liability to tax on profits, income or capital gains for the current or future years; and

- the amount of the tax charge on ordinary activities and on extraordinary items, both analysed into:

  (a) UK corporation tax and the amount by which it has been reduced by the application of double tax relief;

  (b) UK income tax (tax attributable to franked investment income);

  (c) irrecoverable ACT (if material);

  (d) deferred tax; and

INCOME TAXES - PRE FAS 96

latter case, timing differences that do reverse within the normal operating cycle of a business are classified as current and those that do not are classified as non-current.

If deferred tax has not been provided in respect of unremitted earnings of a subsidiary, the reason for not doing so and the amount of earnings involved should be disclosed.

31a.3.2 Income statement

The components of the income tax charge for the period should be disclosed, for example: *APB 11.60*
                                                                                S-X 5-03.11

* income taxes currently payable;

* provision for deferred income taxes;

* the tax effects of operating losses.

These amounts should be allocated to income before extraordinary items and   *APB 11.60,62*
extraordinary items. The amount of the tax charge allocated to discontinued   *APB 30.8*
operations and the tax effects attributable to cumulative effects of accounting
changes, prior year adjustments and capital transactions should be disclosed.

The amounts of any operating loss carry-forwards not recognised in the loss   *APB 11.63(a)-(b)*
period (indicating separately amounts which, upon recognition, would be
credited to deferred tax accounts) and significant amounts of any unused
deductions and tax credits should be disclosed.

TAXATION

      (e)   total overseas taxation, relieved and unrelieved, specifying that part of the unrelieved overseas taxation which arises from the payment or proposed payment of dividends.

SSAP 1.20   Tax attributable to the profits of associated companies should be separately disclosed.

SSAP 15.35   The amount of any unprovided deferred tax in respect of the period analysed into its major components (including unprovided deferred tax assets) should be disclosed.

SSAP 15.36   Any adjustments to deferred tax passing through the profit and loss account which relate to changes in tax rates or in tax allowances should be disclosed.

INCOME TAXES - PRE FAS 96

Reasons for significant variations in the customary relationships between income tax expense and pre-tax accounting income (if not otherwise apparent from the financial statements or nature of the entity's business) should be disclosed. The SEC requires this disclosure in the form of a reconciliation (either in £/$ or % amounts) between the amount of reported total income tax charge and the amount calculated by multiplying income before tax by the statutory tax rate (i.e. the expected tax charge) showing the monetary amount of each of the underlying causes for the difference. A reconciliation need not be provided where no individual reconciling item exceeds 5% of the expected tax charge.

APB 11.63(c)
S-X 4-08(h)(2)

The share of profits of equity accounted investees is disclosed net of tax with no separate disclosure of the tax element required. In the case of an SEC registrant, where the interest in the investee is deemed 'significant', summarised financial information may be required including the disclosure of net and pre-tax income in the notes or even separate financial statements of the investee.

APB 18.19,20
S-X 4-08(g)
S-X 3-09

In the case of an SEC registrant, disclosure is required of:

S-X 4-08(h),(l)

- the components of income before tax as either domestic or foreign and

- the components of the income tax charge such as taxes currently payable and the tax effects of each significant type of timing difference included in the deferred tax element of the charge. For the purposes of ascertaining what is significant, if the amount of the estimated tax effect of each of the various types of timing differences exceeds 5% of the expected tax charge (i.e. obtained by applying statutory tax rate to income before tax), separate disclosure of such tax effects should be made.

Amounts applicable to US income tax, foreign income tax and other income taxes should also be separately disclosed in each case.

31b TAXATION

31b.1 AUTHORITATIVE PRONOUNCEMENTS

- SSAP 8

- SSAP 15

- SSAP 1

- CA 85

31b.2 ALLOCATING TAX BETWEEN PERIODS

SSAP 15 is concerned with accounting for the tax on profits and surpluses which are recognised in the financial statements in one period but assessed in another (i.e. deferred tax). The standard requires the use of the liability method when computing tax deferred/accelerated due to the effects of timing differences and chooses the partial provision approach as its general approach.

31b.2.1 Timing differences

SSAP 15.18-21 Timing differences are differences between profits or losses as computed for tax purposes and results as stated in financial statements, which arise from the inclusion of items of income and expenditure in tax computations in periods different from those in which they are included in financial statements. Timing differences originate in one period and are capable of reversal in one or more subsequent periods.

Some specific timing differences are discussed, as follows.

A loss for tax purposes which is available to relieve future profits from tax constitutes a timing difference.

The revaluation of an asset (including an investment in an associated or subsidiary company) will create a timing difference when it is incorporated into the balance sheet, insofar as the profit or loss that would result from realisation at the revalued amount is taxable, unless disposal of the revalued asset and of any subsequent replacement assets would not result in a tax liability, after taking account of any excepted rollover relief.

Retention of earnings overseas creates a timing difference only if:

- there is an intention or obligation to remit them; and

- remittance would result in a tax liability after taking account of any related double tax relief.

302

INCOME TAXES - FAS 96

31b.1 AUTHORITATIVE PRONOUNCEMENTS

- FAS 96

- FAS 103

- Guide to Implementation of FAS 96 - Q&A booklet

31b.2 GENERAL APPROACH UNDER FAS 96

Deferred tax should be provided on all temporary differences using the liability method (there are exceptions to this basic principle) and enacted tax law and rates at the balance sheet date. This liability approach assumes that the only items of future taxable income or tax deductions are the reversals of temporary differences existing at the balance sheet date.

FAS 96.7-8,16

The tax consequences of events that have not been recognised in the financial statements at the end of the current year should not be anticipated when accounting for deferred tax.

31b.2.1 Temporary differences

Temporary differences are differences between the book basis and the tax basis of an asset or a liability which at some future date will reverse thereby resulting in taxable income or tax deductions. They include conventional timing differences as well as other differences such as those arising in business combinations (see section 2.4.2).

FAS 96.9

The only exceptions in applying the basic principles of FAS 96 are :

FAS 96.8

- the Statement does not amend the provisions of APB 23 which deals with accounting for income taxes in respect of undistributed earnings of subsidiaries, investments in corporate joint ventures and bad debt reserves of savings and loan associations. Thus, for instance, if the presumption that all undistributed earnings of consolidated subsidiaries will eventually be transferred to the parent is overcome, the parent is not required to accrue deferred taxes on the undistributed earnings of consolidated subsidiaries.

- FAS 96 also specifically prohibits recognising deferred taxes for temporary differences arising from goodwill or negative goodwill.

TAXATION

31b.2.2 Method of computation

SSAP 15.24-26
SSAP 15 App Para 4

Tax deferred or accelerated by the effect of timing differences should be accounted for to the extent that it is probable that a liability or asset will crystallise. Tax deferred or accelerated by the effect of timing differences should not be accounted for to the extent that it is probable that a liability or asset will not crystallise. For this purpose, the combined effect of all timing differences should be considered rather than looking at individual categories in isolation.

SSAP 15.27-28

The assessment of whether deferred tax liabilities or assets will or will not crystallise should be based upon reasonable assumptions which take into account all relevant information available up to the date on which the financial statements are approved by the board, and also the intentions of management. Such information will usually include financial plans or projections covering a period of years sufficient to enable an assessment to be made of the likely pattern of future tax liabilities. A prudent view should be taken in the assessment of whether a tax liability will crystallise, particularly where the financial plans or projections are susceptible to a high degree of uncertainty or are not fully developed for the appropriate period.

SSAP 15.29

The provision for deferred tax liabilities should be made after taking account of any deferred tax debit balances arising from separate categories of timing differences and any advance corporation tax (ACT) which is available for offset against those liabilities. Best estimates of the tax rates that will be payable on the taxable profits when the timing differences reverse should be used. This need not be the enacted tax rates. For example, if a change of rate is announced after the year end but before the financial statements are finalised, the effect will be reflected in the year which has just ended.

The difference in the total deferred tax calculated at consecutive year ends gives the deferred tax in respect of the intervening year.

INCOME TAXES - FAS 96

31b.2.2 Method of computation

The computation of the deferred tax liability or asset involves scheduling the *FAS 96.17* cumulative temporary differences at the balance sheet date by the years they would be expected to reverse, assuming no other taxable or deductible amounts will occur in those years. Separate scheduling is necessary for each different tax and also for items which are subject to the same tax but assessed under different headings (e.g. in the UK, income assessed under Schedule D Case I and capital gains and losses).

Such detailed scheduling may not be necessary for all companies; for instance, a company with temporary differences that reverse to give net taxable amounts in each future year and which do not have any loss carry-forwards to deal with. An aggregate calculation is permitted for those companies.

FAS 96 requires that a hypothetical tax return be prepared for each future year to compute the taxes payable or refundable at the balance sheet date due to taxable or deductible amounts arising in those future years from existing temporary differences. Apart from the recovery of assets at their book values and the settlement of liabilities at their recorded amounts, no assumptions can be made about any other future events when computing the deferred tax liability or asset. Tax rates and tax laws enacted as of the balance sheet date are then applied to each year's scheduled net taxable or deductible amounts to compute the deferred tax, after giving effect to certain tax loss and tax credit (i.e. ACT) carry-forwards.

A liability or an asset is recognised currently for the deferred tax consequences of all temporary differences. The deferred tax expense or benefit for the period is the difference between the deferred tax liability or asset at the beginning and end of the year.

When computing the deferred tax liability or asset, tax planning strategies *FAS 96.19* that would alter the particular future years in which temporary differences *Q&A;Q56* result in taxable or deductible amounts should be considered. However in order to be considered in measuring the deferred tax liability or asset, tax planning strategies have to satisfy certain criteria. Qualifying tax-planning strategies that reduce the deferred tax liability or increase the recognised amount of tax benefits for net deductible amounts in future years as much as possible must be incorporated when calculating the deferred tax balance.

Note that use of such tax planning strategies in deferred tax calculations would not impose upon management an obligation to actually implement the

TAXATION

31.b.2.3 *Deferred tax assets*

SSAP 15.30   Deferred tax net debit balances should not be carried forward as assets, except to the extent that they are expected to be recoverable without replacement by equivalent debit balances. This is simply the obverse of the same rule for liabilities. Under SSAP 15, a liability is not provided where there is a 'hard core' of timing differences which represent a postponement of tax; correspondingly, a hard core of timing differences which represents a permanent acceleration of the tax liability should not be regarded as an asset.

SSAP 15 App 14-15   Tax losses may be regarded as recoverable assets if the following conditions are satisfied:

- the loss has resulted from an identifiable and non-recurring cause;

- the enterprise, or predecessor enterprise has been consistently profitable over a considerable period, with any past losses being more than offset by income in subsequent periods; and

- it is assured beyond reasonable doubt that future taxable profits will be sufficient to offset the current loss during the carry-forward period prescribed by tax legislation.

There are corresponding rules and conditions relating to capital losses.

SSAP 15.31-32   Debit balances arising in respect of ACT on dividends payable or proposed at the balance sheet date should be carried forward to the extent that it is foreseen that sufficient corporation tax will be assessed on the profits or income of the succeeding accounting period, against which ACT is available for offset.

Debit balances arising in respect of ACT other than on dividends payable or proposed at the balance sheet should be written off unless their recovery is assured beyond reasonable doubt.

INCOME TAXES - FAS 96

strategies in the future. The issue is whether management would implement the strategy to reduce taxes payable or to increase a tax refund if the need to do so actually arose.

Unlike APB 11, FAS 96 requires that deferred tax liabilities or assets that are recorded in the balance sheet be adjusted for the effect of a change in tax law or rates. Any adjustment that is necessary should be included as part of income from continuing operations for the period that includes the enactment date.

fas 96.20

31b.2.3 Deferred tax assets

Deferred tax assets are recognised only if future net deductions could be carried back to reduce:

FAS 96.17

- a current deferred tax liability; or

- taxes paid in the current or a prior year.

Loss carry-forwards or tax credits may not be recognised as assets if, because of the provisions of tax law, they cannot be applied as reductions of net taxable income scheduled to arise from the reversal of temporary differences of any year (regardless of the level of probability that sufficient income will be generated in future years).

TAXATION

31b.3 DISCLOSURE

See corresponding section in comparison with APB 11 (see section 31a).

INCOME TAXES - FAS 96

31b.3 DISCLOSURE

The disclosure requirements in FAS 96 broadly follow the requirements in APB 11. However, there are some additional/amended disclosures required.

A deferred tax liability or asset should be classified between current and non-current amounts. The current portion generally relates to the tax effects of temporary differences that will reverse during the next year. Deferred tax liabilities and assets attributable to different tax jurisdictions should not be offset. The types of temporary differences that give rise to significant portions of a deferred tax liability or asset should be disclosed.

FAS 96.24

The amount of the tax charge allocated to continued operations, discontinued operations, extraordinary items, the cumulative effect of accounting changes, prior year adjustments and capital transactions should be disclosed for each year for which those items are presented.

FAS 96.26

The significant components of income tax expense attributable to continuing operations should be disclosed for each year presented in the financial statements or in the notes. Those components would include for example:

FAS 96.27

- current tax expense or benefit;

- deferred tax expense or benefit;

- government grants (to the extent recognised as a reduction of income tax expense);

- the benefits of operating loss carry-forwards;

- adjustments made to the deferred tax liability or asset in the balance sheet to reflect changes in enacted tax law/rates.

A reconciliation of the reported amount of income tax expense attributable to continuing operations to the amount of income tax expense calculated by applying statutory rates to pre tax income from continuing operations should be presented. a numerical reconciliation may be omitted but the nature of the significant reconciling items should be disclosed.

FAS 96.28

The amounts of loss and tax credit carry-forwards for financial reporting purposes and for tax purposes must be disclosed. Loss carry-forwards for financial reporting purposes are amounts not already recognised as a reduction of a deferred tax liability, for instance, amounts of future tax deductions expected from existing temporary differences for which a tax benefit has not been recognised in the financial statements. The amounts of loss for tax purposes are the actual tax losses available to reduce taxes payable in future years.

FAS 96.29

32 SHARE CAPITAL

32.1 AUTHORITATIVE PRONOUNCEMENT

- CA 85

32.2 ORDINARY SHARE CAPITAL

32.2.1 Accounting

CA 85 s 100,130(1)

Under CA 85, a company cannot allot shares at a discount to par value. If shares are issued at a premium, whether for cash or otherwise, a sum equal to the aggregate amount or value of the premiums on those shares must be transferred to an account called the share premium account (equivalent to additional paid-up capital in the US). The share premium arising on an issue is measured by reference to the fair value of the consideration received for the shares issued.

No-par value shares cannot be issued by a company incorporated in Great Britain.

CA 85 s 131-134

Limited relief ('merger relief') is available from the general requirement to account for share premium under section 131 of CA 85, where an issuing company has secured at least a 90% equity holding in another company.

Where merger relief is available, the shares issued may be recorded at par (i.e. no premium is accounted for). However, companies often credit the amount that would otherwise have been accounted for as share premium to a non-statutory "merger reserve".

Merger relief is available whenever the above conditions are satisfied, irrespective of whether the acquisition is accounted for as a merger or an

CAPITAL STOCK

32.1 AUTHORITATIVE PRONOUNCEMENTS

- ARB 43

- APB 6

- APB 10

- APB 12

- APB 29

- Regulation S-X

- SABs 40, 64, 68

32.2 COMMON STOCK

32.2.1 Accounting

Common stock issued by an enterprise is recorded at par value. Differences between the fair value of the proceeds of the issue and the par value are recorded as additional paid-in capital.

When no-par value stock is issued, the common stock account is credited with the entire proceeds of the issue. Some States permit the issue of no-par stock and either require or allow such stock to have a stated value, usually the minimum price at which the stock may be issued. Any excess of proceeds received from the issue over stated value is credited to additional paid-in capital.   *S-X 5-02.30*

The only exception to the general requirement to account for additional paid-in capital is when accounting for common stock issued to effect a business combination accounted for as a pooling (see section 2.3.2).

SHARE CAPITAL

acquisition. The relief is however available only in respect of shares issued in the transaction which takes a holding to at least 90% (not of shares already held and which count towards the 90%).

32.2.2 *Disclosure*

The aggregate amount of a company's share capital should be disclosed on the face of the balance sheet.

CA 85 Sch 4.38(1)   The following information should be given in a note:

- the authorised share capital; and

- if shares of more than one class have been allotted, the number and aggregate nominal value of shares of each class allotted.

CA 85 Sch 4.39   If a company has allotted shares during the year, it should disclose:

- the reason for making the allotment;

- the classes of shares allotted; and

- for each class of shares, the number allotted, their aggregate nominal value and the consideration received.

CA 85 Sch 5.10,29   Additional disclosures are required where, during the financial year, the company has allotted shares subject to merger relief.

32.3 PREFERRED SHARES

32.3.1 *General*

The disclosure required to be made in respect of ordinary share capital also applies to preferred shares.

CA 85 Sch 4.49   If any fixed cumulative dividends are in arrears, the following should be disclosed:

- the amount of the arrears; and

- the period for which the dividends are in arrears (for each class of share).

CAPITAL STOCK

32.2.2 *Disclosure*

For each class of common shares, the following information should be disclosed:

- the number of shares issued or outstanding and the dollar amount thereof on the face of the balance sheet;

- the title of the issue and number of shares authorised;

- the dollar amount of any common shares subscribed but unissued. The amounts receivable should be presented as a deduction from stockholders' equity; and

- for each period for which an income statement is presented, the changes in the class of common shares.

Disclosure of changes in common stock and in the number of shares outstanding for at least the most recent year should be presented either as a separate statement or in the notes.

32.3 PREFERRED STOCK

32.3.1 *General*

Enterprises should disclose the preferential rights of preferred stockholders in the event of a liquidation, in the stockholders' equity section of the balance sheet.   *APB 10.10*

Disclosure is also required of the following, either on the face of the balance sheet or in the notes:

- the price at which preferred stock may be called or redeemed through sinking fund requirements or otherwise; and   *APB 10.11*

- the aggregate and per share amounts of cumulative preferred dividends in arrears.   *APB 15.50 fn 16*

Changes in preferred stock and the number of shares outstanding for at least the most recent year should be disclosed.   *APB 12.10*

SHARE CAPITAL

32.3.2 Redeemable preferred stock

A Accounting

There is no authoritative pronouncement dealing with this subject.

B Disclosures

Redeemable preferred stock is included as part of shareholders' equity (i.e. in share capital) in the balance sheet.

CA 85 Sch 4.38 The following disclosures should be made:

• earliest and latest dates of redemption;

• whether redemption is mandatory or at the company's option; and

• the premium (if any) payable on redemption.

32.3.3 Non-redeemable preferred stock

Such stock should be included as part of shareholders' equity. The disclosures to be made are the same as those required for ordinary share capital in 32.2.2 above.

CAPITAL STOCK

32.3.2 Redeemable preferred stock

A Accounting

The initial carrying amount of redeemable preferred stock should be its fair value at the date of issue. The difference between the fair value at the date of issue and the mandatory redemption amount should be accounted for by making periodical charges (using the interest method — see section 5.3) against retained earnings so that the carrying amount will equal the mandatory redemption amount at the mandatory redemption date. These periodical charges should be deducted from earnings for EPS purposes.

SAB 40

SAB 64

B Classification

Preferred stocks which are subject to mandatory redemption requirements or whose redemption is outside the control (no matter how remote the event might be) of the issuer should not be included under the general heading 'stockholders' equity'.

S-X 5-02.28

ASR 268

The following disclosures should be made:

S-X 5-02.28

- the title of each issue, the carrying amount and redemption amount, on the face of the balance sheet;

- the dollar amounts of any shares subscribed but unissued and the deduction of subscriptions receivable therefrom;

- the accounting treatment of the difference between the carrying amount and the redemption amount;

- the number of authorised shares and the number issued or outstanding;

- in a separate note captioned 'Redeemable Preferred Stocks';

  (i) a general description of each issue including its redemption features;

  (ii) the combined aggregate amount of redemption requirements for all issues each year for the five years following the date of the latest balance sheet; and

  (iii) the changes in each issue for each period for which an income statement is presented.

32.3.3 Non-redeemable preferred stock

Non-redeemable preferred stock may be included with common stocks and other equity accounts under the general heading 'Stockholders' equity'. The disclosures to be made in respect of such stock are similar to those required for common stock (see 32.2.2 above).

S-X 5-02.29

SHARE CAPITAL

32.3.4 Increasing-rate preferred shares

There is no authoritative pronouncement dealing with this subject.

32.4 RELATED TOPICS

32.4.1 Purchase of own shares

CA 85 s 162-169   A company is permitted, if authorised to do so by its articles, to purchase its own shares. However, unlike the position in the US, when a purchase takes place the shares purchased must be cancelled and the capital of the company must be maintained.

A purchase of own shares by a company can be effected out of:

- distributable profits and/or

- proceeds of any fresh issue made in connection with the purchase.

CA 85 s 171-173   However, a private company is permitted in certain circumstances to redeem shares out of capital.

CA 85 s 170   In order to maintain fixed capital, the following accounting treatment is applied:

- a transfer is made to the capital redemption reserve (a statutory reserve, see section 33.6) equal to the nominal value of the shares being purchased less the proceeds of any fresh issue; and

- the total cost of the redemption (including any premium payable) must be debited to distributable profits except in certain cases where there is a fresh issue of shares, when part of the premium may be debited to the share premium account.

CAPITAL STOCK

32.3.4 Increasing-rate preferred stock

Dividend costs of increasing rate preferred stock (e.g. non-redeemable *SAB 68*
preferred stock with gradually increasing dividends in the first few years of
issue preceding commencement of the perpetual dividend) should not be
based on the stated dividend schedule. Instead, SAB 68 requires imputation
of a market rate dividend during the initial period. A discount will be
recorded at the date of issue of such preferred stock (being the present value
of the difference between the dividends in the early years and the perpetual
dividend for that same period, using a discount rate based on the market rate
for dividend yield on comparable preferred stocks) and should be amortised
directly to retained earnings over the period preceding the commencement of
the perpetual dividend using the interest method (see section 5.3).

The discount should be shown separately as a deduction from the applicable *S-X 4.07*
account.

32.4 RELATED TOPICS

32.4.1 Treasury stocks

In the US, an enterprise may acquire shares of its own capital stock for
purposes other than retirement subject to state laws and the requirements of
listing agreements. In such situations, the status of such shares is akin to that
of authorised but unissued capital stock.

If treasury shares are reacquired for a purchase price significantly in excess *TB 85-6*
of the current market price of the shares it is presumed that the total purchase
price includes amounts for stated/unstated rights or privileges (this will only
apply when the shares are reacquired as a result of an offer to a limited group
of shareholders as opposed to the whole class). In such circumstances, the
total purchase price should be allocated between the cost of the treasury
shares and the cost of the rights/privileges (which is charged to income)
based on their fair values at the date of the purchase agreement . If no rights
or privileges can be identified, the entire purchase price should be allocated
to the cost of the treasury shares.

A Retirement of treasury stock

When treasury stock is acquired with the intention of retiring the stock, the *APB 6.12a*
excess of the price paid for the treasury stock over its par or stated value may *ARB 43*
either: *Chap 1B*

(a) be charged entirely to retained earnings; or

(b) allocated between additional paid-in capital arising from the same class
of stock and retained earnings.

SHARE CAPITAL

32.4.2 Scrip dividends

There is no specific pronouncement dealing with this subject. However, a common practice is to:

- record the dividend at full cash value in the year of declaration; and

- in the following year (when the number of shareholders choosing the scrip option is known) issue the shares as a bonus issue (see below) recorded at nominal value, with the difference between nominal value and cash value being adjusted in the dividend charge for that year or as a movement in reserves.

Bonus issues may be made out of any reserve (see section 33) of a company (subject to any restrictions contained in the company's own articles of association).

32.4.3 Dividends-in-kind

There is no specific pronouncement dealing with this subject. However, they are generally accounted for at the book value of the distributed assets.

CAPITAL STOCK

If the price paid is less than its par or stated value, the difference is credited to additional paid-in capital.

The original capital balances relating to the shares acquired are eliminated

B   Treasury stock acquired for purposes other than retirement
Treasury stock acquired for purposes other than retirement should be separately disclosed in the balance sheet as a deduction from stockholders' equity or alternatively accounted for as retired stock.

APB 6.12(b)

A gain on the sale of treasury stock should be credited to paid-in capital. Losses may be charged to paid-in capital but only to the extent of available net gains from previous sales or retirements of the same class of stock. Any excess should be charged against retained earnings.

The dividends on treasury stock should not be credited to income.

ARB 43 Chap 1A

32.4.2 Stock dividends
Stock dividends should be accounted for by transferring from retained earnings to capital stock and additional paid-in capital an amount equal to the fair value of the additional shares issued.

ARB 43
Chap 7B.10-11
ASR 214

However, if the number of additional shares issued as a stock dividend is more than 25% of the number previously outstanding the transaction should be accounted for as a stock split and there is no need to capitalise retained earnings.

32.4.3 Dividends-in-kind
Dividends-in-kind are distributions of non-monetary assets (other than an enterprise's own capital stock) to stockholders as dividends. Such dividends should be recorded at the fair value of the asset transferred and a gain or loss recognised on the disposition of the asset (see section 16.5 for exception to this rule).

APB 29.18

SHARE CAPITAL

32.5 SHARE PREMIUM

CA 85 Sch 4.8 This should be disclosed separately on the balance sheet.

CA 85 s 130(2) The uses to which the account may be put are severely restricted by law. However, the following events may result in an entry to the share premium account:

- issue of shares in excess of par or stated value;

- bonus issues;

- conversion of loan stock or preference share capital;

- preliminary expenses of the company;

- the expenses of any issue of shares or debentures of the company (or commission paid or discount allowed); and

- the premium payable on redemption of debentures of the company.

There is no requirement to record assets donated by a related party or expenses or liabilities paid by a principal shareholder in the financial statements of the company unless failure to record such transactions would result in the financial statements not giving a true and fair view. However capital contributions received would generally be recognised directly in other reserves.

CAPITAL STOCK

32.5 ADDITIONAL PAID-IN CAPITAL

This should be disclosed as a separate item on the face of the balance sheet.   *S-X 5-02.31(a)*

The following is a list of events that may result in an entry to additional paid-in capital:

- stock issued in excess of par or stated value or in a business combination;

- stock dividends;

- sale of treasury stock at a gain or loss;

- conversion of convertible preferred stock;

- issue and exercise of detachable stock warrants;

- donated assets from a related party (e.g. capital contributions);

- forgiveness of a debt from a stockholder; and

- expenses or liabilities paid by a principal stockholder.

Occasionally, common stock is issued below par or stated value. The holder of shares issued below par may nevertheless be required to pay the discount in the event of a liquidation where creditors will sustain a loss. The enterprise may either create a 'discount on stock' account or charge such amount to additional paid-in capital to the extent available from the same class of stock.

33 OTHER SHAREHOLDERS' EQUITY

33.1 AUTHORITATIVE PRONOUNCEMENTS

- CA 85

- SSAP 6

- SSAP 20

33.2 PROFIT AND LOSS ACCOUNT RESERVE

This should be separately disclosed on the face of the balance sheet.

SSAP 6.35 A statement of movement on reserves should be given either immediately following the profit and loss account or reference should be made on the face of the profit and loss account as to where it can be found.

The following items may be included in the movements on retained earnings:

- retained profit or loss for the financial year;

- write-off of goodwill;

- prior year adjustment;

- bonus issue of shares;

- exchange differences arising on retranslation of net investment in overseas subsidiaries;

- net amount of exchange gains and losses offset in reserves under the 'cover' method;

- accounting for mergers in circumstances where the accounting periods of the combining companies do not match each other; and

- transfers from other reserves such as the revaluation reserve.

33.3 FOREIGN CURRENCY TRANSLATION RESERVE

This is not required to be disclosed separately and in practice is generally merged with profit and loss account reserve or other reserves.

OTHER STOCKHOLDERS' EQUITY

33.1 AUTHORITATIVE PRONOUNCEMENTS
- Regulation S-X

- APB 12

- FAS 5

- FAS 12

- FAS 52

33.2 RETAINED EARNINGS
This should be disclosed separately on the balance sheet. Details of changes *S-X 5-02.31(a)*
in retained earnings for each period presented should be presented either *FAS 5.15*

- in a separate statement, or *APB 12.10*

- by combining the changes as part of the income statement.

Separate identification of appropriated (e.g. for loss contingencies) and
unappropriated amounts is not prohibited. The following is a list of events
that may result in an entry to retained earnings:

- net income/loss for the year

- dividends declared in the year

- prior-period adjustments

- stock dividends

- changes in the fiscal year of a combining company accounted for as a
  pooling of interests.

33.3 FOREIGN CURRENCY TRANSLATION RESERVE
Translation adjustments which result from retranslating a foreign enterprise's *FAS 52.13,20,31*
financial statements for consolidation purposes should be taken to a separate
component of equity, which should be separately disclosed. Also exchange

OTHER SHAREHOLDERS' EQUITY

33.4 VALUATION ALLOWANCE

This reserve does not arise in the UK (see section 28.4).

33.5 REVALUATION RESERVE

CA 85 Sch 4.34   This is a statutory reserve, which may not be reduced, except as specifically permitted by CA 85. It arises when assets are revalued above depreciated cost and generally may be reduced either by the excess depreciation charges made in respect of the revalued amount (by a transfer of these charges from profit or loss account reserves) or when the revalued asset is sold (see section 27.2.2). Separate disclosure on the face of the balance sheet is required.

33.6 CAPITAL REDEMPTION RESERVE

This, like the share premium account, is a statutory reserve but is subject to even more restrictions on its use (see section 32.4.1).

33.7 MERGER RESERVE

In practice, this reserve arises in the following ways:

- where share premium relief has been claimed on an issue of shares (see section 32.2.1) yet the shares issued have still been recorded at their fair value rather than their nominal value;

- when merger accounting has been adopted and there is a difference between the carrying value of the investment in the issuer's books and the total amount of capital recorded in the investee company's accounts (see section 2.3.2).

Often, companies use it for writing off goodwill. There is no statutory requirement to disclose this reserve separately (it forms part of 'other reserves' - see 33.9 below).

OTHER STOCKHOLDERS' EQUITY

differences attributable to hedges of foreign investments and other intercompany foreign currency transactions that are of a long-term investment nature should be taken to this reserve (see section 10.2.3). All movements in this reserve should be separately identified.

33.4 VALUATION ALLOWANCE
This reserve should be disclosed separately in the balance sheet and reflects the net unrealised losses on the portfolio of non-current marketable equity securities (see section 28.4 below).

FAS 12.11

33.5 REVALUATION RESERVE
Since asset revaluations are not generally permitted under US GAAP, a revaluation reserve will not arise.

OTHER SHAREHOLDERS' EQUITY

33.8 GOODWILL WRITE-OFF RESERVE

This reserve has arisen out of the practice adopted by some companies of establishing a separate reserve as the destination for all goodwill write-offs. Usually disclosed as a separate item within shareholders' equity (see section 27.1.3). In statutory terms it is an 'other reserve' (see 33.9).

33.9 DISCLOSURE

CA 85 Sch 4.8 The following reserves should be shown in the following order on the face of the balance sheet:

- share premium account;

- revaluation reserve;

- other reserves; and

- profit and loss account.

CA 85 Sch 4.8 'Other reserves' should be further analysed, either on the face of the balance sheet or in the notes to the accounts, between:

- capital redemption reserve;

- reserve for own shares;

- reserves provided for by the articles of association; and

- other reserves.

CA 85 Sch 4.46 For each reserve, the movements for the current year should be disclosed showing:

- the transfer to and from the reserves during the year;

- the source and application, respectively, of such transfers; and

SSAP 20.60 - the net movement on reserves arising from foreign currency exchange differences.

OTHER STOCKHOLDERS' EQUITY

34 FINANCIAL INSTRUMENTS

This is not the subject of a specific accounting standard.

FINANCIAL INSTRUMENTS

34.1 AUTHORITATIVE PRONOUNCEMENTS

- FAS 105

FAS 105 is the first standard emerging from the FASB's major project on financial instruments and off-balance-sheet risk which commenced in the Spring of 1986. It is the product of the first phase of the project dealing with disclosure of information about financial investments. Recognition and measurement issues are currently being considered in other phases of the project. The Standard is effective for financial statements issued for periods ending after June 15, 1990.

34.2 SCOPE

FAS 105 applies to all entities. The disclosure requirements apply to: *FAS 105.5*

- financial instruments with off-balance-sheet credit or market risk (see 34.3.2 below)

- all financial instruments with concentrations of credit risk (see 34.3.3 below)

Certain financial instruments are exempted from these requirements *FAS 105.14* primarily because they have been dealt with in previous accounting standards e.g. lease contracts, employers' and plans' obligations for pension, post-retirement health and life benefits, employee stock option and stock purchase plans etc.

34.3 DEFINITIONS

34.3.1 Financial Instruments

A financial instrument is cash, evidence of an ownership interest in an entity *FAS 105.6* (e.g. common stock, warrants or options etc) or a contract that both:

- imposes on one entity a contractual obligation (1) to deliver cash or another financial instrument to a second entity or (2) to exchange financial instruments on potentially unfavourable terms with the second entity; and

- conveys to that second entity a contractual right (1) to receive cash or another financial instrument from the first entity or (2) to exchange other financial instruments on potentially favourable terms with the first entity.

The above definition is recursive but not circular. A financial instrument *FAS 105.31-33* may be a link in a contractual chain with other financial instruments, but the

FINANCIAL INSTRUMENTS

FINANCIAL INSTRUMENTS

chain must end eventually with the delivery of cash or an ownership interest in an entity. Contracts that require or permit settlement by the delivery of goods (e.g. commodity futures) or services are excluded because they do not represent a contract to deliver cash or an ownership interest in an entity. Similarly, contracts that entitle the holder to receive from the issuer either a financial investment or a physical asset (e.g. a specified amount of gold or oil) do not meet the definition of a financial instrument (regardless of the possibility of settlement in cash rather than in goods or services).

34.3.2 Financial instruments with off-balance-sheet risk

Financial instruments with off-balance-sheet risk are identified as those having a risk of accounting loss exceeding the amount recognised in the balance sheet.

'Risk of accounting loss' is defined as including: *FAS 105.7*

- the possibility that a loss may occur from the failure of another party to perform according to the terms of the contract (credit risk);

- the possibility that further changes in market prices may make an instrument less valuable or more onerous (market risk); and

- the risk of theft or physical loss.

FAS 105 addresses credit and market risk only.

An example of a financial instrument that has off-balance-sheet risk is an interest rate swap providing for net settlements of cash receipts and payments that conveys a right to receive cash at current interest rates; but such an instrument may impose an obligation to deliver cash if interest rates change in the future.

34.3.3 Group concentrations of credit risk

Group concentrations are defined as counterparties which are engaged in similar activities and have similar economic characteristics that would cause their ability to meet contractual obligations to be similarly affected by changes in economic or other conditions. Counterparties in the same region or same industry are examples of groups. Identifying concentrations by regions and industries may therefore provide a useful first step in identifying relevant groups of counterparties representing concentrations of credit risks. Concentrations are defined more broadly than just regions and industries, however, in order to include other types of concentrations. For example,

FINANCIAL INSTRUMENTS

FINANCIAL INSTRUMENTS

loans to highly leveraged entities may represent a concentration as might loans to entities dependent upon government spending (which may include several industries and regions).

34.4 DISCLOSURES

34.4.1 Financial instruments with off-balance-sheet risk

The following disclosures should be made either in the body of the financial statements or in the notes by class of financial instrument:

FAS 105.17

- the face, contract or notional principal amounts; and

- the nature and terms including, at a minimum, a discussion of credit and market risk, cash requirements and accounting policies.

Additional disclosures are required for financial instruments with off-balance-sheet credit risk. These are:

FAS 105.18

- the amount of accounting loss the entity would incur if any party to the financial instrument failed completely to perform according to the terms of the contract and the collateral or other security, if any, for the amount due proved to be of no value to the entity; and

- the entity's policy of requiring collateral or other security to support financial instruments subject to credit risk, information about the entity's access to that collateral or other security, and the nature and a brief description of the collateral or other security supporting those financial instruments.

34.4.2 Disclosure of significant concentrations of credit risk of all financial instruments

Disclosure should be made of all significant concentrations of credit risk arising from all financial instruments (even those not included in the balance sheet) whether from an individual counterparty or groups of counterparties. In respect of each significant concentration the following information should be given:

FAS 105.20

- information about the (shared) activity, region, or economic characteristic that identifies the concentration;

- the amount of the accounting loss due to credit risk the entity would incur if parties to the financial instruments that make up the

FINANCIAL INSTRUMENTS

concentration failed completely to perform according to the terms of the contracts and the collateral or other security, if any, for the amount due proved to be of no value to the entity; and

* the entity's policy of requiring collateral or other security to support financial instruments subject to credit risk, information about the entity's access to that collateral or other security, and the nature and a brief description of the collateral or other security supporting those financial instruments.

The standard does not provide quantitative thresholds for determining 'significance'. Guidance may be sought by considering analogies to other standards targeting disclosure of significant risks (e.g. FAS 14, see section 21) or the 'Background Information and Basis for Conditions' accompanying the standard.

FINANCIAL INSTRUMENTS

concentration failed completely to perform according to the terms of the contracts and the collateral or other security, if any, for the amount due proved to be of no value to the entity; and

• the entity's policy of requiring collateral or other security to support financial instruments subject to credit risk, information about the entity's access to that collateral or other security, and the nature and a brief description of the collateral or other security supporting those financial instruments.

The standard does not provide quantitative thresholds for determining 'significance'. Guidance may be sought by considering analogies to other standards targeting disclosure of significant risks (e.g. FAS 14, see section 21) or the 'Background Information and Basis for Conditions' accompanying the standard.

35 SOURCE AND APPLICATION OF FUNDS STATEMENT

35.1 AUTHORITATIVE PRONOUNCEMENT

- SSAP 10

COMMENT

In July 1990, the ASC issued ED 54 — *Cash flow statements* which, if it becomes a standard, will require a cash flow statement (very similar to that required by FAS 95) rather than a funds flow statement as required by SSAP 10.

SSAP 10.9   SSAP 10 applies to all entities whose accounts are intended to give a true and fair view, other than those whose turnover or gross income is less than £25,000 per annum.

35.2 OBJECTIVE OF THE FUNDS STATEMENT

SSAP 10.2-3   The objective of such a statement is to show the manner in which the operations of a company have been financed and in which its financial resources have been used.

It should show clearly the funds generated or absorbed by the operations of the business and the manner in which any resulting surplus of liquid assets has been applied or any deficiency of such assets has been financed, distinguishing the long term from the short term.

35.3 MEANING OF FUNDS

SSAP 10.8   SSAP 10 does not define the term 'funds'; the only term defined in the standard is that of 'net liquid funds' which is defined as 'cash at bank and in hand and cash equivalents less bank overdrafts and other borrowings repayable within one year of the accounting date'.

Of the numerous possible interpretations of the term 'funds', the most commonly used are:

- net liquid funds;

- working capital;

- net borrowings; and

- total external financing.

COMMENT

The ED 54 definition of cash equivalents is similar to the FAS 95 definition. However, whilst the FAS 95 definition is generally restricted to investments with original maturities of 3 months or less, the ED 54 definition is broader; for example, where an enterprise uses short-term bank borrowings, either in part or in whole, as an integral part of its treasury management, the borrowings so used are included in computing the balance of cash and cash equivalents.

STATEMENT OF CASH FLOWS

35.1 AUTHORITATIVE PRONOUNCEMENTS

- FAS 95

- FAS 102

- FAS 104

35.2 OBJECTIVE OF A STATEMENT OF CASH FLOWS

A statement of cash flows explains the change during the period in cash and cash equivalents. The total amounts of cash and cash equivalents at the beginning and end of the period shown in the statement of cash flows will be the same amounts as presented in the balance sheets as at these dates.

FAS 95.7

35.3 DEFINITION OF FUNDS

Cash equivalents are short term, highly liquid investments that are both:

FAS 95.8

- readily convertible to known amounts of cash.

- so near their maturity that they present insignificant risk of changes in value because of changes in interest rates. Generally, only investment with maturities of less than three months at the date of purchase qualify under this definition.

Not all investments that qualify are required to be treated as cash equivalents. The policy for determining which items are treated as cash equivalents should be disclosed.

FAS 95.10

SOURCE AND APPLICATION OF FUNDS STATEMENT

35.4 FORM AND CONTENT OF FUNDS STATEMENT

The standard does not prescribe the order nor form of presentation of the disclosures required to be made, and, as a result, a variety of presentational formats have emerged. These formats can be grouped into three broad types:

*   *Balanced* — sources and applications of funds are shown separately but with equal totals

*   *Remainder* — applications are deducted from sources, leaving a residual amount which usually represents the change in net borrowings, working capital or net liquid funds, whichever is used as 'funds'

*   *Reconciling* — an analysis of the increase/decrease of funds for the period in terms of sources and applications, reconciled with the company's opening and closing fund balances.

It is more usual to start with profit before tax and show tax paid as an application, but it is permissible to start with profit after tax and show tax as a movement in working capital.

SSAP 10.11   The statement should show:

*   the profit and loss for the period together with the adjustments for items which did not use or provide funds;

*   dividends paid;

*   acquisitions and disposals of fixed assets;

*   funds raised by increasing, or expended in repaying or redeeming, medium or long-term loans or the issued capital of the company;

*   increase or decrease in working capital sub-divided into its components;

*   movements in net liquid funds.

SSAP 10.5   It is generally necessary to summarise the effects of any acquisition or disposal of a subsidiary by way of note.

338

STATEMENT OF CASH FLOWS

35.4 FORM AND CONTENT OF THE STATEMENT OF CASH FLOWS

The statement of cash flows should classify cash receipts and payments as resulting from investing, financing or operating activities.

FAS 95.14

Investing activities include making and collecting loans, and acquiring and disposing of debt or equity investments and property, plant and equipment and other productive assets.

FAS 95.15

Financing activities include obtaining resources from investors and providing them with a return on and a return of their investment; borrowing money and repaying amounts borrowed; and obtaining and paying for other resources obtained from creditors on long-term credit.

FAS 95.18

Operating activities include all transactions and other events that are not defined as investing or financing activities above (including interest charges). Cash flows from operating activities are generally the cash effects of transactions and other events that enter into the determination of net income.

FAS 95.21

The direct method of computation (i.e. reporting gross receipts and payments on operating activities) is encouraged along with a reconciliation of net income to net cash flow from operations. However the indirect method (i.e. reconciling net income to net cash flow) is also permitted for operating activities. If the indirect method is used, interest paid (net of that capitalised) and taxes paid should also be disclosed.

FAS 95.27-30

COMMENT

ED 54 adopts a neutral attitude towards the two methods of presentation. Under the ED's proposals, cash flows may be reported using either method.

Cash receipts and payments from purchases and sales of debt or equity securities carried at market value in a trading account which are held principally for resale and certain loans that are acquired specifically for resale should be classified as operating activities in the statement of cash flows.

FAS 102.8-9

Cash flows resulting from futures contracts, forward contracts, option contracts, or swap contracts that are accounted for as hedges of identifiable transactions or events may be classified in the same category as the cash flows from the items being hedged provided the accounting policy is disclosed.

FAS 104.7b

SOURCE AND APPLICATION OF FUNDS STATEMENT

35.4.1 Netting off of transactions

SSAP 10.4 The explanatory note to the standard emphasises that there should be a minimum of netting off in the funds statement and that the figures from which the funds statement is constructed should be identifiable in the profit and loss account and the balance sheet.

35.4.2 Foreign currency differences

The treatment of foreign currency differences in funds statements is not addressed by SSAP 10.

35.4.3 Non-cash transactions

There is no disclosure requirement in SSAP 10 similar to FAS 95.32 .

STATEMENT OF CASH FLOWS

35.4.1 Netting off of transactions

Generally cash receipts and payments should all be shown gross; however *FAS 95.11-13* certain items may be presented net because their turnover is quick, their amounts are large, and their maturities are short. These items will be cash flows relating to investments, loans receivable, and debt, providing their maturity at the date of purchase is less than three months.

Banks and savings institutions are not required to report gross amounts of *FAS 104.7a* cash receipts and cash payments for:

*   deposits placed with other financial institutions and withdrawals of deposits;

*   time deposits accepted and repayments of deposits; and

*   loans made to customers and principal collections of loans.

However, if such institutions constitute part of a consolidated group, those net amounts should be separately disclosed in the consolidated cash flow statement from gross amounts of cash receipts and payments arising from the other investing and financing activities of the consolidated group.

35.4.2 Foreign currency differences

Foreign currency transactions should be reported using the rate ruling at the *FAS 95.25* date of the transaction, or an appropriate average rate (i.e. that used for income statement purposes). Any exchange differences arising on cash balances held in foreign currencies should be reported as a separate part of the reconciliation of the change in cash and cash equivalents during the period.

35.4.3 Non-cash transactions

Non-cash investing and financing transactions should be separately *FAS 95.32* disclosed. Examples of these transactions include converting debt to equity, obtaining an asset by entering into a capital lease etc.

SSAPs, SORPs, Franked SORPs and EDs in the UK

STATEMENTS OF STANDARD ACCOUNTING PRACTICE

No

1   Accounting for associated companies (revised)

2   Disclosure of accounting policies

3   Earnings per share (revised)

4   Accounting for government grants (revised)

5   Accounting for value added tax

6   Extraordinary items and prior year adjustments (revised)

8   The treatment of taxation under the imputation system in the accounts of companies

9   Stocks and long-term contracts (revised)

10 Statements of source and application of funds

12 Accounting for depreciation (revised)

13 Accounting for research and development (revised)

14 Group accounts

15 Accounting for deferred tax (revised)

17 Accounting for post balance sheet events

18 Accounting for contingencies

19 Accounting for investment properties

20 Foreign currency translation

21 Accounting for leases and hire purchase contracts

22 Accounting for goodwill (revised)

23 Accounting for acquisitions and mergers

24 Accounting for pension costs

25 Segmental reporting

STATEMENTS OF RECOMMENDED PRACTICE

No

1   Pension scheme accounts

2   Accounting by charities

FRANKED STATEMENTS OF RECOMMENDED PRACTICE

Issued by

OIAC   Disclosure about oil and gas exploration and production activities

OIAC   Accounting for oil and gas exploration and production activities

OIAC   Accounting for abandonment costs

CIPFA   The application of Accounting Standards (SSAPs) to Local Authorities in Great Britain

CIPFA   Local Authority Accounting

CVCP   Accounting in UK Universities

BBA   Accounting for securities by banks

ABI   Accounting for insurance business

EXPOSURE DRAFTS

No

46   Disclosure of related party transactions

47   Accounting for goodwill

48   Accounting for acquisitions and mergers

49   Reflecting the substance of transactions in assets and liabilities

50   Consolidated accounts

EXPOSURE DRAFTS (continued)

ARBs, APB Opinions and FASB Statements in the US

ACCOUNTING RESEARCH BULLETINS
(issued between 1939-1958)

No

43   Restatement and Revision of Accounting Research Bulletins

Chapter 1A	Rules adopted by Membership
1B	Profits or losses on Treasury Stock
Chapter 2A	Comparative financial statements
Chapter 3A	Current Assets and Current Liabilities
Chapter 4	Inventory Pricing
Chapter 7A	Quasi-Reorganization or Corporate Readjustment
Chapter 7B	Stock dividends and Stock Split-ups
Chapter 9A	Depreciation and High Costs
9C	Emergency Facilities: Depreciation, Amortisation and Income taxes
Chapter 10A	Real and Personal Property Taxes
Chapter 11	Government Contracts
Chapter 12	Foreign Operations and Foreign Exchange
Chapter 13B	Compensation Involved in Stock Option and Stock Purchase Plans

44   Declining-balance Depreciation

45   Long-term Construction-type Contracts

46   Discontinuance of Dating Earned Surplus

51   Consolidated Financial Statements

ACCOUNTING PRINCIPLES BOARD OPINIONS
(issued between 1958-1973)

No

2   Accounting for the 'Investment Credit'

4   Accounting for the 'Investment Credit' (amending No. 2)

6   Status of Accounting Research Bulletins

STATEMENTS OF FINANCIAL ACCOUNTING STANDARDS (issued from 1973)

22 Changes in the Provisions of Lease Agreements Resulting from Refundings of Tax-Exempt Debt (an amendment of FASB Statement No. 13).

23 Inception of the Lease (an amendment of FASB Statement No. 13)

24 Reporting Segment Information in Financial Statements That Are Presented in Another Enterprise's Financial Report (an amendment of FASB Statement No. 14)

25 Suspension of Certain Accounting Requirements for Oil and Gas Producing Companies (an amendment of FASB Statement No. 19)

27 Classification of Renewals or Extensions of Existing Sales-Type or Direct Financing Leases (an amendment of FASB Statement No. 13)

28 Accounting for Sales with Leasebacks (an amendment of FASB Statement No. 13)

29 Determining Contingent Rentals (an amendment of FASB Statement No. 13)

30 Disclosure of Information About Major Customers (an amendment of FASB Statement No. 14)

31 Accounting for Tax Benefits Related to U.K. Tax Legislation concerning Stock Relief

32 Specialized Accounting and Reporting Principles and Practices in AICPA Statements of Position and Guides on Accounting and Auditing Matters (an amendment of APB Opinion No. 20)

34 Capitalization of Interest Cost

35 Accounting and Reporting by Defined Benefit Pension Plans

37 Balance Sheet Classification of Deferred Income Taxes (an amendment of APB Opinion No. 11)

38 Accounting for Preacquisition Contingencies of Purchased Enterprises (an amendment of APB Opinion No. 16)

42 Determining Materiality for Capitalization of Interest Cost (an amendment of FASB Statement No. 34)

43 Accounting for Compensated Absences

99   Deferral of the Effective Date of Recognition of Depreciation by Not-for-Profit Organizations
(an amendment of FASB Statement No. 93)

100   Accounting for Income Taxes—Deferral of the Effective Date of FASB Statement No. 96 (an amendment of Statement No. 96)

101   Regulated Enterprises—Accounting for the Discontinuation of Application of FASB Statement No. 71

102   Statement of Cash Flows—Exemption of Certain Enterprises and Classification of Cash Flows from Certain Securities Acquired for Resale (an amendment of FASB Statement No. 95)

103   Accounting for Income Taxes—Deferral of the Effective Date of FASB Statement No. 96
(an amendment of FASB Statement No. 96)

104   Statement of Cash Flows—Net Reporting of Certain Cash Receipts and Cash Payments and Classification of Cash Flows from Hedging Transactions
(an amendment of FASB Statement No. 95)

105   Disclosure of Information about Financial Instruments with Off-Balance-Sheet Risk and Financial Instruments with Concentrations of Credit Risk